The Future of the Highlands

CONTRIBUTORS

Ian Grimble
F. Fraser Darling
John A. Smith
Farquhar Gillanders
Kenneth D. MacDonald
Derick S. Thomson
Magnus Magnusson

THE FUTURE
OF THE
HIGHLANDS

Edited by
Derick S. Thomson and
Ian Grimble

London
ROUTLEDGE & KEGAN PAUL

First published 1968
by Routledge and Kegan Paul Ltd
Broadway House, 68–74 Carter Lane
London, E.C.4
Printed in Great Britain
by Richard Clay (The Chaucer Press), Ltd.,
Bungay, Suffolk
Ian Grimble and Derick S. Thomson 1968

SBN 7100 6052 1

Contents

v

Biographical Notes
on the Authors

DARLING, FRANK FRASER

Born 1903. Educated at Midland Agricultural College and Edinburgh University. Senior Lecturer in Ecology and Conservation, Edinburgh University 1953–58. Director of the West Highland Survey 1944–50. Rockefeller Special Research Fellow 1950. Vice-President and Director of Research, Conservation Foundation. Author of books including *A Herd of Red Deer* (1937), *The Seasons and the Farmer* (1939), *Island Years* (1940), *The Seasons and the Fisherman* (1941), *Wild Life of Britain* (1943), *Island Farm* (1943), *Crofting Agriculture* (1945), *Natural History of the Highlands and Islands* (1947) (new edition, with J. M. Boyd 1964), *Some Thoughts of an Ecologist on Industrialisation* (1956).

GILLANDERS, FARQUHAR

Born in Applecross, Ross-shire, 1923. Graduate in Economics and Political Science of Glasgow University: on its teaching staff from 1950 until 1966, when he became Assistant Registrar of the University. Served during the war in the Royal Scots Fusiliers and in the 7th Gurkha Rifles. Contributor to journals, on Scottish and Highland economic questions, and on aspects of adult teaching.

GRIMBLE, IAN

Born in Hong-Kong 1921. Williams History Exhibitioner, Balliol College, Oxford, where he graduated. Ph.D., Aberdeen University. F.R. Hist. S. Lieutenant in the Intelligence Corps with service in India 1943–46. House of Commons Library 1947–55. B.B.C. producer 1955–59. Author of *The Harington Family* (1957), *The Trial of Patrick Sellar* (1962), *Chief of Mackay* (1965), *Denmark* (1966). Radio and Television broadcaster.

Biographical Notes on the Authors

MACDONALD, KENNETH D.

Born in Applecross, Ross-shire, 1937. Educated at Applecross Primary School 1943–48, Dingwall Academy 1948–54, and Glasgow University 1954–58 where he graduated with Honours in Celtic. Graduated in the Anglo-Saxon Tripos at Emmanuel College, Cambridge, 1958–60. Assistant Lecturer in the Department of Celtic, Glasgow University, from 1960, and Lecturer since 1963. Appointed Editor of the *Historical Dictionary of Scottish Gaelic* 1966.

MAGNUSSON, MAGNUS

Born in Iceland 1929 and still an Icelandic citizen. Brought up in Edinburgh, and educated at Edinburgh Academy. Graduated in English at Oxford University. Journalist on the staff of *The Scotsman*, and an Assistant Editor. Television broadcaster. Translator with Herman Pálsson of *Njal's Saga*, *The Vinland Sagas*, *King Harald's Saga* and *Laxdaela Saga*. Translator of the Icelandic novels of Halldor Laxness.

SMITH, JOHN ANGUS

Born at Lochmaddy in North Uist 1911. Educated at Tobermory Higher Grade School, Oban High School, and St Andrews University, where he took first-class honours in English and was a triple blue in athletics, football and hockey. Lieutenant Commander in the Royal Navy 1941–46. Lecturer at Moray House College of Education 1947–49. Assistant Director of Education, Fife, 1949–52, H.M.I.S. 1952–55, Vice-Principal of Jordanhill College of Education since 1956.

THOMSON, DERICK S.

Born in 1921. Educated at Bayble Primary School and the Nicolson Institute in Lewis. Graduated with honours in Celtic and English at Aberdeen University, and took the tripos in Archaeology and Anthropology at Cambridge. Assistant in Celtic at Edinburgh University 1948–49, Lecturer in Welsh at Glasgow University 1949–56, Reader in Celtic at Aberdeen University 1956–63, Professor of Celtic at Glasgow University since 1963. Gaelic poet (Ruaraidh Mac Thómais), author of *An Dealbh Briste* (1951), *Eadar Samhradh Is Foghar* (1967). Author in English of *The Gaelic Sources of Macpherson's 'Ossian'* (1952). Author with J. L. Campbell of *Edward Lhuyd in the Scottish Highlands* (1963). Gaelic broadcaster. Editor of *Gairm* and *Scottish Gaelic Studies*.

Acknowledgments

Grateful acknowledgments are made to *The Times*, for permission to publish a letter to this newspaper in the chapter on 'Unsceptered Isles', and also to the letter's signatories. Thanks are extended likewise to Mr P. H. Newby, Head of the Third Programme of the B.B.C., for the quotations from the studies on 'Land Use in the North' produced by Mr Christopher Holme for the Third Programme, which have been used in the same chapter.

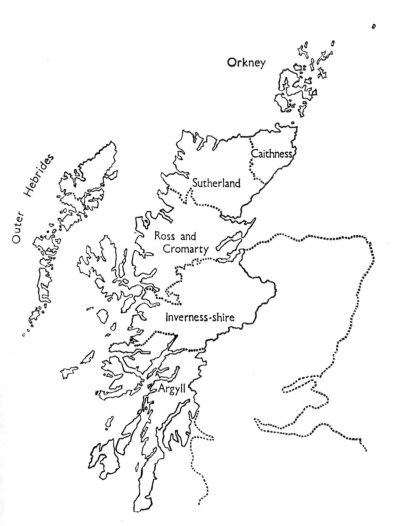

Shetland

Orkney

Outer Hebrides

Caithness

Sutherland

Ross and
Cromarty

Inverness-shire

Argyll

The Crofter Counties

Introduction

Ian Grimble

Introduction

When the Roman administration was withdrawn from Britain at the beginning of the fifth century, the rule of these islands passed into the hands of their Celtic inhabitants. For the only time in Britain's history the Celtic people were in control, and this period lasted for two hundred years.

In Ireland the inhabitants were called Scots, and they spoke an older form of the Celtic tongue than their neighbours in Britain and Gaul, called Gaelic. The Scots in Ireland were never subjugated by the Romans, and soon after the legions left Britain, they began to establish colonies up and down the British mainland to their east.

Here they were resisted by the Celtic princes who had inherited the Roman power, and by Vortigern in particular, the most powerful of them. But Vortigern was also troubled by the landings of Saxons in Kent, illiterate heathens who were enabled to settle by the weakening of the Roman fleet that had for so long guarded its shores. In the annals of the Saxon conquest, Vortigern became the villain who had permitted them to enter Britain; and Arthur the Celtic hero who led the resistance to Saxon expansion.

The civilisation which he fought to protect is best exemplified by his contemporary Saint Patrick, the son of a Romano-Celtic official who spent much of his life in missionary activities among the Gaelic-speaking Scots of Ireland. During the lifetime of the two men, Scottish colonists founded a settlement on the northern mainland, beyond the principalities of the Solway and Strathclyde in which British dynasties had held the frontier in Roman times. The new colony which gave its name to Scotland was called Dalriada: and it was thus that the oldest form of the

Celtic language was brought to the country as late as the mid-fifth century. But it was the tongue that prevailed there long after Pictish and Welsh disappeared, and that is spoken there still in the areas where the Scots first settled a millennium and a half ago.

Scottish Dalriada lay north of the rock of Dumbarton, where a dynasty of Welsh leaders had been holding the frontier against the Picts since the fourth century. The Picts were regarded by the Romans in the latter days of their administration in Britain as a formidable military power, and Christianity had reached the Picts before the Romans withdrew. The Picts left sculptured monuments which attest that they were also a highly artistic people. But alone of all the Celts they have left no written records, so that even the precise form of their language has remained a subject of debate. Their kingdoms extended down the eastern side of Scotland as far south as the Forth, where they faced the chain of Welsh principalities that the Romans had nurtured along the Clyde–Forth frontier.

Throughout the fifth century, Celtic Gaul was the most intellectually vigorous region in the Roman Empire. Its inhabitants looked upon their provincial cousins in Britain as relatively philistine, and indeed the literary remains from this century in Britain do not compare favourably with those of the Continent, either in quality or in quantity. But Saint Patrick's Confession, simple as it is, does show a knowledge of the European conventions of his day in that literary form. His letter to Coroticus does protest against the practice of slavery. In Britain, Pelagius rejected the doctrine of original sin, and such were the links with European thought that his heresy spread beyond Gaul, and Rome was forced to adopt stringent measures against Pelagianism. The Celto-Roman culture of fifth-century Britain may have appeared provincial by continental standards, but it was linked to the European tradition, both through the Welsh and through the Irish intelligentsia. Only the Picts beyond the Firth of Forth stood aloof.

In the Celtic languages themselves, the pre-Christian learning had been preserved and embellished by the three orders of druids, seers and bards; and these orders continued to flourish into Christian times in Britain and Ireland as in Gaul. But their arts were oral ones, and their libraries were prodigious memories. Much of their pagan learning was bound to be rejected

4

when the art of writing was introduced with Christianity, and in fact no Welsh literature survives earlier than the poetry of Aneirin and Taliesin composed late in the sixth century, over a hundred years after the compositions of Saint Patrick in Latin. It is all the more astonishing that the Scots in Ireland should have preserved in Gaelic such a vast and unique corpus of traditional literature, salvaged from the pagan Celtic world, transcribed down the ages by Christian clerics.

By the sixth century the new Christian and the old Celtic learning were being planted in western Scotland by the men of Ireland at a time when the Romano-Welsh principalities were gradually crumbling. Aneirin was composing his elegy on the defeat of the Gododdin heroes in the province south of Edinburgh at the time when Saint Columba was carrying out his missionary activities from Iona. While the Dalriadic Scots were making the decisive advances which turned Pictland into Scotland, the Angles from the east coast were taking the first steps which made an England out of Britain.

An illiterate heathen called Ida had established himself on the rock of Bamburgh Head in about 547. His descendants achieved one of the most fruitful fusions of the Celtic and English peoples ever seen in these islands. Out of it grew the golden age of the Northumbrian kingdom, presided over by one of the most brilliant of all our dynasties. Lindisfarne commemorates its links with Iona and the civilisation that had travelled by way of Gaul and Ireland before it reached Northumbria from the Hebrides.

But Lindisfarne marks the final stage in the process by which a primitive race was civilised by the Celtic peoples whom it defeated. In the first phase of this process the Celtic and Germanic people—Angles and Saxons—settled down beside one another. The dynasty of Ida inter-married with Welsh princes such as the house of Urien which produced such distinguished scholars, and whose capital at Carlisle Saint Cuthbert admired, with its city wall and 'fountain wondrously constructed by the Romans'. The same dynasty married into the Pictish royal house, whose matrilinear rules of succession gave the Northumbrian house claims beyond the Forth. Finally, in 633, a Northumbrian prince returned from exile in Iona to succeed to his father's throne. Within months he had invited Saint Aidan to found the Columban monastery and bishopric of Lindisfarne. Although Saint Cuthbert was an Englishman, reared in the province of south-east Scotland that the Celtic peoples had lost, he was educated by Gaels, to become one of the greatest ornaments of the Celtic Church. His Bible is the earliest remaining book in Britain, its binding the earliest surviving example of craftsmanship in leatherwork. The stole presented to his shrine after his death is by far the earliest treasure of insular needlework: his coffin at Durham is covered with Celtic portaiture. And the Celtic art of the Lindisfarne gospels created one of the most beautiful books the world has ever seen. The two centuries of Celtic control were over in Britain, but they had given place to two more centuries in which the Celtic peoples retained the cultural initiative, until the Angles and Saxons were as civilised as themselves. In the case of Northumbria the links were with Iona. In the case of the southern kingdom to which Alfred ultimately succeeded as the greatest scholar-king of all, the centres of instruction were supplied directly from Ireland, and the principal one was at Malmesbury.

It might easily have happened that the Northumbrian kings would have succeeded in asserting their claims to Pictland, until they had created a single kingdom of eastern Britain from the Moray Firth to the Humber. But in fact they were defeated in a succession of decisive battles. It was the Gaels of Dalriada who finally succeeded under Kenneth Mac Alpin in 864 in uniting east and west in a kingdom of the Picts and Scots north of the Forth. By then, however, the blossoming civilisations of Anglo-Celtic Britain were menaced by the depredations of a new wave of illiterate, heathen Germanic barbarians far more terrible than their predecessors. It was these who, four centuries after the departure of the Romans, destroyed Iona and Lindisfarne and brought the dark age to Britain. They took children to sell as slaves in the eastern Mediterranean, and church ornaments as trinkets for their women. They never preserved a book: the earliest author whose work survives among them is Ari, and he was born six hundred years after Saint Patrick wrote his expostulation against the practice of slavery. At the hands of the Vikings the Celtic civilisation suffered a blow from which, politically, it never recovered.

When the Vikings destroyed the library at York, known to

be one of the finest in Europe, many of its treasures had already reached the Continent. It was observed at the court of Charlemagne that the Gaels were especially welcomed among the refugees, because of the numbers of scholars among them, and of those who had escaped with books in their luggage. And one book that reached the safety of the Continent is to be remarked upon in particular because it is the earliest survivor out of Scotland, Adamnan's *Life of Saint Columba*.

Adamnan appears to have come from Donegal, and he was eighth abbot of Iona in succession to the founder. His *Life* follows a literary convention already centuries old. It has been suggested that these hagiographies of the saints owed much to the influence of the Greek novel. Adamnan's *Life of Columba*, completed before the author's death in 704, is judged to be one of the outstanding masterpieces among them. This and another of Adamnan's surviving works provide proof of the high standard of Gaelic education in Scotland at this time, its close links with the European tradition and the libraries at its disposal. It remains a matter of doubt whether that other wonder of Celtic book production, the book of *Kells*, was made on Iona or in Ireland where it remains today.

The Norsemen established the kingdom of Dublin and won control of the islands from Man to the Faroes and Orkney. They dominated much of the coastal mainland of Scotland by the planting of fortified camps known as ness sites. They won Northumbria and much of eastern England to the south. They reached their zenith when Canute became king of England and Scandinavia. Their principal achievements were to plant towns, introduce mercantile practices, and graft new codes of law and judicial practice upon the ancient legal systems of Britain and Ireland. Since the Vikings were largely exogamous, successive generations of them were reared by Celtic slave mothers. Saint Sunniva proved to be one of the most indomitable of these women: when she was carried off with her companions by the Vikings of north Norway she organised a resistance ending in mass suicide and thus supplied north Norway with a Gaelic patron saint. But others reared the sturdy Celto-Norse stock which contributed so much to the commerce and arts and politics of northern Europe for centuries to come.

The relics of Saint Columba were removed from Iona to Dunkeld, where a bishopric was established. Brechin was handed to the Church, and the round tower of Ireland still stands in the heart of old Pictland. The oldest surviving Scottish Gaelic prose was written in the *Book of Deer* in Buchan. The Norsemen had severed the umbilical cord between Ireland and her Scottish colony. But the Scottish Gael survived the Viking era; to some extent because the kingdoms of Pictland north of the Forth had not been allowed to fall to the English, and therefore remained as a Celtic bastion against the menace of the Norsemen.

But towards the end of the Viking period the whole future of Scottish history was affected as profoundly by internal dynastic events as it ever had been by invasion or by religious organisation. The Pictish rule of matrilinear succession had provided the Northumbrians with their dynastic claims, and finally enabled the Scots of Dalriada to succeed to the high kingship of the Picts and Scots. In the house of Kenneth Mac Alpin kings were not succeeded directly by their descendants but by adult collaterals. In 1034 Malcolm II's new law of succession came into effect at his death. It gave descendants precedence over collaterals, and as Malcolm's direct heir was Duncan, his daughter's son, its effect was to place a new dynasty on the throne. But even under the old law of succession, the title would have had to pass through a female. The heirs under the old law were Gruoch and her son Lulach, and Macbeth who married her when her first husband died. Under the new law Earl Thorfinn of Orkney's claim stood close to that of Duncan. The strife between these cousins lasted from the succession of Duncan in 1034 until his son Malcolm Canmore succeeded in 1057.

What had happened by then was that the crown of the Picts and Scots had virtually passed out of Celtic and into English hands, the seat of government out of Scotland proper into English Northumbria. Lulach was, in fact, the last Ard Righ or High King in Scotland. Although Malcolm Canmore had passed his upbringing in England and his successful invasion was a Northumbrian one like those of an earlier age, he might have re-established a Celtic dynasty. But he did not do so. He took as his second wife Margaret, sister of Edgar the Atheling, and at his death the throne passed to her sons, to the exclusion of the High King Lulach's descendants, or of the offspring of Canmore's first marriage within the Celtic royal house. Only his younger brother Donald Ban succeeded for a short time in reasserting the former law of succession at his brother's death, in an attempt to prevent what amounted to the completion of the Northumbrian conquest, using the crown of the Scots as a camouflage. By the time Margaret's three sons had reigned in succession, most of the alternative heirs had been killed and the Anglo-Norman feudal order had established itself firmly in the northern half of the territories in which the English had overcome the Gododdin over five hundred years earlier. There was no Aneirin to compose a second elegy.

The preoccupations of Margaret's immediate descendants were with the territories of the former Northumbrian kingdom of which the Lothians had been the northernmost province, and with such feudal possessions as the Honour of Huntingdon that her youngest son David enjoyed before he succeeded to the Scottish throne. In due course the kings of Scots abandoned their claims on north England, and agreed upon the frontier that remains today. They concentrated increasingly on reducing the real Scotland beyond the old Forth–Clyde barrier to subservience to the Scottish crown. Gradually they and the Anglo-Norman nobility they had brought north with them became anti-English patriots: just as the Norman aristocracy in England were gradually transformed into English, anti-French patriots. But the Scottish crown was never again the apex of Gaelic society and culture after the death of Lulach the last High King. The earliest surviving Gaelic poem is about the kingship. It was composed in the eleventh century. The next surviving poem is from the thirteenth century and its theme is the Gaelic resistance to the royal government of Scotland. The Scottish Gaels had ceased to be linked politically with Ireland, their country of origin, and had also lost the crown of Scotland.

For a time they enjoyed instead a more limited principality of the Western Isles and the western seaboard where the first settlers from Dalriada had established themselves and Saint Columba had planted the cross on Iona. This most Gaelic region had been controlled by the Norsemen for centuries, leaving a hiatus at the end of the Viking age. After Haakon

Haakonson had failed, in 1263, to restore Norse suzerainty in the Hebrides, they were ceded to the Scottish crown. A mixed Celto-Norse stock reverted wholly to the Gaelic culture. A Norman overlord, owing his title to a Norman king of Scots, became a Gaelic patriarch, just as the Norman king became a Scottish patriot. The lordship of the Isles, administered from Islay, may have been the happiest period in the history of Scottish Gaeldom. It is hard to tell, because the entire muniments of the lordship have disappeared without a trace. Only one solitary Gaelic charter survives to bear witness that the vernacular was used for official purposes. No Gaelic library at all survives from this period, in the country that had produced the finest masterpieces of book production and Scotland's first book.

But one such library was listed before it disappeared, and some of its fifteenth-century manuscripts are preserved in Scotland's national library. They include much of the ancient literature of Ireland, the first translation into any European language of the story of Troy, the medical treatises of Averroes and of the Salerno school translated into Gaelic likewise. The library belonged to the Beaton family, in which this learning was hereditary. Another such family were the MacVurichs, whose origins and learning were Irish, and who preserved their library and learning in Scottish Gaeldom until the end of the eighteenth century.

Before the lordship of the Isles was abolished at the end of the fifteenth century by the king of Scots, the clan structure of Gaelic society had taken its final shape. Some clan names are generic, and of these there are the religious ones: MacTaggart, meaning son of the Priest; MacNab, son of the Abbot; Maclennan, son of the servant of Finnan. Mackintosh means son of the *Tòisech*, a form of senior official. The MacEcherns were sons of a Horse-lord. But others such as the Mackays, sons of *Aodh*, took their name from a supposed common ancestor, whose actual identity is in many cases uncertain. The Frasers and Chisholms are examples of Gaelic clans that adopted the name of a feudal Norman overlord whose descendants became assimilated into Celtic society like the Butlers and Burkes in Ireland. In the most northerly parts of Scotland that never became Gaelic, the Norman Sinclairs did not obtain their title until the fifteenth century, yet the name of Sinclair is commoner in Orkney and Caithness today than any other. Since these earldoms were well populated before the fifteenth century and were not resettled then, it is evident that the name which dominates them today is that of a feudal overlord, not of a common ancestor.

But in Gaeldom the situation was complicated by the grafting of feudalism on to a patriarchal society. The crown granted charters which gave feudal rights over both the land and its inhabitants. A man might find himself owing a divided allegiance to a feudal superior and a clan chief who were not the same person. The tribal connection was naturally the more binding of the two, but it was not the one recognised by the Scottish crown. Some of the most terrible conflicts in Gaeldom resulted from this, and several of them were deliberately fomented by the Scottish administration during the fifteenth and sixteenth centuries. The situation was further aggravated by the weakness of the crown's authority during much of this period, and the fact that two families, the Campbells and the Gordons, were granted lieutenancies which virtually empowered them to conquer and divide Gaeldom between themselves.

The MacGregors are probably the most famous of the clans that found themselves in the first place under Campbell vassalage, and finally reduced to the status of 'broken men' after being totally expropriated. By the end of the sixteenth century their very name was proscribed and anyone bearing it could be hunted like an animal. However, the practice of genocide was being practised fairly systematically by this time, so that the fate of the MacGregors was by no means unique. In 1605 the head of the Gordons offered 'to take in hand the service of settling the North Isles . . . and to put an end to that service by extirpation of the barbarous people of the Isles within a year'. The king of Scots accepted this offer, though it failed: because Hebrideans were better able to defend themselves than MacGregors in the middle of Campbell country.

The sixteenth century saw, in fact, a disintegration of the Gaelic society of Scotland based on the clan system and on the authority and patronage of the vanished lords of the Isles. It was in this century that two MacGregor scholars made the collection of Gaelic poetry known as the *Book of the Dean of*

Lismore. Its Scottish verse covers a period of over two centuries back in time, while much of the collection reveals how strongly men's minds were still influenced by the ancient literature of Ireland. Shortly after the Dean's book was completed, the first Gaelic book was published in Scotland. It is a translation of the Calvinist liturgy of John Knox, and Carswell's introduction contains an attack on the secular traditions and legends that had entertained so many generations of men, and dominated the repertoire of poet and story-teller. While feudalism was playing its part in destroying the patriarchal society of Gaeldom, Calvinism took its first steps towards destroying the cultural links with Catholic Ireland that had somehow survived for over a thousand years.

To some extent it was Calvinism in the end that fulfilled the dreams of conquest of the Northumbrians, and realised the aspirations of England-loving Edgar's sister. For the conflict between two ethnic groups was fought with new weapons once the printing press had been invented and the Bible was translated into the vernacular. In Scotland the Catholic religion was abolished by Act of Parliament in 1560. The Liturgy of John Knox was printed in Gaelic in 1567. Metrical versions of the psalms followed, while Calvin's Catechism was published in Gaelic in 1631. But the Bible itself, which it was the principal objective of the Reformers to make available to Christians in the vernacular, was withheld from the Gaels in their own tongue. The complete translation was not published, in fact, until the nineteenth century. The very king to whom the authorised version of the English Bible is dedicated is the man who authorised the indiscriminate massacre of Celtic peoples and the resettlement of their lands by English speakers. But the new weapon probably proved more effective in the long run than the old. One of the most literate peoples in Europe was reduced to almost total illiteracy.

The statutes of Iona formulate this policy clearly. In 1609 King James launched an expedition which inveigled a number of chiefs on board a ship upon the pretence that they were to listen to a sermon from a bishop. They were carried to the mainland and imprisoned, and only obtained their freedom by signing the statutes of Iona. These provided that masterless vagabonds were to be expelled from the Hebrides, beggars to be treated as thieves. The greater number of Gaels could by this time be fitted into either category. Bards were to be first placed in the stocks and then driven from the country; a measure that struck at the popular culture of the Gaels, even if it was not aimed to destroy Gaelic literature and learning. These were perhaps more effectively undermined by the provision that the eldest sons of the aristocracy were to be sent to receive an English education in the Lowlands. For this measure was calculated to create a separate class of alien landowners over the Gaelic peasantry of the Highlands.

It succeeded ultimately, but not immediately. For centuries the Celtic peoples of Britain and Ireland had profited by the fact that the English-speaking peoples were as disunited as themselves. The intensification of an anti-Celtic policy was made possible by the union of the English and Scottish crowns in 1603. When the rule of Charles I was rejected both in Edinburgh and in London by his English subjects, he turned increasingly to his Celtic subjects for support. He did so unwillingly and after fatal delays, so that he earned the greatest opprobrium from the English with the minimum of advantage from his Celtic subjects. But this conflict enabled Ireland to set up an independent government for several years before Cromwell took his terrible revenge at Wexford and Drogheda. And in Scotland King Charles gave his commission to one of the greatest soldiers the country has ever produced, and this man became the leader of a Gaelic resistance movement, the first to possess royal authority for over five hundred years.

Montrose was a Lowlander, but the pages of history are filled with the Löhengrin legend come true. He was a leader of genius and he possessed the king's commission, and that was enough. Perhaps the appearance of Iain Lom Macdonald as his accredited bard is less surprising in the circumstances of the time than the emergence of Montrose himself. Iain Lom descended from the first lord of the Isles and he was a Catholic and he identified himself in searing poetry with the dispossessed Macdonalds, the Iro-Scottish culture and the proscribed religion. He celebrated the victories of Montrose and lashed his opponents with anathema. Above all, he witnessed the defeat of the Campbells and the occupation of their lands, and was pitiless in his exultation. When Montrose was finally defeated and betrayed, Iain Lom composed his most famous cry of bitterness.

The statutes of Iona, in fact, had been followed by a Gaelic renaissance. This may have been due partly to the failure of the Stewarts to maintain good relations with their English subjects, and consequently to pursue their anti-Celtic policies. But until the Gaelic aristocracy were anglicised, it was natural that they should have continued to patronise their own culture, and this now blossomed in the pibroch compositions of the MacCrimmons and in the new poetic forms that Iain Lom Macdonald and Mary Macleod popularised. Another bard did lament at the death of Rory Macleod of Dunvegan in 1626 that the last of patrons had died in that ancient centre. But the MacVurich scholar of the day was still using the ancient Irish script in his chronicle of the Montrose wars, while the bards experimented in new forms and the pipes were made the instrument for a more sophisticated music than any had attempted for them before. If the writing was on the wall, its lettering was not very large.

The Gaelic links with Europe had never been altogether severed, and in the seventeenth century they were strengthened. The Reformation led to an exodus of men of religion and learning, many of whom carried muniments with them. The largest collection of these were deposited at the Scots College in Paris, where they survived until the French Revolution. Other Scottish centres were established at Valladolid in Spain, and in Rome. But an altogether different kind of link was established with Europe by the mercenary regiments that the Stewart kings allowed men to recruit from the Gaels of Scotland and Ireland to fight in continental wars. Mackay's Regiment is the most famous of these, partly because it possessed the only regimental chronicler in the entire annals of the Thirty Years War, and partly because its men earned such fame by their courage. These men were Protestants, fighting for Lutheran kings, while opposed to them were innumerable Gaels fighting in the Catholic cause. It was in Germany that the Scottish Gael was first depicted in his Highland dress. It was here, too, that Gaels destroyed the monastery and library of Würzburg which their forebears had created nearly a thousand years earlier.

Mackay's Regiment, first recruited in 1626, is the precursor

14

of the 'family' regiments of a later century. The survival of the clan system made such a system of recruitment possible, and it might be thought that the survival of a clan spirit made it easy. But evidence for this is by no means certain. Mackay's clansmen were by this time vassals in a hierarchy of sub-infeudation. The relationship as Martin described it in the Hebrides later in the century might be a kindly one. But it contained the sanction of absolute power. The fact that the Scottish Government issued instructions for rounding up deserters from the regiment and drafting them into another one proves that some men attempted to escape. When Mackay had bled his own lands of their young men, he raised them in England and tried to obtain permission to recruit in Ireland as well. This is the beginning of the commerce which traded peasants for cash as cannon-fodder, and dressed the transaction in the colours of patriotism and family attachment. Many Gaels settled in Europe with distinction, but the overwhelming majority of them were just left to fight on until they died or were disabled.

But this military connection with the Continent was one of the decisive elements of the revolution of 1688 that turned the Stewarts off the throne. For William of Orange was able to bring his own British troops under a General Mackay whom he made his commander-in-chief in Scotland, so that his usurpation did not have the appearance of a foreign invasion. The presence of a Gael as revolutionary leader did not, however, prevent the majority of Highlanders from choosing the Jacobite cause, with all the disastrous consequences that were to follow.

The Stewarts sought, and received, the support of the Gaels of Scotland and Ireland only when they were rejected by the English speakers of these islands. They never identified themselves with Gaelic interests except to serve their own. During the centuries of their rule in Scotland they were either indifferent or hostile to Gaeldom, and the record of their government is outstanding in its enormity, so far as its treatment of a minority ethnic group is concerned. In particular, it is interesting to compare the Stewarts with the Tudors, who continued to patronise their Welsh kinsmen and culture for long after they obtained the English throne. In Scotland the Stewarts were sovereigns of a bi-lingual country, as the Tudors were in England.

The Revolution Settlement of 1688 struck a particularly effective blow at what remained of the religious and cultural connection between Scottish and Irish Gaeldom. Franciscan missions from Ireland had been active in the Hebrides earlier in the century. But now even the Protestant Episcopal Church bowed to the final triumph of Calvinism in Scotland. The owner of the Beaton library, an episcopal minister, was deprived of his living. It was in Ireland that Edward Lhuyd from Oxford met this last representative of the ancient learning, and noted the contents of some of his books. They disappeared without any of the four universities of Scotland exhibiting the least interest in their existence. In Ireland itself, Ulster had been the strongest bastion of Gaeldom when the century opened. By the time it closed, this province within sight of Campbell's kingdom across the water had been replanted with English-speaking Calvinists.

Jacobitism therefore became to a large extent identified with the Catholics, persecuted by Calvinists, who were at the same time the Gaels expropriated by the English speakers. These possessed the apparent advantage that the legitimate sovereign, although in exile, was on their side. The identification of the Stewart cause with the interests of Gaelic society had been expressed in poetry by Iain Lom Macdonald earlier in the century, and it is to be found in the Ross-shire collection of poetry made by Duncan Macrae in 1688. But it received its fullest expression from Alexander Macdonald, a convert to the Catholic faith who personally welcomed Prince Charles Edward in 1745 and who was inspired by this cause to write Scotland's most distinguished Gaelic poetry.

But this identification between the cause of the Stewarts and of Gaeldom proved to be fatal. It brought together the three principal sources of human cruelty, greed, religious intolerance and racial hostility in a policy of genocide in both Ireland and Scotland that gathered momentum throughout the eighteenth century and continued into the present one. In particular, it encouraged the English establishment in Edinburgh to use religious proselytisation as a political weapon. The Society for the Propagation of Christian Knowledge was designed to promote English and Calvinism equally. Highland ministers had no option but to preach to their monoglot congregations in

Gaelic. But they were without education in their own tongue and they expounded from an English Bible. When Samuel Johnson visited Scotland he observed that the Lowlanders were still as ignorant of the Highlands as they were of Borneo and Sumatra: and he stated as a fact that they had denied a Gaelic Bible to the Highlanders deliberately, lest these should possess any monument to their native tongue. By this time the English speech of the Scottish Lowlands, which descends from the northern English of the Northumbrian kingdom, was being called the 'Scots' tongue, while the actual language of the Scots was referred to as 'Irish'.

But there were extensive areas of Gaeldom from which the Catholic religion had disappeared before the eighteenth century and in which Jacobitism never took root. As many Gaels fought for the Hanoverian as for the Jacobite cause at Culloden. The Act proscribing Highland dress and disarming the population was especially insulting to those districts that had sent forces to support the Government, but they suffered no more than insult in the aftermath of the Forty-Five. And it is in some of these areas that the Gaelic way of life can be evaluated best during the century before the Highland clearances.

The population of the Highlands was estimated in 1747 to be about 230,000, which is approximately the number of people living in this half of Scotland today. In the second half of the eighteenth century the population rose steeply, especially in the western Highlands, and there were massive waves of emigration. The exodus to America in particular rose to a peak in 1774 and only declined upon the outbreak of the American War of Independence in the following year. Among the emigrants was John Macrae from Kintail, the only Gaelic bard whose American compositions survive in his country of origin. The most famous of the emigrants were Allan and Flora Macdonald of Kingsburgh, and it may be their story that has helped to give rise to the myth that the flight to America was a consequence of the failure of the Forty-Five. It occurred a generation later and was due to different causes.

The economy of the Highlands was, in fact, predominantly pastoral and based upon the export of cattle. It could not support the population increase that occurred, although the introduction of the potato in the second half of the century helped to ease the food problem.

This was due partly to the paucity of natural resources, but it was also caused largely by the structure of society in the Highlands. In the eighteenth century this was still enmeshed in the tribal framework upon which a feudal system of landowner-ship had been imposed. 'This is truly the patriarchal life,' as Samuel Johnson observed in 1773; 'this is what we came to find.' It remained, rigid and archaic, an anachronism in the times in which he lived. The only recent development was that the patriarch, stripped of his local jurisdiction after Culloden, was ceasing to be a Gaelic tribal father and becoming trans-formed into an English absentee landlord.

Beneath the feudal superiors of the Highland estates lived the leaseholders, generally known as tacksmen from the most usual form of title by which they held their land. The tacksmen gener-ally sprang from cadet branches of the chief's own family, and they frequently provided the officers in the Highland regiments, and the factors of a chief's estate. These were the men who earned such compliments abroad as those of Daniel Defoe, who found them 'as polite and as finished gentlemen as any from other countries, or even among our own'. At home they might live in a low thatched house without modern windows or chimneys, but many of them were travelled and well educated, and they helped to maintain the standards of the small rural societies in which they spent the greater part of their lives. It was from the ranks of the tacksmen that some of the best ministers were recruited, so that the first published collection of Highland airs in 1784 evolved from the love of music shared by tacksman and minister near Cape Wrath.

But the position of the tacksmen was being debated before 1730, and as the century of improvement advanced, criticism of them increased. Too many of them did not engage in agricul-ture at all, but lived upon the labour of sub-tenants who were compelled to give almost unlimited periods of servile labour in return for their own holdings. The money spent on travel and education might contribute to the grace of rural life, but it did not help to improve cultivation, when this alone could solve the problems of increasing population.

Nevertheless, some tacksmen did engage efficiently in local

agriculture and husbandry, and one of them was described in fascinating detail by a Gaelic monoglot among his own sub-tenants. It is perfectly clear from Rob Donn's portrait of the little world of Iain Mac Eachainn that the old order could be economically viable as well as an extremely happy way of life even to the poorest members of the community. Rob Donn's record of a conversation between the tacksman's two daughters about the relative pleasures of that life and the amenities of Lowland towns tells us that this topic was not discussed only by outsiders.

Their father engaged in the cattle trade which formed the crucial economic link between Highlands and Lowlands, and he was accompanied on his droving expeditions by the chief's son and by the sub-tenant's son, Rob Donn, who composed his unique portrait of their lives.

Cattle represented the principal capital of a Highland estate. Every peasant upon it, whatever the nature of his holding, possessed cattle. He never ate beef, but reared his animals for sale, to pay his rent and to buy the few essentials that required cash payment. On an average he sold about a fifth of his stock every year, and it was generally a tacksman such as Iain Mac Eachainn who, acting as factor for the chief and as broker to his tenantry, drove the cattle to the great fairs of Falkirk and Crieff. The Highland peasant was as completely dependent on the whim of chief and tacksman in marketing the product of his labour as he was for the privilege of living on the estate at all.

He did not live in a village, in the Lowland sense, but in a township that consisted of scattered houses among strips of fields that were used for arable or pasture and reallocated among the members of the township from time to time. As the population rose, the share of each member of a township was bound to diminish, and there were members of it who possessed little more than the hut they occupied. But beyond the township stretched the great hill grazings where the animals were pastured during the summer months, and where even a tacksman's daughter did not scorn to live the simple life of the shieling, tending the cattle and making butter and cheese. When they returned at harvest time, the pastures around the township had enjoyed a respite from grazing, and might provide enough food for the animals that had not been sent south to be sold. But this was the weakest part of the Highland economy. A rising population required an increase in the cattle stocks, and the larger the stock, the greater the danger of disaster in a severe winter. Although the introduction of turnip and artificial grass spread throughout the second half of the eighteenth century, there could be little attention to the winter feeding of animals in those parts of the Highlands in which the people could hardly grow enough to feed themselves. But one economic fact served to support the precarious Highland economy from without. The price of cattle rose consistently throughout the century. At least the cash return for the animals that were driven south was relatively secure.

There were Highland landlords who cared for the welfare of their dependants, as well as those whose only concern was to squeeze as much money as possible out of their estates to spend abroad. There were tacksmen who ran their townships efficiently and with an eye to improvements, as well as those who lived idly upon the proceeds of servile labour. But the social order contained too large a superstructure for the resources of the land to support. It was too rigid to permit the efficiency required to solve its problems. There was not enough capital to finance improvements, and too much of it was drained out of the Highlands altogether. The population rise led inevitably to the massive emigrations of the 1770s.

Some landlords and tacksmen sought to obstruct these emigrations. Others assisted their peasantry to leave, and even accompanied them to their settlements in North America. Some Gaels, such as Rob Donn, saw the crisis as one that a little patience and sound planning would solve. Others like his neighbour Donald Matheson and the Hebridean John Mac-Codrum decided that the only solution was to emigrate *en masse*, and build a new society beyond the Atlantic. What might have occurred if the outbreak of the American War of Independence had not put a stop to emigration in 1775 is hard to surmise.

It was now that landlords began to revolutionise the structure of Highland townships, and to abolish the communal system of run-rig in favour of independent peasant holdings. In areas of large and rising population these holdings were often extremely small. But at least they became the exclusive responsibility of the individual crofter, and he still possessed his share of cattle in the hill pastures, while he was able increasingly to feed his family on potatoes. The fatal flaw in the rearrangement was that the peasant obtained no security of tenure such as the Swedish peasant had always enjoyed, and much of the peasantry of Europe had by this time obtained. The Gael could still be evicted at the whim of his feudal superior, and his rent could be raised as soon as he was seen to have improved his land.

At the same time, a change in the structure of animal husbandry began to occur in the parts of the Highlands nearest to the plains, and to extend gradually to the remotest parts of Gaeldom. It substituted sheep farming for the old cattle economy.

There had always been sheep among the horses and goats and dogs of the old run-rig townships. It has been estimated that there were generally as many sheep as cattle beasts. But the sheep were of a small and peculiar breed, kept mainly for their wool and to be milked. They were not marketed like the cattle, and they were left to fend for themselves in the routine based on the harvesting of crops for human consumption and on the herding of the cattle in their summer and winter pastures. The five hundred pages of Rob Donn's poetry reveal a society almost as closely related to cattle as mountain Lapps to reindeer: he hardly mentioned the existence of sheep.

But south-country farmers began to cast speculative eyes on the vast pastures of the Highlands. They offered landlords a higher rent than the old economy could provide. Theoretical economists applauded the change as a contribution to progress in an area that had contributed little hitherto except men to win Britain's wars. And there was an ecological factor to support the economic one.

One of the ways in which Highland landlords had been able to obtain sums of capital at short notice in the past had been by the sale of forests. Since the seventeenth century the felling of trees had gathered momentum, especially when the use of timber for smelting was forbidden in England owing to the ravages it had caused to English woods. The iron ore was carried by ship into Highland sea lochs, and here whole forests were destroyed for the most wasteful of all purposes—to be used as a smelting fuel. In the Spey valley, great areas of forest were destroyed likewise by the York Building Society.

But the areas that had lain under trees for so many years preserved a residual fertility that enabled plant life to grow where the forests stood no longer. It was this that enabled the landlords to secure one further cash crop before the land was finally ruined. They did it when they placed upon the old forest lands the one animal which could tear up the new growth and destroy the remaining fertility of the hills. But Professor Nassau Senior wrote from Oxford that it was the proper course. Improving farmers promoted the change and offered the high rents. Financial need advised acceptance. A whole literature agreed that this was the march of progress, at last embracing the backward Highlands: an English literature, indeed, but nobody except a Gael knew what Gaelic literature had to say about it.

What Gaelic literature had to say was what is now generally agreed to be the truth of the matter. The coming of the sheep involved the expulsion of a minority ethnic group from the country they had inhabited since time immemorial, without the slightest consultation, and frequently with little warning. Not only were the hills on which they pastured their cattle in the summer required by the sheep farmers, but the valleys that they cultivated were needed equally for the wintering of the sheep. These valleys consisted in many cases of relatively poor ground, but they had been cultivated intensively for centuries, and consequently they too possessed a residual fertility for the sheep to destroy. Today the ratio of sheep to cattle is sometimes as much as seventy to one in areas in which it was once one to one. The full devastating effect of the coming of the sheep has now materialised in one of the most mutilated regions of Europe.

The Highland clearances did not lead immediately to depopulation. The population continued to rise in Gaeldom throughout the first half of the nineteenth century. The evicted peasantry, torn from the only way of life they knew, were driven into overcrowded communities on barren coastlines. Often they had to build new homes without access to the necessary materials, such as timber for roof and doors. They had to dig ground that had never been worked before, since it was utterly unsuitable for cultivation. People who had never been on the sea were compelled to take up fishing without equipment. In these centres of galloping destitution the Gaels saw their land being exploited by foreigners who spoke a different language. The policy of genocide could scarcely have been carried farther.

A number of landlords protested. Sir John Sinclair of Ulbster in Caithness, one of the most enlightened agriculturists of his generation, expostulated in 1791: 'the first thing that is done is to drive away all the present inhabitants. The next is to introduce a shepherd and a few dogs.' David Stewart of Garth in Perthshire published a book in 1822 condemning this policy in detail. The Duke of Argyll consistently opposed measures which deprived the people of the Highlands of any part in the development of their own land. And *The Times* of London was sufficiently well informed a hundred years ago to take its views from Highlanders, rather than from men who had come to the Highlands to make their own fortunes while they preached the gospel of economic progress. But the logic of the great sheep farms proved unassailable, and opposition to it was described as the selfish attempt of the tacksmen to preserve their idle, privileged position. The improvers even claimed that they were acting in the interests of the evicted peasantry, and that their victims were grateful.

By the end of the nineteenth century a new interest in the Highland estates had been created by the growing enthusiasm of the very rich for grouse shooting, deer stalking and salmon fishing. This enthusiasm gave a fresh value to the devastated terrain, and brought new proprietors who generally had even less interest in the social life of the region than the old. The old hierarchy which had preserved some sort of connection between a patriarchal chief, his junior relatives among the tacksmen, and his clan or children, was finally dismantled. The landlord might be as enlightened as the Duke of Westminster, but between him and the Lowland sheep farmers, and the most destitute peasantry in Europe whose land they owned, there was less connection than between a Russian nobleman, his estate managers and his serfs.

In 1886 and 1892 Parliament intervened decisively in the Highlands by passing the Crofters' Acts. For the first time the Gaelic peasantry were given security of tenure by statute in the limited areas of their homeland that they still occupied. They could no longer be evicted at the whim of their feudal superiors. But neither could they buy and sell among themselves and thus evolve holdings of a size suited to twentieth-century farming requirements. The amount of hill grazing available to them on the sporting estates has been progressively increased. New holdings have been made available, first under the auspices of the Congested Districts Board, and subsequently by the Scottish Department of Agriculture. Nevertheless it has proved that the measures designed by Parliament for the benefit of the crofters has created a system as rigid and obstructive to progress as the old run-rig system of the eighteenth century. It has frustrated every attempt to solve the Highland problem during this century.

The Gael has in fact reached the end of the road along which he first began to retreat when Celtic Britain was first invaded by English-speaking settlers over a millennium and a half ago. Just as the Lapps retreated north through Scandinavia until they reached the rim of the Arctic and could go no farther, so the Gaels in Scotland have reached the peripheries of the Atlantic and remain there as a protected species, their affairs ordered for them by strangers with scarcely any reference to their wishes or requirements. The final step in this process was the creation of a Highland Development Board having as little connection with Highland society as the American Control Commission of 1945 to the Japanese. The Board may prove as beneficial to Gaeldom as the American Control Commission to Japan, or the Norwegian, Swedish, Finnish or Russian administrations to the Lapps under their control. The relationship is identical. What is different is that the Gaels have a past history, a literature, a connection with the main stream of European civilisation altogether different from the Lapps. Unlike the Japanese, they were not defeated by a foreign power. They have simply been squeezed by degrees out of a country which they once owned, and their language reduced from one of the most literate in Europe to the status of a redundant peasant dialect.

Today there are about 3,000 people who can still be said to belong to the Lappish culture and ethnic group in Finnish Lapland, out of a population of nearly a quarter of a million. In the Scottish Highlands the population is about the same, but the Gaelic element has not yet been reduced to 3,000. Some people believe that it would be a disaster and a disgrace to our civilisation if this should occur, and that even at this late hour there is no reason why the Highlands should not be recovered culturally, ecologically and economically by their native inhabitants, and under their own control.

Ecology of Land Use
in the
Highlands and Islands

F. Fraser Darling

Ecology of Land Use in the Highlands and Islands

I
What is Ecology?

Ecology is generally defined as the study of the organism in relation to its environment, of the relations of organisms between themselves and between different species. It is possible to infer from this definition that ecology is concerned with process, but it is not emphasised, whereas process is of the very quality of ecology. Baldly put, ecology studies causes and consequences in the world of living things, but in practice we find ourselves up against complexity, and causes and consequences rarely present themselves sharp and clear. Complexity of biological communities of plants and animals and their inter-relationships makes for reserve in the ecologist's pronouncements: he tends to speak of influences, he deals with *nuance* in animate nature, and socially he almost invariably seeks time before being definite about his interpretations. This is one reason why the ecologist has been late to come to the council table in governmental administrative problems. Indeed, we are at a point where the notion of ecology has captured public imagination and the reticent student of this science is being called upon to fulfil his social role.

The social role is a significant phrase: ecology had of necessity to cast its net wide, observing the dynamic inter-relationships of communities of different living things, whereas the tendency of so much scientific research has been towards specialisation, knowing more and more about less and less. Ecology, looking wide, could become so diffuse as to mean little and that would never do. The science was first conceived in terms of animal communities, but the botanists really developed it. Animal ecology came later and when herbivorous animals were studied an integrated and single ecology was imperative. It is interesting to note that a scientific journal of *applied* ecology has reached only its fourth volume. Ecologists studied nature, or thought they did, and most of them fought a losing battle against the biological fact that man was part of nature; and what is now becoming apparent, there are not many parts of the earth's surface that have not been influenced in some way or other by the presence of man at some time or other.

Now, most of us are ready to include man as one of the species in our observational study of communities of plants and animals, however disturbing and complicating he may be to a nice little bit of natural history. The term natural history is an old one with a connotation which may have tended to degenerate in common parlance to 'nature and all that'. But the ecologist finds that natural history is still history and though political history seems far away from it and social history too full of its urgent problems to bother about natural history, the three histories have numerous links with each other and are, in more ways than we realised, interdependent. What we have come to call the problem of the Highlands and Islands is a fragment of history which lends itself particularly to the ecological approach in its examination and attempted solution.

The word ecology has obvious links with economics through the derivation from the Greek root of *oikos*, the home. If economics deals with income and expenditure symbolised in money, ecology deals with income and expenditure in terms of energy flux in communities of animals and plants. Between the two there is the matter of wealth: economists today are tending to move away from the notion of wealth in money terms, by which they have been too long obsessed, to see wealth as availability of resources, often natural and renewable organic resources, and rate of flow within the economic system. At this stage economists and ecologists are coming quite close together and seem in good shape to be able to help each other in a particular socio-ecological economic problem so well typified by that of the Highlands and Islands. Economic system and ecosystem have characteristics in common which should be comprehensible to men of sense and sensibility.

The ecosystem 'digs' its wealth primarily from sunlight, water and carbon dioxide, providing the basis of organic compounds through the phenomenon of photosynthesis. Inorganic nitrogen, phosphorus and potassium as well as several more elements are taken up by plants as inorganic salts. Even the most theoretical economics is nonsense without the biochemical basis. From this point we can go forward to find out what the Highlands and Islands have in the way of climate and geological character to supplement the fundamental gifts of air, water and light.

II
The Climate

There is no need to go into detail: the climate is cool and wet. The winters are not in general cold, especially on the Atlantic shore and zero temperatures Fahrenheit are not common even in the Central Highlands. Rainfall in the whole Highland area varies from around 45 inches to over 150 inches deep in western glens. Considerable variations in rainfall can occur within a few miles. The summers are cool and yet I have known occasional days of 93° F. in western deer forests. Winds are common and strong. The North-West Highlands are the windiest area of Europe. As south-west winds are commonest they tend to carry rain, yet the rain is rarely of such force as to exceed one or two inches a day even in the wettest parts. May is generally the driest month.

III
The Bare Bones of Geology

The Highlands and Islands are mainly composed of old or very old rocks. The Outer Hebrides, Coll and Tiree and the north-western mainland parishes are of Archaean gneiss, the oldest rock of all. It is very hard, and glaciation has in no way smoothed its extremely rough physiography. Torridonian Sandstone in much of Wester Ross and some of Sutherland has produced spiry hills, such as Suilven, Slioch and An Teallach; Cambrian quartzite, of extreme hardness, often caps the Torridonian Hills. Undifferentiated Metamorphic schists of varying hardness cover great areas of the mainland Highlands; Granite occurs sporadically as isolated bosses sometimes 20 miles across, as in Skye, Morvern, Lochaber, Rannoch and Loch Etive. Lochnagar is an eastern boss of granite. The Cuillin Hills, part of Rhum and part of Ardnamurchan are of the hard igneous rock gabbro. Much of Mull, Morvern and Skye are of Tertiary Basalt, a young volcanic rock a mere 30 million years old. All of these rocks except the Tertiary Basalt are acid rocks short of basic chemicals and in the Highland situation they yield very little soil. The basalt does not reach in general as high as the other rocks and can break down to good brown soil. Other formations to be found in small areas are Cambrian Limestone along the line of that geological expression, the Moine Thrust, between Durness and Loch Slapin in Skye; Metamorphic Limestone occurs in strips, in Lismore, Lochaber and south of the Great Glen. There is more of it in Perthshire. Soil-making, base-rich serpilaceous grits run across the Highlands through Breadalbane, which make Ben Lawers and the other Breadalbane hills a wonderful country for the botanist and the sheep farms are good. Old Red Sandstone, the basis of Orkney's fertility, is found in part of the Great Glen, in Cowal and southern Kintyre. Old Red Sandstone reaches down the eastern side of the Highlands through Caithness, Sutherland and Eastern Ross, and provides the rich farming country of eastern Scotland. Graphite schist and slate appear at Ballachulish and at some of the inner Argyll islands. Cornbrash, Lias and Cretaceous rock appear fragmentarily being scarcely more than of academic importance.

IV

Masking Influences on Geology

This bare geology of the Highland region is sometimes masked incrementally or detrimentally as far as conditions for plant growth are concerned. The tops of the hills may be bare and rocky or they may carry surfaces of fine gravel and even true soil which are free of peat. The herbage on such areas may not be profuse by agricultural or woodland standards because of the elevation and exposure at anything up to 4,400 feet in a very windy part of the world. The alpine herbage may also be unavailable to such mammals and birds as may wish to eat it, but the vegetation itself has its roots against the rock and by the solvent action of the root tips extracts its mineral nutrition directly, and the water supply is the direct rainfall or flushes out of the hill itself, untainted by the acid peat which has formed on the lower slopes of the hills. It is a fact of plant physiology that unless plants get an adequate mineral nutrition they cannot synthesise protein efficiently into their tissues. The alpine vegetation is indeed more nutritious weight for weight than that of the areas covered with blanket peat, and it is eagerly sought by deer and sheep which will move up to it whenever the going is good.

The flora of the peat slopes and bogs is sedgy in general character, as would be expected in such highly acid conditions. The growing season is short and protein synthesis is poor. The roots of the plants do not in general reach the bedrock. Small and rather less acid bogs of predominantly *Eriophorum* sedge do provide an early bite in late February and March for sheep and deer, but on the whole these slopes of blanket peat are the poorest grazing, often dominated by deer's hair sedge, *Scirpus caespitosus*. When we consider the history of the Highland region we shall find that in the past the slopes of blanket bog were the areas where forest of some kind was found, even if only of the poorest scrub birch at the less hospitable points, but often of Scots pine and on the lower north side of sheltered glens even oak forest was found. The roots of these trees went below the peat. The present grazing slopes of blanket peat represent a degraded vegetation expressing less than the potential of even such essentially poor ground.

The floors of glens are of two kinds: the typical U-shaped glacial valley has been scoured by the ice and little alluvium has gathered. There may be small patches along the burn or river and these will grow grass; such grass patches are almost invariably overgrazed by sheep or deer unless the sheep are driven up the hill each evening as a routine of husbandry. These small patches of grass in U-shaped glens become infestation points unless the sheep are kept off them at night and in the early morning. The second type of glen floor is called a strath. The river through time has brought down such quantity of moraine and soil that with the slackening of speed of the water the material has been deposited eventually to form a more or less flat expanse as the floor of the glen. The river meanders, forms oxbows and changes its course from time to time to the confusion of landowners who have the river as boundary. Straths can carry full-scale farms or at least be the arable and low ground pastures of sheep farms on the steeper slopes. Again, the accumulation of soil in the straths masks the true nature of the solid geology.

A further example of this is on some of the seaward-lying land of Lewis where the peat is not unduly thick over glacier boulder till which overlies the Archaean Gneiss. Much of this land was common grazings of the townships and the peat had been cut for fuel for many years, laying bare the boulder till, which was left naturally to green over in its own time, no effort being made to level the surface. The West Highland Survey, of which I was Director, recommended that these 'skinned lands' should be bulldozed into pastures, for in 1944 and subsequently the heavy earth-moving equipment was already in the island making the Stornoway airfield. It would have been a simple thing to get this work going and heavy dressings of phosphate applied to raise the productivity of these common grazings. It is regrettable to state that the Department of Agriculture got around to this way of thinking long after the heavy equipment had left the island. However, we must be thankful that the *quondam* poverty-stricken skinned lands have at last been seen as a potential and positive natural resource which needed only the application of the modern technology now available to make them into the productive grazings they are now becoming increasingly.

Lastly, the *machairs* of the Outer Isles and of a few places on the mainland shore show the masking influence on bed rock of calcareous shell sand thrown up the long beaches by the ocean and blown inland by the winds on to the platforms of gneiss at the sea's edge. The shell sand made a lime-rich soil landward of the dunes of a quarter mile to a mile across.

V

An Ecologically Adapted Subsistence Culture

The *machair* provided arable and pasture for the Outer Hebridean townships. The religious and intellectual cultures of East and West Hebridean townships may have been the same, but

34

their husbandries were quite different. While Hebrideans were dependent on their environment for their whole subsistence a very beautiful ecological adaptation to circumstances took place and is worth recounting, as it is also necessary to state that when a culture is beginning to break down, its disciplines of existence also begin to fail and the empirical conservation of habitat at which the people had arrived breaks down into exploitative attrition of natural resources.

The Outer Hebrideans grew primitive six-rowed barley or bere as their bread corn on their arable strips of the *machair*. Quite empirically these people had gained the knowledge that the barley for bread grown on the *machair* needed the best of their husbandry. In the first place the ocean cast up periodically on their beaches vast quantities of *Laminaria* seaweed or tangle which is relatively rich in potash, an element singularly lacking in the shell sand soils. The tangle was carted on to the *machair* land in huge quantities as manure. It was a principal task after each winter storm.

Barley as bread corn should have the highest possible protein content, whereas the East Coast farmer growing barley for distilling or malting works for low protein and high carbohydrate content. The Hebridean knew nothing about protein but so complex and little understood is the empirical process in human cultures, we think it remarkable and extraordinary that these people should have arrived so surely at fitness of method. The limited animal manure available was beautifully conserved. Divots of turf were laid on the floor of the byre in late fall when the milk cow was brought in. The turf as a base helped to soak up the urine. All manner of rough vegetation—though there was then little bracken—was used as litter put down on the accumulating dung. Even the human excrement was not lost, for the women went to the byre and the men to the stable. (Here was no squalor; indeed, the West Highlander hearing of water closets inside houses was shocked. 'Are they still babies, that they must remain in the house?')

The barley ground was carefully worked by the *cas-chrom*, the manure of the winter being dug in. The thatch from the house, if it needed renewal, would also be used as manure for the soot content was nitrogenous. The barley had had the best a subsistence husbandry could give and that without waste. The

35

short-strawed crop did not go down under rain and wind as would a farmer's two-rowed barley given nitrogenous fertiliser. Barley bread from the *machair* as one of the staples of life gave the Hebridean the best teeth in Europe.

One more example of empirical arriving at truth, long before the physiology of mineral nutrition was opened up by John Boyd Orr at Aberdeen, was in grinding up the bones from the ling fishery. This was done by women, the *cosnaiche cnàmhan*, and the bone meal was fed to the cow in the winter. The *machair* soil is deficient in phosphorus however rich it may be in calcium, and the cattle may still be seen chewing bones they find cast on the shore. The husbandry was ecologically integrated and a naturally poor terrain was made fruitful by gathering through labour the gifts of the ocean.

The Eastern Hebridean coasts have no *machair*; they are often steep and are much indented by the sea. The soil, if there is any, is peaty. No casts of tangle are deposited on the beaches. Here the soil must often be built up, the extreme example being at Manish, on the east coast of Harris, where terraced patches a few yards long and a few feet wide grew both potatoes and straw crops well within my own memory. The seaweed of the inlets is wrack (*Fucus*) and this must be cut, brought ashore to dry a little and then be carried up on the back by creel and head-strap. Different methods dictated by environment, but still the empirical approximation to a sound use of natural resources on a continuing non-exploitative basis. Elsewhere on the peaty soils the potatoes were grown on lazy beds (*feannagan*), a series of ridges and furrows which provided drainage.

Another factor of importance in conservation of the Hebridean and West Highland habitat was the close understanding by the people of carrying capacity of the land for grazing. Each croft carried a *souming*, a tally of stock based on the grazing of a cow. Soumings varied from place to place, depending on the human density, but the total tally of stock for any given area could not vary. Thus was prevented the overgrazing of the tender grassland of the *machair*, dunes and adjacent moors. The tally could be varied in content by equating the various classes of stock (*coilpeachadh*). A constable elected by the township was responsible for discipline. This was good native democracy. The Napier Commission Report of 1886 changed the order from an elected constable to a grazing committee, which has not been so successful, though perhaps we should remember the crofting life and communalistic pattern was breaking down anyway and as I have said, ecological adaptations to living successfully in any habitat tend to fall away when the discipline of nature is discarded without thoughtful replacement. Overgrazing has been common for years throughout the crofting areas of the Highlands, to the further detriment of the habitat. A good sheep farmer who reaps the full consequences of any foolish action is particularly careful to keep his sheep stock just below an estimated carrying capacity.

Unfortunately, subsistence cultures are brittle, and small changes, as they may appear, exert wide consequences. That of the old Hebridean crofting life was dependent on a few staples of food. During the population explosion in the Highlands in the nineteenth century there was too much dependence on the potato, a crop which, by its disease failure and intrinsic nutritional inadequacy, gravely failed the Highlander. The advent of steam-baked white bread caused a further descent and the ling fishery failed at the time of the First World War. Even milk became scarce except in summer, so that at present caries are as common in the Hebrides as elsewhere in Scotland. Social anthropology and ecology are inevitably mixed as culture and habitat interact.

A History of Devastation

The Highlands and Islands of Scotland have suffered for some hundreds of years by being a second-class neighbourhood of little importance to a dominant South. When southern government ultimately and belatedly accepted its administrative responsibility for the Highlands, the patterns of administration were not those adapted from the indigenous culture but were those of a quite foreign and in general urban culture. Before then, the Highlands after subjection were treated, as were colonial areas at a later date, as a ground for exploitation of such resources as there were.

The coastal areas of the Highlands had suffered even as early as Viking times when the woodlands were burned either in offence or defence during raids. Then the Wolf of Badenoch in the Central Highlands, a terrible destroyer; General Monk did not like forest either, for it hid 'rebels and mossers'. Even the deep hatred of the wolf as a wild creature caused forest to be burned to help in extirpation. The seventeenth century saw Highland forests, particularly on the West Coast, being felled to provide heat for the smelting of iron, the ore being shipped from England to the long sea lochs. There are places called Furneis (furnace) far up Loch Fyne and on the north shore of Loch Maree where there was good oak forest. The Rising of 1715 broke the Highlands; the Forty-Five was really little more than an irritation to the government though it gave a good excuse for finishing off what had begun after the Fifteen, i.e. a systematic exploitation of natural resources and a change of order. The forests took another blow and after the Forty-Five the newly greened hills after the fellings were new country for the Southern Upland sheepmasters who made epic journeys northwards. The more remote forests now met their ignominious end, to be destroyed to provide more sheep grazing. Today we prize our fragments of the Caledonian Forest as National Nature Reserves, and one or two more are in the careful hands of proud private owners who are doing a splendid work of conservation. Two centuries of extractive sheep farming in Highland hills have reduced a rich natural resource to a state of desolation, and sheep farming itself is declining and was sustained for a long time only by subsidisation.

Even the Hebrides and Inner Isles held woodland in the long past, but human occupation before and since Megalithic times made heavy demands if only for fuel. The last fragment of hazel scrub in the Hebrides is round a narrow inlet on the east side of South Uist, certainly no more than an acre in extent. Hazel scrub, like *maqui*, can still be found in Mull and Morvern, and there is even a tiny patch in Ardnamurchan.

These two centuries of constant grazing have prevented regeneration of all woody growth other than some birch which has persisted in some of the deer forests. The Highlands then are a deforested country, which has suffered all that a country of steep slopes, acid rocks and high rainfall can suffer after such an event.

VI
The Course of Reduction in Fertility

Peat is no new thing in the Highlands, but after the last Ice Age and a period of tundra conditions, a forest of birch, pine and hazel grew in what is called the Boreal period from about 8000 B.C. This is known as the Lower Forest of Scotland. It spread to Shetland and St Kilda. Then followed a period of wet and cold which allowed dense growth of sphagnum moss, cotton grass (*Eriophorum*) and crowberry (*Empetrum*), but was too cold to allow decomposition of these plants. They formed a rising layer of peat which destroyed the forest. The warmer but still wet Atlantic period followed from around 6000 to 4000 B.C. and produced a new forest of birch and pine, though peat was still forming in places. In the cooler and drier sub-Boreal period which followed until 500 B.C., hardwood trees appeared and pine and birch reached as high as 3,200 feet on Scottish hills.

The Megalithic immigrants to the islands had now arrived and raised such monuments as Callanish in Lewis and Stenness in Orkney. Climate is no set piece, for a retrograde trend set in just before the Christian era. Peat formation began afresh and killed vast areas of the higher forest. This is the time of the formation of blanket bog we know today, except that its extent was not so great as now. When Sir John Matheson excavated Callanish in 1857–58 he removed a depth of 5 feet of peat. The Tertiary Basalt of the Inner Hebrides having produced a more basic soil was able to oxidize more of the decaying mossy vegetation and peat deposition was prevented much better than on the older, more acid rocks. Though forest undoubtedly receded over much of Scotland, an immense amount persisted, possibly 50 per cent of the land surface so remaining. Reduction since then to at most one-twentieth of that figure is entirely the result of human activity.

Development of blanket bog was outlined by G. K. Fraser at the Macaulay Soil Research Institute, Aberdeen (1943). The rainfall leaches out the plant nutrients and there is development of acid-loving plants. Fraser said, 'The relative shallowness of blanket moss is due in large measure to the fact that the surface of the peat is soon raised above the range of the mineral

39

nutrients.' This is a statement of fundamental importance implying that the blanket peat flora does not reach the stratum of mineral decomposition. In short, no basic salts are brought into biological circulation and growth may be so slow that even deposition of peat is insufficient to replace erosion. Acres of sterile gullies and haggs are common on the middle heights of Highland hills.

Here we are at a point where we should like to know much more than we do about the circulatory system of the natural forests of the Highlands, the differences between nutrient flow of oak, birch and pine on soils which are in general acidic. Since I wrote the chapter on ecology of land use in *West Highland Survey* the Nature Conservancy has been concerned with such fundamental studies and the work of McVean and Radcliffe and of Ovington has been published. The workers at the Merlewood Research Institute of the Nature Conservancy have also worked on the invertebrate animals concerned in the conservation of organic detritus of woodlands to simpler forms for the ultimate recycling as plant nutrients. McVean has emphasised the incidence of fire in the pine forests and the subsequent regeneration. All of them have confirmed by elegant experimentation what was in some sense adumbrated in earlier years following the work on forest soils by the Scandinavians such as Romell, Börnebusch and Overgaarde-Nielsen.

Examination of forest soils and forest fauna and flora in macroscopic fashion in the spirit of ecological reconnaissance has impressed on me a fact of great scientific and philosophical beauty: that even with essentially poor geological conditions of acid rocks and glaciated slopes and not very kind climatic conditions of coolness, cloudiness, high precipitation and windiness, the edaphic array and the regenerative power of the forest represented the development of a state of natural wealth, diversity and energy flow far greater than geology and climate would have indicated.

Brown forest soil is rich and active in that conversion of organic matter is rapid. The nearest approach we have to it in the Highlands is in the very few surviving patches of oak wood, but all deciduous woods tend to bring about this kind of soil in greater or less degree and even in a Highland natural pine wood the peaty, podsolised soil is ameliorated by the interspersion of rowan (*Sorbus*), birch (*Betula*) and willow (*Salix*). The trees get their roots down below the blanket peat and bring up to the leaves the mineral nutrients which have leached from the surface or which are dissolved each season from the rock. See what happens in spring if a birch tree falls: the young leaves are stripped almost immediately by deer or other livestock, for the leaves are mineral rich.

There is a fair amount of defoliation by caterpillars each spring, and the droppings of these creatures are consequently mineral rich and also charged with cellulose-splitting organisms. These droppings are eagerly consumed by earthworms which themselves are preyed upon by soil-living beetles and by birds. The action of the worms and beetles in the forest keep it light and aerated and the circulation I have outlined means that such minerals as are brought from below the blanket peat through the trees are deposited in the field layer as organic detritus which is broken down further to humus and nutrient salts. A wooded island in a loch, which has thereby escaped fire, will be found to have a richer flora than the indurated blanket peat of the land round the loch which is frequently burned. The soil itself will be granular and less rubbery than the blanket peat and a crop of annual plants will be found that ameliorates the soil. It is even possible to find plants, usually considered as lime-loving, growing in old woodland soil overlying such refractory bedrock as Archaean gneiss.

The larger animal life which may feed in part from the plants of the field layer of old forest benefits greatly. An animal as plastic in size as the red deer is a good biological indicator. It is common to say that the red deer have degenerated when present-day antlers are compared with specimens from earlier centuries. The deer themselves have not degenerated (except in so far as importations of foreign blood has damaged the gene pool of the stock), so much as the edaphic conditions of which the deer are a sensitive expression or indicator species. Deer which gain access to old natural forest for some part of the annual feeding cycle enjoy better mineral nutrition than do those existing on the *Scirpus* dominated blanket bog character-istic of so many moors and deer forests.

Reduced to basic ecological and chemical terms, we can see that a country of acid rocks, steep slopes and high rainfall is primarily by nature a cellulose-producing area; in short, timber. Any protein crop is secondary, e.g. a limited number of deer. But what has been attempted through two centuries, with continuing declining success, has been to draw a double protein crop, of mutton and wool, from a degraded vegetation over-lying blanket peat on acid rocks. Such a proposition is not ecologically sound, nor is it good chemistry.

Fire as a coup-de-grâce

Fire used by man has been one of the most potent ecological factors in world history and prehistory in changing the vege-tational face of the earth. Fire created the savannahs of Africa and man made much of it and still does. Man-made fire ex-tended the prairies of the United States beyond their natural bounds. More savannahs not comparable with the African ones for biological productivity have been made more recently in South America. Man-made fire has made a desert of the High-lands from the time the Hallstadt Celts came to the east and the Vikings to the west. The present population grossly misuses fire to produce an early bite of grass.

When an increase in treeless ground has been created and it is decided that is how it is wanted, fire can be used responsibly to preserve the *status quo*. If the geological formation is a good one and the rainfall moderate, the triennial to quinquennial or even decennial use of fire can maintain a vigorous growth of heather which is good food for sheep and grouse. The Yorkshire moors are well maintained by frequent burning; the sheep country of the Southern Uplands of Scotland has withstood a régime of careful burning for 400–500 years, though deterior-ation is now becoming apparent. The Highlands on poorer geological formations have not well endured the two hundred years of too frequent burning, especially since all social discip-line in its use has gone from the crofting areas.

Fire as a clearing agent puts climax vegetation back to a pioneer stage of succession which is much less able to withstand flood and overgrazing. Fire and tooth between them are invincible in preventing regeneration of forest. After fire alone, perhaps once in two centuries, a forest may come back rapidly, but the continual, sometimes annual burning for the early bite pushed many Highland hills back to an unproductive tundra-like condition of *Scirpus* moors. Burning on this principle is an admission of failure in husbandry in that the potential food grown in the previous season has not been eaten and must now be burnt to let the new leaves through. Many herbaceous plants cannot withstand a burning régime so the diversity of the vegetation is impoverished and reduced to a few fire-resistant dominants. The soil, or peat, is laid bare to erosive influences; indeed, I have seen the peat itself burning slowly for weeks when burning has been done too late in a dry spring. The peat when not injured by fire tends to become tough and indurated and water is shed laterally from it, water acid-laden and subjecting lower slopes to frequent baths of carbonic acid.

Burning on crofting grazings is worst where the cattle and sheep ratio has become too wide and grazing is therefore unbalanced. In much earlier days the cattle–sheep ratio was probably around unity. Even at 1:4 a *Holcus–Agrostis–Festuca* sward of grass will persist, especially on Tertiary Basalt. A cattle–sheep ratio of 1:20 is dangerous for the herbage and when one finds parishes with 1:40 and even 1:70 not only the vegetation is ruined but the social state of the people is also in a bad way. This is never sufficiently realised by governments and civil service departments, that economic and social collapse cannot be considered apart from and unconnected with ecological conditions in the habitat.

The spread of bracken in the Highlands is intimately bound up with the practice of burning and particularly overburning. It is perhaps ironical that the discipline of proper rotational burning over perhaps fifteen-year intervals is least observed in the West Highlands where the milder winter climate so greatly favours the growth of bracken. This fern grows best on better drained sites such as old arable land, alluvial pans, talus and drift slopes, and on Tertiary Basalt soils reaches a luxuriance not seen elsewhere. Bracken is properly a fern of light woodland which supplies some shade, but in the West Highlands the general cloudiness is itself shade from the sun, so that bracken may become a climax vegetation of itself.

Burning favours bracken because competition is relieved and a dressing of ash has been appreciated by the fern. Many examples may be seen of bracken colonising to the absolute edge of

43

an earlier burn. Here is a good example of what may be called an ecological vicious circle: unbalanced grazing practices necessitate burning; falling away of social discipline makes for too frequent and uncontrolled burning; and burning greatly favours the spread of bracken. Any remedial answer is not to be found in the head-on approach for much of the ground is too rough for heavy machinery and the terrain is not good for aerial spraying of herbicides. Any cure must start at the causes, pastoral and social.

VII

Erosion

There is a prevalent notion that erosion is something that happens somewhere else rather than in one's own country. Gullying, landslips, scree slopes and blow-outs in dunes and *machair* are 'natural' when they occur at home. Impartial inquiry in the Highlands could scarcely support such a view and we find numerous examples of erosion directly attributable to wrong land use.

Overgrazing is a common cause of setting the conditions for erosion by wind and water, and even frost in the terraces of glacial drift in the Central Highlands. Overgrazing is a prime cause of erosion by wind in dunes and *machair*, and it is again remarkable that the social disciplines of communalistic subsistence life are necessary for conservation of the habitat. Cutting of 'bents', i.e. marram grass (*Psamma*), was prohibited in many communities liable to high winds in the dunes; the consequences of a blow-out are not merely the sterile patches *from* which the dunes have blown, but the sterile patches *over* which the dunes have blown. Overgrazing means a pulling and dragging of the rhizomes by which marram and sand sedge creep and bind the soil, as well as the actual damage caused by too many hooves. The rabbit is another cause of erosion in the isles through breaking the surface of the dunes. Unfortunately, myxomatosis has not really hit the rabbit in the isles because the animals do not carry the profusion of fleas to be found on mainland rabbits and the disease is a density–dependant one, working through the fleas as intermediate host.

The Tertiary Basalt formations of talus slopes and loose hillsides are intensely subject to erosion if the hazel scrub has been removed. Sheep make lying-places which are loci from which erosion can spread. The same phenomenon may be seen on some slopes of old red sandstone in the eastern Highlands and in the Southern Uplands of Scotland, e.g. the Lammermuirs. Rabbits also like the drier easier burrowing conditions of basaltic talus and they start slips and screes. Erosion of this nature may be seen in Mull, Morvern and Ardnamurchan, and I have thought that the spread of bracken may well be one natural way of checking erosion, but I do not know whether bracken is a continuing climax or a long stage of biological repair. I wish I could live long enough to know.

Wild-life Conservation

The Highlands of Scotland have been a country in which human asininity—to put it as mildly as possible—has expressed itself with flamboyant, ostentatious and utterly ignorant extravagance. Nowhere is it more apparent than in the 150 years or less of sporting amusement with the wild creatures of the Highlands. In that time the rich occupied the region in a big way and undoubtedly helped the economy with their building of some of the most uncomfortable living-places which passed as shooting lodges, castles and what not. As a whole the owners and tenants of deer forests and grouse moors and salmon fishings were quite a humane lot. Were not the Earl and Countess of Dunmore responsible for setting up the Harris tweed industry? The clearance of Knoydart for a deer forest was an isolated blot, but it is fashionable in this era of proletarian glorification to make these isolated incidents a generalisation. It should be repeated that the clearances had to do with sheep farms, but after the passage of a century the demagogues of the masses have found it convenient to link clearances with deer forests. Their vinegary irk has even been so illogical as to apply the class system to the fauna: red deer and blue blood, grouse and gourmandising, salmon and satiety.

The ecologist can never ignore politics and political idiocies as profound environmental factors, but here he must remain detached and academic, possibly amused, though the man of feeling cannot be amused for long with political influence on the world of living things—including the suffering human being.

To return to wild-life conservation in the Highlands: sporting owners, being men the same as the proletarian demagogues, could be just as silly. Deer, grouse and salmon being desirable, were good animals; hawks, owls, foxes and polecats were bad animals. It never occurred to the owners and their minions to inquire into the habits of living things in the spirit of science. The natural hunters of the Highlands who became gamekeepers were so good at the job that, obeying orders, they almost made extinct some species. Finishing the osprey was not a game-keeper's achievement: it remained for a man of family, Charles St John, author of classics of Highland natural history, to do that.

Red deer had occupied the Highlands since the ice receded a dozen millennia since. The coming of the sheep in the late eighteenth century made them grazing competitors rather than accepted facts of life, so their range was restricted to the wilder areas. William Scrope altered all this by publishing his *Days of Deer Stalking* in 1838, which book described his wonderful life in Atholl. The notion took on, much helped no doubt by the Sovereign's delight in the Highlands and the building of Balmoral and all its balmorality. To entice deer back into grounds from which they had been evicted called for keeping the ground quiet. This philosophy long outlived its usefulness and even when I was working on the red deer in the early 1930s, freedom from disturbance was thought a first necessity in deer forests. I have since learned, through experience in Alaska and Africa, that some disturbance of herds of grazing and browsing animals is a good thing for the herbage and for the animals themselves. The shepherd putting the sheep up the slopes of the glen each evening with his collie dog is in effect being an artificial wolf.

There was some hind shooting in the winter to be sure, but not much, and the forests were stocked to capacity and more with an adult and elderly lot of deer. The Highland sheep farmer casts his ewes after three crops of lambs and is never sentimental about numbers. The deer forest owner did not grasp that wild herbivores were subject to the same physiological laws as domesticated ones. The herds built up to an unwieldy strength and their productivity was poor. They became a political factor, both in and out of the Highlands.

It is unfortunate that science could not have come earlier into the deer forests. Mathematicians have helped ecology enormously by their analysis of the data of experimental animal populations and this work has been extended to the study of wild stocks. We know now the nature of the asymptotic or S curve applied to animal populations, that after a slow start of increase in a population in an ample habitat there is a sharp rise in increase or productivity until near saturation of the habitat, whereafter the curve flattens out, making the numbers of the population more or less static. The animal manager gets ready for a catastrophic fall if he has read the signs. The deer forest owners rarely did, though the sheep farmer had arrived empirically at this truth long before.

Deer forests can be just as productive of high-class protein as sheep farms and with a good deal less trouble, except for the time of harvest when it is truly hard work to take off a sufficient number of stags from 1 September to 15 October and hinds from 15 November to 15 January, to keep the population pruned down to the steep phase of productivity on the S curve. Any considerable die-off in the deer herd in winter is a sign of mismanagement, for the die-off represents an excess of stocking which should have been removed earlier when the animals were in flesh.

The most significant event in the Highlands in relation to wild-life management, bringing the subject out of politics into the calmer consideration of the country's natural resources, has been the establishment of the Nature Conservancy in 1949. This body, answerable to the Privy Council, always operated in the Highlands as being concerned with *management* of wild populations rather than by throwing a blanket of absolute protection over them. This fact and the derivative attitudes were not always grasped by the growing band of nature lovers.

The Conservancy was the body which brought about reconciliation between forest owners and farmers and resulted in establishing legal close seasons and setting up the Red Deer Commission. The Conservancy achieved this desirable end by making it plain that it looked upon red deer as a valuable natural resource of the Highlands which was not being well managed and that proper management enjoying legal close seasons demanded a very considerable reduction in the number of deer, probably to two-thirds or a half of numbers then existing.

The spirit of science in ecological research conducted by the Nature Conservancy has blown like a clean wind through the archaic sportsmen's world of the Highlands which crumbled in the Second World War, and through the fuddy-duddy thinking of the Scottish Department of Agriculture which had been the most powerful governmental body in the Highlands. The linking of wild-life management with reality has been further demonstrated in the work of the Unit of Grouse and Moorland Management, a research unit based by the Conservancy under the Department of Zoology in the University of Aberdeen. The Nature Conservancy's Report of 1962 said:

'. . . it has become apparent that the numbers of grouse on the study areas are not directly governed by external accidents of recruitment and mortality, although these are of course secondarily involved, but rather that they depend upon and reflect underlying changes in the primary productivity of moorland vegetation. A possible implication therefore is that the long-term decline in numbers has resulted from a gradual overall impoverishment of the moorland itself. For this there seem to be three likely causes: first, that the climate is changing, making the environment less suitable for heather growth; second, that moor management is less efficient than formerly; third, that existing methods of moor management are causing a run-down of moorland fertility. Research on grouse is consequently bringing the ecologists involved into close contact with practical problems of land management, and with primary aspects of moorland ecology including the study of micro-climate, and of the mineral content of soils.'

The Nature Conservancy has conducted many researches *ad hoc* as contemporary problems have arisen, e.g. on the diet of the golden eagle, the ecology of the fox and on vole populations in relation to forestry.

The West Highland Survey Report, published as *West Highland Survey* (Oxford University Press) was completed in 1951, but publication was not sanctioned by Government until 1955. The ecological approach to land use had been the foundation on which that Survey had been initiated, and the wild life of the Highlands had been emphasised as a valuable natural resource of the region, but I could not have imagined, in those days of the Survey, what valuable contributions ecological study would make in these twenty years to general appreciation of Highland affairs. A further example of the advent of ecology into management of natural resources was the establishment of the Brown Trout Research Laboratory of Pitlochry in 1948, now the Freshwater Fisheries Research Laboratory. Fundamental advances in knowledge have been gained.

It should also be recorded with appreciation that the Forestry Commission has developed a much more ecological policy in recent years, not only in connection with planting and forest management but also in the attitude to wild life. It is plainly seen that wild life is a complex, and interdependent with the whole environment. No longer is it possible to categorise and produce simple answers of no validity. There has been no time in the recent past of say two centuries when the outlook for integration of the natural history of the Highlands with current management and development of Highland affairs was more promising.

I repeat, the Highlands are a devastated countryside, and from that understanding we should be able to embark on a century of rehabilitation in return for a thousand years of accelerating misuse. Ecological understanding working as a policy of conservation can show a few short cuts, but not many, and certainly no wonder cures. Ecological studies conspicuously can prevent making mistakes in policies of rehabilitation and development.

VIII
Some Thought of the Future

I have gone through a long story of thoughtless devastation and exploitation, of unknowing misuse, of some beautiful native and empirical ecological adjustment to a difficult environment, and a whole host of cock-eyed failures to respond to what would have seemed to be obvious co-operations and co-ordinations. These have got worse instead of better until the last ten or fifteen years, since when have come glimmerings of hope. The last considerable gesture has been the appointment of the Highland Development Board with executive powers. The West Highland Survey recommended such a body twenty years ago but was told flat that such a thing could not be because it would cut across the democratic process and the autonomies of county councils. The Government of the day must have had such ideas in mind when it made English National Parks by definition non-national and in Scotland the notion of a series of national parks removed from county council control was baulked altogether. These days of holding absolutely by a human administrative machinery that served its end in its own time, are passing; the Highland Development Board is a reality in a time when an increasing amount of research on land use is becoming available as a basis for policy making.

Those who think everything will come right in the economic condition of the Highlands by promoting 'industry', always a woolly term, are either ignorant rustics dissatisfied with their lot or urban types reflecting the restricted pattern of their own minds. Some industry will come and the projected development of the Moray Firth area makes good sense. There are excellent harbour facilities, a good surrounding countryside which could help service the area and a reasonably dry climate. There is good hope that such development can escape the squalor of that going-in-the-face-of-nature example of Kinlochleven.

This is the cornerstone of land-use ecology as one of the foundations of administrative policy, that you try to work with nature and gain the advantages of such action rather than arrogantly push nature the way you think she ought to go. The land-use ecologist will be no sentimentalist looking back over his shoulder, but one intensely aware of modern trends and of changes taking place in technology. There are even changes in styles of thinking which can profoundly affect what happens to a countryside, without involving any abrupt change of intention in land use. The earlier Forestry Commission concerned itself with its first narrow remit, to grow sticks of timber. There were numerous, almost unbelievable examples of failure to think of co-ordinated land use on the areas of estates bought for afforestation that could not grow trees anyway. Forestry wanted the lower slopes, not the tops or the bottoms. In those days there was no consideration whatever for sterilisation of more than half an estate, or that the winter feeding grounds of deer herds had been taken away. Deer should live on the tops and practical men could not be bothered about them. All that has changed. Broad rides are now left so that sheep or deer can naturally move up and down. If necessary, as is usual, the stocks are humanely cut down to match the available grazing. Even the planting patterns have changed from the great black blocks of Norway spruce to the more varied ones of planting different species according to the indications of each square chain of ground. The Forestry Commission in Scotland was also ahead of any committee on national parks appointed by the Secretary of State for it established National Forest Parks which recognised the reasonable potential of wooded hill country for recreational purposes, and actually spent money building facilities for tourists in the National Forest Parks.

The whole subject of recreation has changed the land-use picture in the Highlands and needs some discussion here. It was extraordinary that a forward-looking, experimentally-minded Socialist Government in 1949 should turn down the idea of national parks in Scotland, and that such a government should have taken some heed of the backwoodsmen and landowners of the opposite side in opposing that decision. Scotland has been left as the only nation of any consequence, civilised or not, that is without a system of national parks. Such a system would have had a stabilising, directional influence on tourism in Scotland, a phenomenon which has caught the country quite unprepared. Not only is accommodation for tourism quite inadequate and the road condition a source of constant irritation to tourist and native alike, but planning, land apportionment and landscaping are being neglected to the detriment of the working capital of the Highlands, which is its scenery.

On the planning side the county councils are either so ignorant or unheeding that corrugated iron is still thriving as a building material; asbestos sheeting runs it a close second. The most atrocious architecture for petrol stations, lodging houses and snack bars is being allowed; this in sublime scenery to which the coach-encapsulated tourists may lift their eyes on a fine day, but many days are misty and rainy and the tourist gets a concentrated vision of the ramshackle building going up so rapidly.

To put it quite baldly, scenery is money, and the Highlands are throwing away their capital.

As a further example of lack of co-ordination and of failure to see where the money lies, we may take that kind of land reclamation which would cut down a birch wood and erect a barbed-wire fence to establish a few acres of indifferent pasture that will soak up fertilisers till the ardent reclaimer (who has drawn a 50 per cent grant from the Department of Agriculture) gets tired or bankrupt. That birch wood was of more tourist value to the Highlands than the vision of the barbed-wire fence. Any Highland natural woodland should be valued in terms of tourism and recreation, for let it be quite clearly understood, the recreational value of Highland land is now likely to be its greatest commercial value. This fact is one it took me too long to realise, brought up in the conviction that the agricultural quality of land was its criterion of value. I think it was experience in the United States which almost shocked me into a new realisation. The Appalachian woodlands of the East which are now the backcloth to the Megalopolis of the Boston–Washington conurbation are called the suburban forest. Three efforts at farming the region have gone and the woods have returned to stay. Land value of these 'useless' (*sic*) woodlands are very high. Or go into some steep and rocky canyon of the West: quite useless ground for growing anything will cost $1,000 an acre or even more. It is the wilderness quality which has value, and our Highlands are one of Europe's best bits of wilderness.

It is already obvious to some landowners and such public bodies as the Nature Conservancy and the National Trust for Scotland that, apart from isolated examples such as the Corpach district which is going to develop industrially on timber grown in the Highlands, wilderness and the wild life, however damaged they may be from their pristine state, are the premier asset of the Highlands for recreational purposes. The Highlands and Islands are still one of the great wild-life areas of the world and it is our duty as world stewards to conserve it for posterity. Visitation to the Highlands is increasing much faster than official cognisance of the fact. The National Trust is now running highly successful island cruises each year to those remote islands which were extraordinarily inaccessible only a few years ago and the stupendous beauty of the gannet-haunted pinnacles of the St Kilda group of islands is now known to thousands rather than dozens.

Since the Nature Conservancy has come actively into the field of land-use ecology in the Highlands, it has learned a great deal about effective co-operation in achieving ends. This public body could not buy all the property it wished and it could not get through Parliament all the conservation legislation it would like to see passed. Much has been done by compromise, covenant and easement, so that some hundreds of thousands of acres are now running under a unified and expertly informed policy. We can expect this kind of management to increase, especially as it is growing increasingly difficult and expensive to get private expert management for the smaller blocks of country into which the great Highland estates are being divided through time.

The Nature Conservancy and the National Trust for Scotland are co-operating fully in management of the St Kilda National Nature Reserve. An area in Wester Ross belonging to the Conservancy and several other owners has seemed a suitable block for experimental co-operative management. The deer are being counted co-operatively twice a year to arrive at a scientific basis for culling, and there will be some calf marking to help gain knowledge of deer movement. Most recently the Torridon estate has become the property of the National Trust for Scotland and will join the area of co-operative management. The Ross and Cromarty County Council are improving the road system in the area very markedly. Crofting townships and limited sheep farming exist at the seaward end and around Gairloch, but for the rest of the area the recreational potential is recognised as being far beyond the pastoral. Afforestation can be carried out where it is feasible to the aesthetic advantage of the area as a whole. Here, then, will be a research unit for co-operative regional management on ecological lines.

We may hope that the Highland Development Board will take on some research responsibility for crofting land. Successive governments have log-rolled the Highland problem by appointing bodies such as the Highland Panel and the Crofters Commission, given them little money and little or no executive power and placed them more or less under the long arm of the

Department of Agriculture, which has never had any positive Highland policy.

Some of the inbye land of some crofting townships could be highly productive of fodder, or vegetables for tourist consumption. An intensification of this land is absolutely necessary if the summer potential of the common grazings is to be matched by the inbye land producing the winter fodder. This improvement is quite impossible while archaic methods of township communalistic management are followed. If the township inbye lands are thrown open to all and any of the township livestock on 1 November, few individuals will be so altruistic as to sow down a high-yielding temporary ley and give it adequate dressings of fertilisers. It would be eaten as bare as a board by other crofters' stock. In the course of the West Highland Survey we found one or two townships still balloting annually for the arable strips. No one is going to put more into such land than the current season will give return. We found more than half the 1,040 townships we surveyed were opened for the winter. Obviously there must be consolidation of crofts (no difficulty these days when many croft houses are becoming summer dwellings for townsfolk), then adequate fencing and change of custom to closed crofts in winter, so that the progressive man can reap the fruits of his labour and investment.

Souming of the crofting townships must be rigorously controlled and if a definite reduction in the sheep stock of the souming could be accepted by a township—even with the help of a subsidy for each sheep *not* kept—rehabilitation would be quicker and the fencing would last longer. A hungry and determined Blackface ewe of the western grazings will get through anything!

Lastly, in this period when crofting is less followed as a livelihood and yet tenaciously retained as a way of life, I think it should be possible for a public body having responsible concern, to get research done on getting some tree growth going for purposes of shelter and amenity on the common grazings. There are already promising patches on very inhospitable ground, such as Druim na Fuar near Bad-luachrach on the south side of Little Loch Broom.

Equally, if a new industrial area is set up, vigorous land-use survey and improvement of productivity should be followed in the Kildonan region as a whole. People do not live happily in an isolated and almost traumatic environment. The surrounding countryside, if green and pleasant, has value for the psychosomatic health of folk in a new and possibly unassimilated urban area. This is part of human ecology.

Finally, there is no mystique of science about land-use ecology, for we have seen already how near native wit and experience can arrive at ecological repose for a human habitat. As far as I know, ecology is no more than an open-minded approach to problems, an acute power of comparative observation in order to read the signs, and the practice of informed common sense.

The Position of Gaelic and Gaelic Culture in Scottish Education

John A. Smith

The Position of Gaelic and Gaelic Culture in Scottish Education

It was in 1872 that the central authority of the government in Scotland took over as a duty the task of educating the people which the Churches and other bodies had been undertaking on a voluntary basis for centuries previously. The process which was thus begun of establishing in Scotland a unified, national, statutory system of education, with English as the educational medium of instruction, is now nearing completion. Every stage of education, from infancy to old age, seems to be, if not in practice, at least in legislation, accounted for. Although the principle of voluntary and independent provision has been retained in law and in practice, the system is becoming increasingly one of uniformity and statutory provision. There are even signs that the process of nationalisation will go farther and effect an alignment between the Scottish educational system and the English educational system.

In roughly the same period since 1872 the process of deterioration in the state of the Gaelic language, which in the eleventh century was spoken over most of Scotland but which from that time on has been receding steadily into the north-western part of the country, has continued at an even faster rate than previously. The number of Gaelic speakers in Scotland in this period fell by something like 70 per cent, the most recent census figures showing that the number of persons speaking both Gaelic and English in 1961 was 80,004 as compared with 231,594 speaking it 'habitually' in 1881. The fact that these comparative figures are based on different definitions of 'Gaelic-speaking' is not important here, except to emphasise the truth which the figures reveal, since by the 1881 definition the 1961 figure is a distinct overestimate. In other words, the true fall has been even more than 70 per cent.

Now it is obvious that these two historical processes, the one of the spread of state education and the other of the continuing deterioration of the Gaelic language, have been highly correlated with each other. It could not have been otherwise. Most people would also be willing to admit that there has been some kind of causal connection as well between the two processes, and this is certainly true. Some would go so far as to say that the decrease in the number of Gaelic speakers in that time has been in direct proportion to the spread of compulsory education in the Gaelic-speaking areas. In so far as this is true, it certainly need not and, at least from a strictly educational point of view, should not have been so. It is tempting and it could be helpful to trace the historical connection in further detail, but on this occasion all that can be given is the helpful historical reference from time to time. In any case much research has still to be done before the historical connection can be stated accurately and fully. Perhaps this short introduction is a sufficient reminder for the present that some of the forces which sustained these two processes in the past are probably still at work and driving in the same direction. What we are really concerned with here and what matters most now is the relationship between the two processes at the present time and what that relationship is likely to be and could be in the future.

The Present Position

It should help this effort to be positive, realistic and forward-looking about the position of Gaelic in education if the educational problem is restated, first of all, in its present-day form. For educational purposes the Gaelic-speaking areas are now usually described as, broadly speaking, the Outer and Inner Hebrides, and some of the more remote coastal districts of the counties of Sutherland, Ross and Cromarty, Inverness and Argyll. The rest of the mainland of these counties, like the rest of Scotland in this respect, can no longer be regarded as Gaelic-speaking, and only in the Outer Hebrides, outside the larger centres of population, is the language still strong and vigorous. The percentage of the Scottish population which is still Gaelic-speaking is, therefore, on the most generous interpretation of the term, something of the order of 1·5 per cent, while the number of schoolchildren, whose first language is Gaelic, lies between 0·5 and 1 per cent of the corresponding Scottish total and is falling at the rate of about 0·7 per cent per year.

Moreover, the completion of the process of state education in English has meant almost the complete disappearance of the monoglot Gaelic speakers, who were, in any case, usually illiterate in their own language. The number of persons speaking Gaelic only, and not English, was 974 in 1961. The virtual disappearance of this section of the Gaelic-speaking population which, to some students of bilingualism, is an essential condition for the continued existence of a language, can certainly be attributed directly to the spread of compulsory primary school education.

In the face of these statistics even the most perfervid Gael might be expected to admit that, from a political point of view, the problem has become a relatively minor one. From an educational point of view, on the other hand, the problem cannot be shrugged off so easily. When an educational system has become so highly sophisticated and is in the final stages of its development, like the Scottish educational system, it might reasonably be expected to deal adequately with varieties of situation and circumstance. The accepted philosophy of those who direct and serve it is based essentially on the belief that the system which they operate should be made to do so. Cognisance, therefore, has to be taken in the Scottish educational system of what even the smallest percentages mean in individual terms and what they may signify in less tangible form. In the case of Gaelic the percentages mean that there are still coming annually into the infant departments of primary schools in the Gaelic speaking areas about 1,000 little children whose first language is Gaelic and who have little or no English; that there are in the primary schools already about 4,000 children whose first language is still Gaelic; and that there are at least 2,500 children in the same category in the secondary schools. There are also a great number of children in the schools who know some Gaelic or who live with Gaelic-speaking adults or who live in Gaelic-speaking communities. In addition, the cultural heritage embodied in the language which these children speak and to which it holds the key, is a heritage which belongs not only to these children but also to the whole of Scotland. As long as there are some children coming to school who speak Gaelic or whose parents wish them to learn Gaelic, and as long as there is something worth studying in the heritage of the Gael, it will remain the duty of the educational system, if it is to claim the title of a fully developed system, to make adequate provision for these educational needs.

In such a highly developed and centrally controlled system and with such a relatively small number of speakers of the language, the attitude of officialdom to Gaelic and all that it represents is obviously of crucial importance. It can be said right away that the official attitude at all levels has never been more sympathetic. This is most clearly seen in various memoranda and reports on education that have emanated in recent years from the Scottish Education Department. The fact that there are whole chapters on Gaelic in these documents and that it has been dealt with seriously in detail is historically noteworthy in itself. A comparative study of the statements of policy towards Gaelic that have appeared in such documents over the years since 1872 shows even more conclusively how complete the change has been from an attitude of active hostility to one of warm sympathy. It is a far cry, for example, from the inspector's report of 1878, 'I should regard the teaching of Gaelic in schools in any shape or form as a most serious misfortune,' or even from the report in 1877 of an inspector considered unusually sympathetic to Gaelic, 'English being foreign and more difficult, it could not be acquired to any purpose, if one or two years of the five or six of school life were first devoted to another language,' to the following pronouncement of the Scottish Education Department in 1965, 'It would be absurd that children who come to school speaking only Gaelic should have their early lessons in reading and number in English.' The disillusioned may comment that the official authorities can well afford to show sympathy when the damage has been done, or that sympathy means little if more active measures are not introduced to remedy the position of Gaelic and redress the balance of the old official attitude. There is little doubt, however, that the change in official attitude has sprung mainly from a general change in educational outlook affecting not only Gaelic but also all other subjects. This change is based largely on acceptance of the principle that the education of a child should be child centred and not authoritarian. There has also been some accompanying change for the better in attitude towards Gaelic in other quarters, among teachers, among parents and in the public generally.

Having thus given all credit where it is due, it must now be made quite clear that the official attitude towards Gaelic in Scotland still falls definitely far short of the position in most other countries where the problem of educating a people who are likely to use more than one language in their lives is a familiar one. As an educational problem the position of Gaelic in Scottish education is not new. Indeed, for a variety of reasons which need not be stated here, the incidence of bilingualism is distinctly on the increase throughout the world in this century. In the countries familiar with the problem it is usual to find a definite statement of policy on how the bilingual problem is to be dealt with in the educational system. A distinction is usually drawn between the position of the first language or mother tongue and the position of the second language. By far the most widely accepted principle, although not always the accepted one, is to provide education, first of all, in the mother tongue and to establish literacy there before introducing the second language. Anyone who seeks for such a principle in the educational legislation relating to Scotland will hunt for it in vain. One can only assume that the problem of how best to educate a Gaelic-speaking child who comes to school with no English has not been seen as a problem from this point of view at all. There is simply no reference in the education act to first language or mother tongue. There is no mention even of English itself. It is the official language of the country, the only official language, and as such it is assumed to be the medium, and, officially, the only medium of general instruction, even for those who do not speak it. Curiously enough, the only reference to a specific language is to Gaelic, but this reference carries the clear implication that it is not so much a language as a special subject or circumstance—some may think of it as a handicap—certainly not the general medium. Even in its latest and most favourable references to Gaelic the Scottish Education Department is still far removed from the active policy of fully developed bilingualism with literacy in both languages, which is officially advocated even if it is not fully implemented in practice in countries such as Wales and Ireland where the problem is very similar. The truth is that the possibility of making the bilingual Gaelic speaker literate in his two languages has not yet been seriously considered. In this respect the attitude of the official authorities remains within the original imperialist tradition of providing 'a good English education' for minority or native language groups, a policy long since rejected and abandoned by Britain itself in its dealings with other countries of the Commonwealth.

As to how far such a policy is educationally defensible and open to change that will be discussed later. In the meantime it can be stated that the official educational policy in Scotland towards Gaelic is and has been since 1918 to include Gaelic in the curriculum only as a special subject for Gaelic-speaking pupils. It is not even a second language in the sense of that term as applied to bilingual situations. The duty that has been laid on education authorities since that date has been to make adequate provision for the teaching of Gaelic, and that only in the Gaelic-speaking areas. The governing clause in the Act has thus left considerable freedom to education authorities in the matter of its interpretation, particularly of the words 'adequate' and 'Gaelic-speaking areas', and it has provided plenty of opportunity for disagreement among those concerned with its implementation.

It is, therefore, to some extent a matter of opinion as to how far this so-called Gaelic clause in the Act has been implemented. No one would claim that the expectations aroused by the inclusion of the clause in the Act have been approached, far less realised, but how far the reality has fallen short of what should have been possible is not so easy to judge. There are so many other forces, outside the educational field, affecting the educational position of Gaelic. Within education itself, and quite apart from the matter of interpretation of the intention of the law, considerable difficulties have faced the authorities in implementing this clause to the full. For example, it is not always possible to have Gaelic-speaking teachers available as required, and without them on the spot the clause becomes obsolete even in a strongly Gaelic-speaking area. Again, what was once a Gaelic-speaking area can quite suddenly, as far as the children are concerned, become an English-speaking area. The process of centralisation of schools, forced on authorities for educational or other than educational reasons, can cut across the schemes for teaching Gaelic. There are grave shortages of suitable teaching materials in Gaelic. The greatest difficulties, however, and this should be stated quite clearly without beating about the bush, are encountered in dealing with the children themselves, the parents and the teachers, and the root cause of the trouble lies in their general opinion of the educational value of Gaelic in schools.

The children have been mentioned first, although they, it can fairly be said, take their opinion in this matter from the others and from the status which they see accorded in the world around them to the respective languages. In the face of parental apathy and the varying attitudes of their teachers, which may be one of active, if sentimental, enthusiasm but which is more likely to be one of resigned acceptance of the position or sometimes of active hostility towards the language, it is difficult for the children to form their own conclusions until it is too late. Cut off from their natural heritage in this way, many Gaelic-speaking children never find out what they have been denied and lost.

Of the others, the parents are not, by and large, convinced that the study of Gaelic is at any stage as valuable even to Gaelic-speaking children as the study of English. This outlook is, in part, a legacy from the past and not surprising to those who know something of the former treatment of Gaelic. Only a minority of Gaelic-speaking parents are actively interested in an improvement of the position of Gaelic in schools. The majority of parents, while kindly disposed, are apathetic and some are either secretly or actively hostile. As for the teaching profession, it is fair to say that while they are now more prepared to admit the educational value of Gaelic and Gaelic culture, especially to the Gaelic-speaking child, the majority are still far more concerned to see that the child gets, whatever happens to Gaelic, a good education in English. They are genuinely, if mistakenly, afraid that if Gaelic is given adequate or more than adequate time the English and thus, in their judgment, the whole future of the child may be jeopardised. Faced with the choice, the teachers will make sure that it is literacy in English which is secured, and in this they will be supported by the great majority of parents and the children

65

themselves. It is, of course, very easy to be critical of these attitudes among parents and teachers, and it is noticeable that the further one is removed from the Gaelic-speaking scene and relieved of the responsibility of being the teacher or the parent concerned, the easier it seems to become to criticise.

The stage of education which was most affected by the 1918 clause is the primary school stage, and it is also the stage most crucial for the acquisition of literacy, the formation of attitude towards Gaelic, and, in general, the fate of the language itself. In these latter days it has acquired an added strategic importance. As the language weakens in an area and begins to lose that purity and richness which it had when the community was entirely Gaelic-speaking, only the primary school can take over the functions formerly left to the community of preserving the standards of Gaelic speech and even of using the language orally. As a result of the 1918 clause Gaelic has now come officially into the primary school, admittedly slowly and without the expected general enthusiasm but still it is officially there. In the old days it was seldom used in the primary school unless to help with interpretation of English, or perhaps it would be more correct to say that it was deliberately excluded except as required.

Again as a result of the 1872 Act and the 1918 clause the great majority of teachers at this stage in the Gaelic-speaking areas have themselves some literary knowledge of Gaelic or are, at least, Gaelic-speaking. This is particularly true of the infant departments where a teaching qualification to speak, read, and write Gaelic is vitally important. Indeed, the Gaelic-speaking areas produce more than their share of teachers of young children, and the majority of them seek posts in Gaelic-speaking areas when they qualify. There is official time set aside now in the primary school timetable for Gaelic, usually about two or three periods per week on the average. This is certainly not nearly enough to provide the desired literacy in the language by the end of the primary school and to produce literacy on a corresponding level with what is attained in English. Nevertheless, the conditions for education in Gaelic were never better on paper than they are now. In that sense if Gaelic is viewed simply as another language it has been given an unrivalled position in our educational system as compared to that of second languages in other educational systems. Seldom is a second language introduced as early into the curriculum as the infant room, and seldom is it so closely related to the needs and interests of the child.

All these changes in the primary school relating to the position of Gaelic represent historical improvements, and the general impression of the educational system at this stage would appear to be that, as far as the outward forms go, there has been an honest attempt to fulfil the legal requirement. There is no doubt, however, that within the forms the general situation is most unhealthy. The underlying causes for this have already been implied. Hindering even the enthusiastic teachers are, in addition, two major obstacles. One is the grave lack of suitable illustrated teaching material, graded textbooks and material of contemporary interest for more extensive reading. The infant teacher is not so hampered. She often can and does prefer to make her own material, because so much of her work is oral, spontaneous and creative. But as the child goes up the school this difficulty becomes more pronounced. The tremendous disparity between the growing and changing provision of material in English side by side with that available in Gaelic becomes very marked and very obvious to the child. It is not surprising that the child begins to turn naturally to English and often comes to regard Gaelic as generally inferior in some way. The other major difficulty lies in the lack of time made available for Gaelic, and its comparative isolation as a special subject. The main appeal, for most people, and certainly for children at this stage in learning a language is to use it and apply it. Because of its position in the system, the use made of Gaelic has to be limited so often to saying or repeating it in a formal way, writing it formally, or using it for translation to and from English.

It is seldom that Gaelic is used as a medium of instruction for other subjects or as the language medium which is used to explain and accompany practical activities. Although there is no reason, either legal or educational, to prevent the use of Gaelic in this way, the language of instruction for all other subjects is English, as a rule, and quite often English is the medium of instruction for teaching Gaelic itself. Apart from the loss to Gaelic in this way in terms of skill and prestige, there can be, on occasion, a loss to the subject-matter also, particularly if it is of a kind where Gaelic is obviously the better or more relevant medium. Only in the case of religious instruction is there a tendency to prefer Gaelic as the medium to English, and here the reason is obvious. It may not be good either for Gaelic or for religious instruction or for English that the two subjects of Gaelic and religious instruction should remain so closely associated in isolation in the child's mind. There are other subjects, for example, music, art, history and geography where Gaelic could often be used more effectively than English as the educational medium, especially in the earlier years of schooling.

It is difficult in leaving the subject of the primary school to know whether to finish on the note of disappointment or to point at the glimmers of hope. If one makes comparisons with Wales and Ireland, the disappointment is intensified, but surprisingly enough there is the consolation that, to judge from what has happened in the more favourable circumstances in these other two countries, disappointment should not be unexpected and is certainly not unique. It is obviously a difficult, perhaps an impossible task, to revive faith in a language where the spirit is not really willing or cannot be convinced. There are, however, glimmers of hope. In recent years there has been a special effort made in certain areas to improve the place of Gaelic in the primary school and to encourage its use orally. The two education authorities most concerned with Gaelic, Inverness and Ross and Cromarty, have made special appointments of Gaelic organisers to move round the schools, helping the teachers and encouraging the parents. Their work has resulted in a renewal of faith and enthusiasm, an improvement in quality, and keener general interest. It has been hampered by lack of suitable books and teaching materials, the apathy of parents and the lack of faith among teachers. Continued headway will call for great patience and abiding enthusiasm. It is possible already to find schools where literacy is attempted first in Gaelic, where English has benefited from literacy in Gaelic, and where progress in making pupils literate in Gaelic and enthusiastic about Gaelic is quite remarkable. This is not the first, but it is certainly the boldest, most imaginative, and best-organised attempt as yet to deal positively and directly within the terms of the act with what has become, to many of those involved, an intractable problem, a moribund state of affairs or a lost cause. It has come late, perhaps too late, but it is a fine and admirable gesture to which everyone should wish well.

It is hardly necessary to say much here about the position of Gaelic in primary schools outside the Gaelic-speaking areas. The topic should be mentioned because it illustrates very clearly how closely the education act has limited the meaning of Gaelic culture to the language and to the area where it is spoken. The first real attempt to teach Gaelic in the primary school outside the Gaelic-speaking area was made some years ago in Glasgow, and more recently the language has been introduced into primary schools in the town of Inverness. Apart from these instances there has been no real effort to make use of the language in the education of non-Gaelic-speaking pupils at this stage. If it is educationally sound to introduce pupils to a second language in the primary school, and from the enthusiasm with which French, a foreign language at that, has been introduced into many Scottish primary schools in recent years this view is apparently widely accepted, it might have been expected that Gaelic which was once spoken all over Scotland and which is a native and not a foreign language, could have provided a profitable and appropriate subject of study for selected primary school pupils in, at least, some Scottish schools, especially in those schools situated in districts where Gaelic was spoken within living memory. The teaching of Gaelic to non-Gaelic-speaking children in primary schools could provide all the educational advantages which the teaching of a modern foreign language can give with such added advantages as the easier opportunity to use the language with native speakers and the access which it can provide to the culture of our own country of Scotland. There has been no such development in Scottish schools, but there has been talk of introducing French into primary schools in Gaelic-speaking areas. The reason for this extraordinary state of affairs is not far to seek. Gaelic does not have the prestige or status or value of French in the eyes of the teachers and parents concerned. It is thought to have no commercial or utilitarian value, and the well-known fact that the vast majority of these who already study a foreign language in the primary and later in the secondary school are not going to obtain sufficient command of it to use it in its spoken or written forms does not apparently affect the issue at all. It is to be hoped that the experiment just begun in selected primary schools in Inverness to teach Gaelic to pupils at this stage within school hours will meet with the success and support which it deserves. Educationally it is a sound experiment.

In the secondary schools of the Highlands and Islands Gaelic has been an established subject in the curriculum since long before 1918. At present it is taught in about seven senior secondary schools and in about thirty-five junior secondary schools, to a total of approximately 2,500 pupils. Most of the senior secondary schools, and three of the junior secondary schools are located outside the Gaelic-speaking areas, largely for geographical reasons and because of centralisation policy; but no matter where the schools happen to be, the great majority of the pupils who study the language are native speakers. It is true that in the south of the country, in Glasgow, Edinburgh and Greenock, there are also courses in Gaelic available in certain selected secondary schools. Here the majority of pupils involved are not native speakers although the courses have appeared in these schools because the cities have a strong Gaelic-speaking population. Apart from these instances, however, Gaelic is not studied in the other secondary schools of Scotland and, as a general rule, never has been. The language does have its due place in the secondary school external examination system although the number of presentations is necessarily small as compared with those in most of the foreign languages taught in Scottish schools. Until very recently these examinations seemed to presuppose that Gaelic is to be taught and examined largely through the medium of English, but now the Ordinary paper for native speakers is set in Gaelic, while the forthcoming Higher paper for native speakers will also be set in the same way.

Much of what has already been said generally in the way of critical commentary on the place of Gaelic in the primary school is also applicable at this stage. The underlying apathy towards the language and its lack of prestige have their effects on even the most enthusiastic pupils and teachers of the subject, not to speak of the other pupils and teachers who have no such connection with the language. Among the languages taught in the secondary school Gaelic is a poor relation, and it is often paired off with one of the others at a particular period in the timetable to its disadvantage. For example, in most of the schools concerned Gaelic can be taken only to the exclusion of another subject, usually another language, and the abler pupils particularly are advised and feel it safer to choose the other subject. These clashes of timetable have had unfortunate effects on Gaelic. Not only have they caused it to be compared unfavourably in terms of educational and utilitarian value with other subjects, they have deprived a number of Gaelic-speaking pupils of qualifications in a subject which they were entitled to exploit, and what is much more serious, they have cut off a steady and rich supply of pupils from taking a further qualification in this subject at an establishment of higher education. This is one of the reasons for the present grave shortage of Gaelic students at the University and of specialist teachers qualified in Gaelic. It all arises out of a school timetable limitation which, if it can be avoided in one or two schools, could surely be avoided in most of the schools concerned.

The teaching of Gaelic in the secondary school suffers also from a number of special difficulties. There is a shortage of well-qualified specialist teachers of the subject. The supply of text-books, while of a satisfactory standard for native speakers, is distinctly limited and lacks variety. A fair criticism of the kind of course offered, which applies particularly to the junior secondary school, would be that the approach is still too traditionally academic. It is reminiscent of the earlier days when Gaelic was taught like the classics and regarded similarly as a dead language. Gaelic is still too closely associated with old unhappy far-off things and battles long ago. To appeal to young people, especially at the junior secondary school stage, when the comparison with English has become critical, Gaelic must be given more relevance to the contemporary world. The provision of more suitable textbooks, the use of Gaelic for other subjects, and the application of modern teaching aids such as tapes and T.V. are all examples of developments which require to be encouraged if Gaelic is to retain interest for the adolescent. There are signs, it is pleasing to record, that a livelier and more realistic approach is developing in some junior secondary schools. Perhaps the appearance of the Gaelic learner at this stage will also help the native speaker. The difficulties of the learner have become so obvious that special examination papers have been introduced for learners, as distinct from native speakers, in the Scottish Certificate for Education examinations. The 'O' level paper has already been introduced, and arrangements are now complete to provide a Higher level paper for learners. This was a reform that was overdue, but the learners still lack suitable textbook material and that rich variety and kind of teaching material which has been provided and found so appropriate for learners of foreign languages.

At the higher institutions of learning the study of Gaelic has been established for many years. For most of that time the provision has been limited to three of the older universities and two of the colleges of education. In more recent years courses in Gaelic have been made available in daytime at three or four colleges of further education, and there should be ample room for development here not only in the study of the language itself but also in the study of Gaelic culture as an aspect of liberal studies. Mention should also be made here of the thriving development in certain areas, although noticeably not so much in Gaelic-speaking areas, in the acquisition of Gaelic by learners at the adult education stage. This work is done in the leisure time of those concerned, usually by evening classes, and some very good and encouraging results have been obtained at this stage, particularly where modern teaching methods based on an oral approach to the learning of the language have been employed.

The most ambitious and scholarly study of Gaelic takes place at the three older universities, two of which have chairs in Celtic, and all three of which provide courses up to Honours degree standard. For the small number of students who come forward to take university courses in Celtic the provision is more than ample, although for the advanced study of Celtic it should be appropriate that all Scottish universities were interested in the subject. The smallness of the number of university students, most of whom are native speakers and come from the Gaelic-speaking areas, reflects not only the general position of Gaelic in the schools but also the lack of suitable opportunities later for graduates qualified in Celtic, and the lack of recognition of the subject in Civil Service and other examinations and in Scottish life generally. It is still true to say that anyone taking a course in Celtic at the university is likely to find an applied use for it only in a teaching or academic post. There is no valid reason, however, why those who specialise in Celtic at the university should have to look for a career only to teaching or academic work connected with their subject unless they wish to do so. An education in Celtic should be regarded as a sound preparation for a variety of careers just like an education in any other language. Nowadays, Celtic can be combined as a subject of university study with another subject, out of a wide range of subjects that includes English, Latin, Scottish History, Mediaeval History and Archaeology. This means that even if a university education is regarded from the strictly utilitarian or vocational angle, a point of view which the university itself deplores, a course in Celtic should lead naturally to many careers. It is fair to claim that a degree which includes Celtic (and especially one involving a wide course of study in Scottish Gaelic) is a most suitable preparation for posts in administration, say, in the central government at the Scottish Office, or in one of the new government agencies connected with Scotland such as the Highlands and Islands Development Board. Celtic is surely as relevant a subject as Classics in some sections of the Civil Service, as relevant as History in some sections of publishing, journalism and broadcasting, and it could be particularly useful in a number of posts in archaeology, librarianship and museum work.

The content of the existing university courses, traditionally dominated by the study of old Irish and old Welsh, has been broadened in recent years in at least two of the universities to give more prominence to Scottish Gaelic. An increase in the university funds available, the provision of modern equipment and a widening of interest have also resulted in the improvement of facilities generally for the study of Gaelic, and the establishment of a number of special studies and activities in and around the universities which are quite central to the well-being of Gaelic. These new studies include various surveys of the language and the compilation of an historical dictionary. The level and output of Gaelic scholarship at the universities, both in linguistic and literary studies, has probably never been higher and the activity of the scholars, small though they may be in number, has probably never been greater than at the present time. The contrast between the prestige and direction of the scholarship in the universities and the state of the language in the schools and in the living form has thus become quite marked. It would do much for the prestige of Gaelic throughout the country and for the encouragement of its use in public and official business if it could be shown that at the university level Gaelic itself can be used as an adequate teaching medium and that, despite statements sometimes made to the contrary, it can sustain intellectual discussion of this order. It is encouraging, therefore, to note that the use of Gaelic as a teaching medium has now been introduced, admittedly on a small scale as yet, into one of the university departments. The charge is also made, and it could be a fair charge, that more money and effort and interest is now being spent on the preservation of the historical remains of the language than on its continued existence in the living form. The answer to that is surely more activity outside the universities, involving different sources of revenue and different interests and individuals.

The other institution of higher learning whose work affects the place of Gaelic in the educational system is the college of education which trains the specialist teachers of Gaelic for the secondary school and the teachers of Gaelic-speaking children in the primary school. The importance for Gaelic of the teachers concerned with it has always been recognised and needs no explanation. It has become all the more important because of the state of the language and the fall in the number of Gaelic speakers from whom this section of the teaching profession is recruited. The training of teachers of Gaelic for the secondary school follows the same lines of training as for teachers of foreign languages. They have all to be graduates who have studied Gaelic for at least two years at the university, but there is this significant omission that these graduates have not the same oral tests to pass nor do they need to fulfil residence of a prescribed length in a Gaelic-speaking area. Presumably this omission relates to a time when every Gaelic specialist teacher could be expected to speak the best of Gaelic. That is no longer the case. It is now possible for a learner of Gaelic, as distinct from a native speaker, to become a teacher of Gaelic by obtaining the necessary academic qualifications and training as a teacher. All this he can do without becoming a fluent speaker of the language. Only one of the colleges of education provides teaching practice in Gaelic itself for students who are to become secondary school teachers and this is done in a city where classes of learners can be made available. Provided that these classes are taught orally in Gaelic, the experience is useful but not adequate. It would be so much better for these students if they had this experience in a Gaelic-speaking area, but such an arrangement, although quite feasible, and sometimes made, is not insisted upon. One benefit has come, however, from the association of this training course with those for teachers of other languages. There is no reason why the oral methods, the modern devices and the specialised equipment now required for other languages cannot be used, with suitable modifications, in the training of Gaelic teachers. The most crucial question, however, overhanging the training of specialist teachers of Gaelic is the question of supply. The position has now become exceedingly dangerous, and the danger has come suddenly because of the small numbers of posts involved. It has been noted for some time that posts requiring high qualification and good experience are proving very difficult to fill. During the next few years, when a number of the most experienced and best-qualified teachers of the subject are due to retire from the schools, there is a real danger that the supply of able pupils in Gaelic to the universities and colleges may be seriously interfered with. This problem requires urgent attention, and one of the first measures to be taken should be to free the school timetable so that as many of the Gaelic-speaking pupils as possible can obtain a recognised academic qualification in the subject before leaving the secondary school.

The training of teachers who are going to make use of Gaelic in the primary school, especially the training of those who are to deal with younger children, is of crucial importance for the future of the language. Only at two of the colleges of education is any particular provision made for the needs of these teachers, and this special course is additional to the normal training course; it is not compulsory, it is held in the student's own time, and it provides the students with no additional official qualification or salary payment. These discouragements are not the responsibility of the colleges, because they have to certificate teachers for duties anywhere in Scotland on the same terms as the other colleges who do not offer this special course at all. It is a distinct reflection on the official status of Gaelic in the system that the primary school teachers who make a special additional effort to prepare themselves in this way receive no official recognition for this. This omission is all the more deplorable, because, in some ways, they are more important for the future of the language than their secondary school counterparts. Despite all these discouragements, this course is well supported by the students and has been very successful. What is more significant, this course has had an appreciable effect in the primary schools, because it has been conducted in line with modern language teaching methods, with particular attention paid to the selection and preparation of material, the study of contemporary literature, and the relevance of the subject-matter to the needs and interests of primary school pupils. As a training for the teaching of Gaelic-speaking children in the primary school the present arrangement, although representing a notable advance on what was formerly provided, is still quite inadequate for its purpose, even for the situation where Gaelic is a second or subsidiary language with only a limited amount of time allocated to it. The current philosophy of the primary school is that it should be child centred, full of purposeful activity, and related to the child's environment. After making allowance for the fact that teachers have to be trained primarily to teach English-speaking children, and for the fact that most of what applies to the one language situation should apply to the other, it seems reasonable to suggest that those who will have to teach Gaelic-speaking children should be encouraged and specially prepared to do for Gaelic-speaking children what they are expected to do for English-speaking children. It can be imagined how unfavourable a comparison of the facilities for training teachers of Gaelic and Gaelic-speaking children in Scotland with the facilities for training teachers for similar purposes in Wales and Ireland would be to Scotland if it were made here in any detail. This particular topic would reflect as clearly as any the many other points of unfavourable comparison which exist between the respective systems as a whole for dealing with the native language. In fact, the comparison is largely pointless and has not been developed anywhere in this commentary on the Scottish system for this very reason. There is really no basis for comparison, because the respective systems are based on such radically different conceptions of what the place of the native language should be.

From what has already been said about the place of Gaelic in the educational system (a special circumstance to be taken into consideration only when dealing with Gaelic-speaking children) it is not surprising to find that little use has been made in Scottish education generally of the worthwhile contribution which Gaelic culture might make. This general criticism has always been applicable to Scottish education that it has not been related closely enough to the native soil, and here it is a particular criticism of the Gaelic clause in the education act which seems to be based on the assumption that Gaelic is simply a language and not the expression of a wider culture which belongs to Scotland as a whole and which could be made accessible even to those who do not speak the language. The influence of Gaelic sources can, of course, be seen quite clearly here and there in school textbooks, particularly among books and story-books, but these contributions are limited, they are often second-hand and romanticised, and they are more likely to be based on derived interpretations than to be introduced direct from the Gaelic source itself. It is fair, therefore, to say that the glorious heritage of Gaelic folk-lore, literature, music, art, archaeology and so forth is not only sadly neglected but also largely unknown to the schools and general public at large. This sad state of affairs is not limited to the educational system which is used both to create and to reflect public attitudes. It was observed long ago that the Scots, for all their professed love of country, knew singularly little of their own heritage. This truth applies to the Scots part of their heritage as well but access to the Gaelic heritage is now even more difficult for the person who does not know Gaelic. To transmit this heritage properly would require enthusiasm, knowledge and imagination throughout the teaching profession as a whole, and before that can be expected there must be large-scale research and preparation of material by scholars and others to make the heritage available. There is a particular duty on teachers of Gaelic and of Gaelic-speaking children to make use of this heritage, and where the language is known and is being studied at school it should be possible for children and students to be made more fully aware of their birthright and to take part in its defence and to make use of it. Teachers of other subjects who have not been made aware of what is actually there in Gaelic culture cannot obtain access to it so easily in a convenient form and cannot be expected to pass it on to Scottish pupils generally until they can do this. That there is a general awareness of the loss that is occurring to the nation as a whole in the continued neglect of Scottish and Gaelic studies is shown by the expansion of faculties at the universities concerned with such studies and especially by the establishment of the School of Scottish Studies for the express purpose of rescuing for posterity as much as possible of what is left of our folk culture. The work of collection is in full swing and it is particularly important for the Gaelic part of our heritage where the oral traditions are exceptionally rich. It is time also that the equally important work of editing the collected material and making it available to the schools and public generally was being prosecuted with the same vigour. If this is not done fairly quickly a great opportunity to help in the work of developing a contemporary culture from the old roots will have been lost and the collection which is already quite considerable will fall into the same condition as the great Irish collection of Delargy, which was assembled with encouraging rapidity in the thirties but which still lies largely unused in the Dublin archives.

Because of the inferior position of Gaelic in the official educational system it has fallen to outside agencies, or it has been assumed by them as a duty, to undertake a considerable amount of educational work outside the system. The most important of these agencies is An Comunn Gaidhealach (The Highland Association) which played a leading part in obtaining the insertion of the Gaelic clause in the education act. Since its foundation in 1891 it has exercised a watching brief over the position of Gaelic in education and continues to do so. It has also contributed notably to the general educational provision, by supplying teachers outside the schools, by preparing and publishing textbooks, by establishing a Gaelic youth movement, in conducting competitions of an educational nature, in arranging summer schools of Gaelic and many other activities. Special mention might also be made here of two other agencies which have given yeoman service to the general cause of Gaelic education, particularly from a point of view which has been refreshingly contemporary and forward-looking. These are The Gaelic League of Scotland, which has done notable work in the teaching of Gaelic to adult students, and Gairm Publications which have demonstrated most successfully that Gaelic can sustain a contemporary periodical and which have published in the last fourteen years more Gaelic than any other organisation. There are many other agencies that could be named as having what is in part an educational function to perform, such as The Scottish Gaelic Texts Society, whose main function is to edit and publish worthwhile literature as yet unpublished, and The Gaelic Society of Inverness, whose publications of learned papers have appeared regularly over the years since 1872; the various clan and territorial societies who conduct annual programmes of talks and music; and agencies which, although not officially educational in aim, do in practice have that kind of effect. Such an agency, for example, is the B.B.C., which through its various services has done so much to stimulate an educational interest in Gaelic. Altogether, there seem to be a great number of agencies and individuals involved in a variety of ways in doing what they can to strengthen the position of Gaelic and to raise its prestige, and they are to be congratulated and praised for this work which they so willingly undertake and pursue in the face of financial difficulty, lack of recognition, and general public apathy.

A Critical Evaluation

Before turning now from what has been a general critical commentary of the whole system to present some kind of evaluation of the place accorded to Gaelic in the pattern of Scottish education it should be made clear that the only fair way to judge the educational system provided is to do so, firstly, in terms of the kind of education which it seeks to provide for Gaelic-speaking children, and, secondly, in terms of the place which it affords to Gaelic culture generally. The second topic can be dismissed very briefly. It belongs to the larger problem of the whole Scottish heritage and enough has been said about this already to indicate that the general attitude of the Scots to their heritage, not only Gaelic but Scots, not only in their educational system but in their national life generally, reflects little credit on them as a nation. It is difficult to say how far the educational system has been in this respect the sufferer and how far it has been a contributory cause. It would seem anyhow that the main causes of this state of affairs are not primarily attributable to the position afforded to Gaelic in the system.

The present educational system is, therefore, to be judged mainly in terms of the provision which it makes for the Gaelic-speaking children, and, before this can be done fairly, certain misconceptions have to be removed about the connection between the education of Gaelic-speaking children and the present state of the language. Everyone will agree that the present state of Gaelic is disheartening, especially after the improvements made in this century in the educational arrangements for its well-being; and some, in their disappointment, have not hesitated to lay most, if not all, of the blame for this, on those responsible for the education of the young. The charge is unfair because while the two are obviously closely connected, there are a number of other considerations to be taken into account. First of all, it is not necessarily the function of an educational system to preserve languages or to destroy them. It can help to do both, and it can be used to do both, for political or for educational reasons. Ultimately the responsibility for the continued existence or the disappearance of a language must rest on those who were born into it and speak it naturally. A second general truth is that, by and large, a nation gets the education which it deserves. The fundamental decisions as to what education is to be provided are made ultimately on political grounds and are effective only with regard to the practical considerations of the time. The present position of Gaelic in the educational system is such that it could be considerably improved if the Gaelic-speaking population made a concerted and sustained demand for such an improvement. Finally, to attribute the present state of Gaelic wholly or largely to the educational system provided is to take a view of bilingualism which is far too simple and naïve. This term does not describe a state which is merely linguistic or purely educational. It represents a state of mind, or a set of attitudes, which is, in itself, the product of many factors both general and individual. Over the pressures which produce these attitudes to the mother tongue and to the second language the education available or provided may have very little influence. Thus, a minority language may have heavy government backing and lose ground; another minority language may have no such aid, may not even have a recognised place in the official educational system, and it thrives. In the case of Gaelic there have been powerful forces at work outside education, some for a very long time, which, in themselves, could account for its deterioration. There is not the slightest doubt but that the position of Gaelic has been adversely affected by the general malaise which has lain for centuries over the area where it is spoken. Hundreds of thousands of Gaelic speakers have been lost through heavy emigration and continuous depopulation, the old ways of life which helped to protect the language have broken up, the urge is on Gaelic-speaking youth as elsewhere to break with the past— in all of these changes the language has grievously suffered. Its comparative isolation has protected Gaelic in certain areas from earlier disappearance, but nowadays with the improvement of transport, the threat of mass pressures like T.V. from the outside world, and the deliberate planting of industrial centres in the Highland area there are new forces at work potentially more powerful and more strategically placed for the obliteration of the language. And so it may come that when the full story is written it will be claimed that the present arrangements for Gaelic in the educational system are also doing something to prolong the existence of Gaelic artificially as well as to make it disappear prematurely.

There is no doubt, however, that the pattern of education has had and is still having adverse effects on the state of the Gaelic language. One of the most obvious of these is the constant draining away into higher institutions of education and into the professions elsewhere of the intellectual cream of the Gaelic-speaking areas. Education in these areas is essentially for export, and even if this process does help afterwards the balance of payments problem in these areas, it takes away, and largely for ever, hundreds of Gaelic speakers. This process has been going on for centuries but increasingly since 1872, and it is somewhat unfair to blame education directly for this. The same process goes on in areas that are not Gaelic-speaking but are similarly placed economically. It is difficult to suggest a remedy for this, and the remedies usually suggested which seem to advocate that education should aim at keeping Highlanders at home content with their lot are quite unsound educationally and quite unacceptable economically. Furthermore, even if Gaelic were the sole educational medium in these areas the process would still go on and perhaps even at an accelerated rate. The fact that to some extent education has ill effects on the Gaelic language does not mean that as a whole the system of education is unsound.

It should also be noted that the educational system in the Gaelic-speaking areas can be criticised from a number of points of view which have little bearing on the position of Gaelic. As compared with other parts of the country, particularly the more prosperous and thickly populated parts, education suffers by having fewer facilities, on the whole less ambitious teachers, a less stimulating educational environment in some ways and other defects of that nature which are directly attributable to the stage of the economy and the geographical position. These factors all combine to increase the movement of Gaelic speakers away from the areas, but they cannot be regarded as the sole or entire responsibility of the education system.

The most serious criticism of the educational system from the Gaelic point of view and from the educational point of view really centres on the type of education given to the Gaelic-speaking children who come to school speaking little or no English. Statistically this is a minor problem, as has been already indicated, but it is the fundamental problem, the touchstone which decides not only the status of the language but also the quality of the system. It should be expected of a fully developed education system that it can make arrangements for the education of children speaking a minority language which are as good and as adequate educationally as those for the children who speak only the official language. In the Gaelic-speaking areas this is not so. The children are not being made literate in their mother tongue either before or after literacy is secured in English. To make children literate and numerate in their own tongue is a primary purpose of an educational system.

The principle that a child should be made literate, first of all, in his mother tongue is a principle that is very difficult to resist on educational grounds. It has been resisted often, on political grounds, but even on these grounds it is now generally accepted as sound and practicable. It is not possible to develop here the arguments in support of this principle but, briefly, they rest on the nature and function of language itself. Language is not only a medium of communication, it is the vehicle of thought and intellect, and it is the embodiment of culture. By forcing the Gaelic-speaking child to become literate in English, first of all, and without ensuring literacy in Gaelic, the educational system is interfering with the natural development of the child, it is making demands in time and effort and adjustment on the child beyond what the English-speaking child has to bear, it is failing to make full use of the child's natural prowess, and it is cutting him off from his heritage quite often so completely that he is unaware of what he has lost. There can be no defence of such a system on educational grounds, and politically it can only be defended if its primary aim is admitted to be still that of turning Gaelic children into English as soon and as securely as possible. If that is its real aim, the system is well conceived and has been remarkably successful.

Although it was originally the primary aim of education in the Gaelic-speaking areas of Scotland to turn Gaelic children into English children, it is certainly no longer true to say this. There has even been to some extent an official repudiation of that aim, but in practice that is what is still largely happening as long as Gaelic is kept in a subsidiary position. Nevertheless, the present educational system for Gaelic retains the support of the majority of the public, of the authorities, of the teaching profession, of the parents involved, and even of the children who have been educated in this way. In so far as they all will admit that there is a real educational problem left unsolved, they would still prefer to see Gaelic kept as a special subject in the educational system. They are not willing to see it given parity and far less priority. This may seem a sweeping generalisation and it can only be put forward as opinion, but it is opinion based on what happens in practice for the most part. This general attitude is based not on theoretical grounds but on practical considerations. It is argued that delay in establishing literacy in English would be to the educational disadvantage of the child. This is the real consideration that weighs with parents, teachers and officials, it is perfectly understandable, and it is honestly held by most of them.

The answer to these fears is a simple one. They are unfounded, and there is evidence from other comparable situations to this effect. In theory there is no reason why the achievement of literacy in Gaelic should retard or hold back literacy in English, and, indeed, there is reason to believe that for Gaelic-speaking children literacy in Gaelic could improve literacy in English. The present arrangement for switching over at such an early stage from one language to the other may well prevent the Gaelic-speaking child from pouring into the development of literacy in both languages the linguistic powers and the natural urge to literacy with which he came to school. Everyone will agree that, in the special circumstances which apply to him, the Gaelic-speaking child requires on educational grounds to acquire literacy in English as early as possible. The disagreement, and it is simply a disagreement, lies in whether this should mean that literacy in Gaelic has to be postponed or, more often, sacrificed. It is tragic for Gaelic and unhealthy for the educational system that there should be this issue or disagreement because it need not exist. In the meantime we are left with an educational system in which Gaelic is a special subject, intended only for Gaelic-speaking children, with all the attendant difficulties of such an inferior position. With the best will in the world, and without some fundamental change in outlook to give Gaelic better status, it is going to be difficult to help the language in this position, or to arouse much enthusiasm for it as an educational medium.

The Future

The position of Gaelic and of Gaelic culture in the educational pattern is not going to be determined in the future any more than it has been in the past or at the present time by educational considerations alone. The Highlands and Islands, which include all the Gaelic-speaking areas, are now receiving particular attention from the planner, the economist and the politician. An official mandate has been given to a statutory body to repopulate and revitalise the Highland area. It will depend very much on the outlook of this new Development Board as to whether, in trying to carry out its mandate, it helps Gaelic to survive or kills it off. At one time it might have been expected that the educational and cultural aspects of the position of less than 1 per cent of the Scottish population would not count for much in the planning of an economic redevelopment, but the modern planner should be well aware that the quickest and most effective way of ensuring regrowth is to grow from old roots as much as possible and to rally and retrain the existing labour force. It would certainly be ironic, although not surprising to the student of Highland history, if one of the main results of the salvage operation now in progress were to finish off a process which began before 1745 and the clearances, and to destroy completely the Highland ways of life and the Gaelic language. Without certain safeguards, and without some change in the present educational arrangements, this could well happen.

In the face of these new dangers to the language, and in the continuing unsatisfactory nature of the present provision, it is obvious that educational changes will have to be contemplated if the language is to survive and the heritage is to be maintained. Without positive action to raise the prestige of the language, encourage its use and develop it as an educational medium, Gaelic will disappear sooner rather than later, and with it will be lost for ever from the world much of the value and the beauty that can exist only in this living form. There are, of course, those who will argue that it is unrealistic to think in any other way. They say that the passing is inevitable, and that if this is to be so the sooner the better, that it is no part of the responsibility of the rest of us to help in the preservation of a language whose speakers can no longer ensure its existence among themselves. The experience of other countries, however, has shown that a strong lead in education can do much to help in such circumstances, and that while it cannot ensure the future it can bear fruit in the bygoing. There is now a moral obligation on the authorities not only to recognise with favour the position of Gaelic but also to show more than favour, since in the past they did much harm to the language and can be held responsible to some extent for its present position. The teaching profession occupies a key role. There is no doubt, for example, that it was the teachers of Wales who raised Welsh from its position as a language of the hearth to a place in the statute book of parity with English. This does not mean that they have saved Welsh for all time: they certainly have not been able to do this, but their leadership has brought much of value into Welsh life in the meantime.

If the leadership could be forthcoming, and there is faith in the value of what is being attempted, there are quite a number of practical measures which can be contemplated for the improvement in the immediate future of the position of Gaelic and Gaelic culture within the present pattern of education. The measures presuppose certain conditions. One is that the existing individual efforts can be linked into a joint co-operative effort. Another is that ignorant fears should be discarded. Such a fear is the doubt as to whether the Gaelic language is still viable as a modern language. Any language can be made viable, if the demands are made on it. Otherwise the practical measures envisaged could all be put into effect fairly easily and without much cost, and they are also all worth putting into effect, irrespective of the effect on the language, because of their soundness as educational measures and their value to the country as a whole. The following seem to be the most urgent of these measures:

(*a*) It is not too late to set up a Gaelic school in the Gaelic speaking area, a primary school, where Gaelic is the first language, into which English is introduced as early as possible, and where the aim of the school is to produce a bilingual pupil fully literate and articulate in both languages, but in his mother tongue first. The purpose of this school would not be to produce bilinguals for their own sake, because there is no particular value in bilingualism as such. The school would be a recognition of the fact that Gaelic-speaking children must master English and that they can do this without sacrificing Gaelic. The experiment, if successful, would convince Gaelic-speaking parents that such an educational arrangement is quite feasible. Proper safeguards could be laid down to deal with the possible failure of the experiment, but there is no particular reason for thinking that it would fail. There were doubts before the first Welsh school was established in Aberystwyth. It is interesting to note that its results in English are very reassuring.

Once this Gaelic school were soundly established it would attract pupils from elsewhere, and its work in Gaelic and the relevant cultural studies related to the language would soon have an influence on other primary schools throughout the Gaelic-speaking area.

(*b*) Crucial as a primary school of this kind would be for the acquisition of literacy in the language, it could come too late in those marginal areas where anglicisation is threatening the future of Gaelic. In such areas the establishment of nursery schools conducted entirely in Gaelic could help children who have Gaelic and English to acquire a stronger grasp of Gaelic at a stage when it is important that they should do so and before the full weight of the anglicising school education is felt. Nursery schools in Gaelic for English-speaking areas where there is some concentration of Gaelic-speaking parents who wish their children to learn the language would serve a similar purpose. At present any statutory provision of nursery schools is not to be expected, unless by special arrangement or by recognition of the special need, but the possibility of establishing nursery schools on a voluntary basis is always possible.

(*c*) Apart from experiments like the above, there could be encouragement given to providing the same type of development within selected existing schools and establishments favourably placed, with the agreement of parents and teachers, and with safeguards laid down to allay their anxieties. There could be a gradual extension of the use of Gaelic and the time allotted to it, with a view to achieving some form of parity for it with English and using it as an educational medium for the other subject-matter to which it is well suited.

(*d*) There is also room for establishing an institution of further education on the model of the Scandinavian Folk High School, with the same original aim of restoring faith and confidence in the national culture and, in this particular instance, in the use of the national language. This establishment would be intended for students from many different parts, its courses would be fitted into the pattern of seasonal activities, and, if successful, it could make a great appeal to Gaelic-speaking youth. To set up this type of further education establishment seems to be a more feasible proposition at the present time than to begin at the top level and establish, as is suggested from time to time, a University or University College in the Highlands, with Gaelic as a central or special study. There are already three Celtic departments in the existing universities, and while there may still be other reasons for contemplating a university-type establishment in the Highlands, even after the establishment of Stirling University, it is certainly not needed for Gaelic. What is now required at this top level is to strengthen and support the existing departments, and to encourage one or other of them to provide extension work at university level in the Gaelic-speaking areas, and perhaps ultimately to establish a base or annexe in the heart of these areas as a focal point for local Gaelic studies.

(*e*) In the study of Gaelic at all levels there could be a general movement towards the greater use of it orally. Greater importance could be laid on the employment of Gaelic as a living language. Modern devices for the teaching and learning of languages could be made more easily available for the learning of Gaelic. The specific problems of the learner should be given special attention, not simply the learner in the Gaelic-speaking area or in the marginal area but in the English area, and not simply the young learner but the adult learner. To encourage the learner there must not only be encouragement of this kind forthcoming from official sources but also from the native speakers themselves. Too often the learner receives positive discouragement from the native speakers, who fail to appreciate his needs and his difficulties.

(*f*) The main weakness of the Gaelic movement outside education is that its attack hitherto has been directed at the marginal areas where Gaelic is disappearing or at Lowland areas where Gaelic speakers are trying to keep in touch with each other. There are historical reasons for this policy which probably explain why at one time this seemed the proper line of action. It has meant, however, that the movement has never established itself securely in the Gaelic-speaking areas, and has thus come to be regarded in some degree as alien or irrelevant to it. This policy now requires to be reversed. From an educational point of view, every endeavour should be made now by the official movement to combine with the education authorities or, at least, to support them in establishing within the Gaelic-speaking areas a comprehensive adult education service in Gaelic. This service could cover a variety of activities, not simply classes for the acquisition of literacy in Gaelic but interesting activities like study groups on contemporary topics, cultural groups and activities of that kind designed to interest the native speakers in the use of their language for other than simply everyday purposes and to show them that it is still a contemporary medium for all levels of language use. Allied to this adult education service there should also be developed a Gaelic Youth movement. Despite laudable efforts by devoted individuals the Gaelic movement has hitherto failed to sustain a thriving youth service. This is very much in contrast to what has happened in Wales where the position of the Welsh language owes much of its success to the support of an active youth movement, led by teachers. It is suggested that the time is opportune to try again and this time from within the education system.

(g) Although it has been conceded that it is not necessarily the function of education authorities to preserve languages, it does not seem unreasonable, for reasons already implied, to suggest that the authorities, particularly the central authority, should take a bolder and more active part in improving the position of Gaelic in the educational system. While still leaving open the question of whether Gaelic should be the first language or the second language, there are two practical measures which could promote a more deliberate movement in the direction of making Gaelic-speaking children fully literate in their own language. One would be official recognition for standards of literacy in Gaelic in the primary school, especially at the promotion stage. This would certainly require strengthening of the inspectorate, where at present the whole responsibility for Gaelic at all stages falls on two inspectors who have many other duties to perform. The other is the provision of a special fund to help school authorities and students of Gaelic generally in obtaining adequate supplies of suitable textbooks and learning materials, including tapes, records and other modern language learning aids for the various levels of learning. For the English language the free commercial market can normally be depended upon to finance the production of learning and teaching materials, but such an arrangement is not possible in the limited Gaelic market. Any real effort to provide an adequate supply of Gaelic materials would require government subsidy, and such an arrangement has been accepted in other countries with similar problems.

(*h*) There is a general need in Scotland, both for the Gaelic and the Scots side of our culture, to make known more accurately and generally to the people the heritage of the Scottish nation. To do this the material has not only to be collected, identified, studied and investigated but it has also to be selected, published, disseminated and popularised. It is contended that the central and local authorities of Scotland have a special duty both within and without the schools to give every encouragement and help of this kind to the agencies and individuals who are prepared to undertake it.

(*i*) Constructive use must be made by all concerned with Gaelic and Gaelic culture of certain forces which will otherwise help to destroy the Highland ways of life and the Gaelic language. The myth that it was the 1745 and forced clearances which began the process of change in the Highland way of life should be exploded once and for all. This process had begun long before 1745 and it was inevitable. The clearances were not all forced on the people: many of them were voluntary movements by the Highlanders themselves. Furthermore, the clearance movement has become far more widespread and continuous in the last fifty years. The underlying forces which have been at work thus for centuries are mainly social and economic. They are not necessarily destructive in aim nor in result. There are certain modern forces such as the replanning agencies and the mass pressures of the Press, radio and television which cannot be gainsaid, and therefore they must be harnessed and used to develop what they will otherwise destroy. Their educational potentialities for the good of Gaelic and Gaelic culture are enormous, and they are not ill-disposed.

These measures have all been suggested as measures to strengthen the present position of Gaelic and of Gaelic culture, and to keep it developing in the required direction. Separately they do not add up to so much, but the success of one or other of them might spark off that upsurge of leadership, joint effort and faith in the value of what is being attempted which is all that is required. Until that upsurge comes it will not be easy to improve the present provision and there is no guarantee that this can be achieved. What is important, however, is that some continuing improvement should be attempted. If it fails no harm will have been caused but much good in the bygoing. Whatever happens, something will have been tried to ease the conscience and redress the balance of the old, to grow a contemporary culture from old roots, and to allow the ancient Gaelic heritage, if it has to go, to pass with honour from the lips of the Scots.

Selected Bibliography

Gaelic-speaking Children in Highland Schools. Vol. XLVII. Scottish Council for Research in Education. U.L.P., 1961.

The Place of Welsh and English in the Schools of Wales. Report of the Central Advisory Council for Education (Wales). H.M.S.O., 1953.

The Problem of Bilingualism in the Schools of Wales and Scotland. Stewart R. Semple. Educational Research Series No. 35, Ontario College of Education, Toronto, 1964.

'Gaelic in Highland Education.' Murdo MacLeod. *Transactions of the Gaelic Society of Inverness,* Vol. XLIII, 1966.

Gaelic in Scottish Education and Life. J. L. Campbell. For the Saltire Society. W. &. A. K. Johnston Ltd., 1950.

The following publications of the Scottish Education Department, all H.M.S.O.:

(*a*) *Junior Secondary Education* (chapter on Gaelic), 1955.
(*b*) 'The Teaching of Gaelic in Secondary Schools' (extract from 1960 *Annual Report*).
(*c*) *Primary Education in Scotland,* 1965.
(*d*) *Education in Scotland in 1965,* 1966.

The Economic Life of
Gaelic Scotland Today

Farquhar Gillanders

The Economic Life of
Gaelic Scotland Today[1]

Two public bodies, recently created—the Crofters Commission and the Highlands and Islands Development Board—came into existence specifically charged by Parliament, to revive the economy of Gaelic Scotland. This chapter will be concerned with the reasons for their creation, their subsequent development and the atmosphere in which they took office, and now work—and the prospects before them in 1967. Historically, therefore, the chapter only covers the period 1945–67, except in its reference to the Napier Commission Report and the important legislation that followed it and which dominated West Highland economic life without significant amendment until the Crofters (Scotland) Act of 1955.

The *current* economic problem in Gaelic Scotland was well defined in the *Programme of Highland Development*[2] presented to Parliament in the summer of 1950. Since then, both Labour and Conservative governments have repeated this same definition, with obvious approval, in subsequent parliamentary documents and reports on the Highland economy.

'Fundamentally the Highland problem is to encourage people to live in the Highlands by making it possible to secure there, in return for reasonable efforts, proper standards of life and the means of paying for them. The depopulation of the Highlands has long been viewed with concern. Commissions and Committees of Enquiry into the Highland problem or into particular aspects of it have been numerous, but the action taken by successive Governments has been on the whole designed to preserve rather than to construct and has been motivated by social rather than economic considerations. This is true even of the notable Crofters Holdings (Scotland) Act, 1886, which conferred security of tenure and other material benefits on the

95

crofting population in the Highlands following the decline of their customary rights when the clan system was broken down. More positive measures were taken in 1897 when the Congested Districts (Scotland) Board was set up with power to aid agriculture, fishing and rural industries, to acquire land for land settlement purposes, and to assist in the provision of public works such as roads, piers and harbours. But the use made of these powers was related more to the preservation of the existing population in their traditional pursuits than to the building up of a new economy.

'For a long time the scope for any more constructive approach was limited. There was little prospect of introducing new economic activity and the agricultural and fishing industries passed through periods of depression which affected their vitality not only in the Highlands but in all parts of the country. In recent years, however, new factors have emerged which provide the basis for a more constructive approach to the Highland problem and for treating it effectively as one *of economic development*. These new factors are the increased importance of home food production, the necessity for a large scale programme of afforestation, the development of hydroelectric power in the Highlands and the greatly increased importance of the tourist trade. The need now is to re-assess the Highland problem in the light of these new factors and to frame plans for securing the full benefits which they make possible.'

The present imbalance of the Highland economy is, in part, the direct result of the Highland history which Dr Ian Grimble has analysed in his introductory chapter to this book. In part, also, it is due to the Napier Commission Report of 1884 and the Crofters (Holdings) Act, which followed it two years later to give the Highland crofter an economic security that he had never known before. The basic intention of the British Parliament in its Crofters Holdings Act of 1886 was to remove the deep-rooted grievances in the Highlands, to which Lord Napier and his fellow commissioners had so vividly drawn their attention. The legislation, largely inspired by the desire to redress the wrongs perpetrated in the Highlands since 1746, was heralded in the Highlands and elsewhere as the panacea for the festering economic malaise that had given rise, surprisingly late, to scattered, sporadic but unco-ordinated rioting following the mass planned eviction of crofters from the land which they had traditionally cultivated and which they had come to look upon as their own. It is my belief, however, that the 1886 legislation heralded the doom of crofting as a way of life, insulating it almost completely from normal economic trends and *legally* ensuring that crofting land could not now be developed into viable economic units. Certainly, the bewildered Highland crofter, after 1886, enjoyed a unique security of tenure, but despite this or more accurately, perhaps, as a direct result of this, the exodus of young men and young women from the seven crofting counties continued, less dramatically it is true, but economically, in the long run, even more devastatingly, than at the time of the evictions. The *current* Highland problem, as I see it, then, is certainly the result of fairly recent history and persistent Parliamentary indifference, but it is also, in my opinion, the direct result of an emotional rather than an economic attachment to crofting as a way of life and to a continuing irrational belief by Highlanders and administrators that land—small scattered patches of land—is the basic economic resource of the Highlands and Islands. Crofting and Gaelic Scotland are synonymous both in the English and Gaelic tongues. It is so for the majority of Highlanders, be they at home, in Glasgow or elsewhere in the British Isles, or in exile; it has been so for the Government in its frequent pronouncements and occasional attempts at formulating an economic policy for the area, and it is largely so for the B.B.C. in its meagre but daily recognition of the Highlands as an autonomous region with a language and culture of its own. Yet, we are told officially in the Autumn of 1966 that only 7 per cent of crofting land is cultivated. Crofting, in my opinion, has very little to do with the serious economic problem that confronts the Scottish Highlands today. But it has proved administratively convenient for governments and their agencies to suppose otherwise and any economic analysis of the area in 1967 must give considerable attention to it. This chapter, therefore, deals with crofting at some length not because of its economic importance to the future of the region but because of its continuing existence as an economic factor and its very considerable influence on the Highland way of life.

Geographically, half the land area of Scotland, or one-sixth of that of Great Britain, is contained in the Crofting Counties.[3] But less than 277,000 people now live in this vast region,[4] and of these an abnormal proportion consists of old-age pensioners.

The basic reason for this imbalance is that successive governments have, negatively, allowed the area to degenerate economically; and depopulation, ageing communities and a
reluctance of young men and women to remain in the crofting
counties are the demographic background to the economic
stalemate that is now the Highland Problem. In the five
important years from 1947–52, for example, when the rest
of Britain was striving desperately to boost the domestic
economy to recover from the effects of the war, agricultural
output from the crofting counties fell by more than 10 per cent.[5]
And the returning, restless, ex-service men and women from the
Highlands and Islands soon realised that for them their native
parishes had little to offer in the economic and social developments that were being discussed and initiated elsewhere in
Britain.

Three important new studies, however, in this period, once
more focused the country's attention on the plight of the Highlands and Islands, and the Conservative Secretary of State for
Scotland in 1954 promised that effective legislation would soon
be enacted to translate the latest recommendations into positive
action. A new deal for the area was, again, being promised.

Dr Frank Fraser Darling's *West Highland Survey*[6] was a
scholarly and scientific analysis of the agricultural potential of
seventy-one West Highland parishes and it was ready to hand to
form the basis of any new postwar plan to improve the West
Highland Economy. Early in his book Dr Fraser Darling
writes,[7] 'the land of the crofts and the common grazings are
used at a low fraction of their potential and are deteriorating,
and the level of agricultural knowledge is extremely low'. Soil
fertility is being reduced, he maintained, by the decline in the
cattle–sheep ratio, by the absence of enclosures of crofts and
townships, and by deliberate neglect due to absenteeism or
because the crofter is preoccupied with another job. In *West
Highland Survey* a scientist and an ecologist analysed the crofting
problem in detail. He did so with an intimacy and a clarity
which commanded immediate admiration. The postwar
problem was clearly stated not just in terms of history but in
keeping with contemporary economic thinking.

A second study, *The Crofting Problem*,[8] by the late Adam Collier was edited by Professor A. K. Cairncross, then of Glasgow

University, and was the first of the series of important Scottish economic studies by the Department of Social and Economic Research of the University of Glasgow. Collier, a Glaswegian, passionately interested in Gaelic Scotland, was killed in a climbing accident in Sutherlandshire in 1945 and at that time his book was still in manuscript and incomplete. On Collier's death, Professor Cairncross undertook to edit the book for publication, because he realised that in 1945 it stood head and shoulders above any extant analysis of the social and economic problems of the Highlands and Islands of Scotland and showed a remarkable grasp of all the developments that might bear on the future of a crofting economy.

A Commission of Enquiry was appointed in June 1951, under the chairmanship of the late Principal Taylor of Aberdeen University to 'review crofting conditions in the Highlands and Islands with special reference to the secure establishment of a small-holding population making full use of agricultural resources and deriving the maximum economic benefit therefrom'.

The terms of the remit presupposed, officially, that it was desirable to maintain a population of crofters in the Highlands and Islands of Scotland. Despite this, we find the Commission[9] recording a unanimous conviction 'founded on personal knowledge and on the evidence we have received, that *in the national interest the maintenance of these communities is desirable*, because they embody a free and independent way of life which, in a civilisation predominantly urban and industrial in character, is worth preserving for its own intrinsic value'.[10] And later, 'We believe that these communities deserved to be saved from extinction and that they were capable of restoration and survival *if the proper measures were taken in time*. We are convinced that with the application of modern knowledge they can be raised to a level of security and prosperity such as they have never known.'[11]

The third important study, then, the *Report of the Commission of Enquiry* was published on 27 April 1954 and made forty-two recommendations. Of these the main ones were:

(1) The establishment of a new administrative authority— a Crofters Commission—with special responsibility for the improvement of crofting conditions: this Commission to be endowed with adequate financial and executive powers;

(2) The enlargement and improvement of holdings by the allocation of new land for the use of crofters and the consolidation of existing holdings into economic units;

(3) The active use by the new Crofters Commission of land settlement powers; and

(4) The establishment of a loans scheme, under the Crofters Commission, on which crofters could draw readily for working capital.

Legislation followed quickly but in some vital respects fell far short of the basic recommendations of the Taylor Commission of Enquiry. Without intending to do so the Act of Parliament[12] made economic progress in the Highlands almost impossible of achievement. Throughout the Highlands and Islands, however, the new legislation was widely acclaimed. There were some who saw the Act of Parliament, however, as a lost opportunity to do something really positive for the economic life of the area. Under the Crofters (Scotland) Act 1955, a Crofters Commission (under the surprising chairmanship of a career diplomat) was established and took office in Inverness on 1 October 1955, and on 3 June 1957 it presented its first report for the period 1 October 1955 to 31 December 1956.[13] From this report a confident and optimistic picture of the future of crofting emerged, and the Scottish Press, in general, and Highland newspapers in particular, enthusiastically welcomed this first survey by the newly constituted Commission. The optimism of the report was infectious, and much publicity was given to its brave assertion that while now, as ever, a stable and healthy crofting population cannot be supported on any acceptable scale on husbandry alone nevertheless 'we are confident that given a chance it (crofting) will re-establish itself as a sane, healthy and independent way of life, one which will repay the effort to preserve it *even if it be in face of the current economic trend*'.

The second annual report of the Crofters Commission, published on 3 July 1958,[14] was a very different document, appearing, virtually, to abandon the main recommendation of the Taylor Committee of Enquiry whose recommendations many had, mistakenly, thought were embodied in the Crofters (Scotland) Act of 1955, under which the Commission functioned administratively. The Taylor Committee had explicitly recommended that the Commission's primary function should be to expand crofting agriculture by means of enlargement of individual holdings. But this, apparently, the Commission was now unwilling or unable to do and in its report it concentrated on a review of more general matters outside its intended scope of action, and gave the appearance of being rather more concerned with ancillary occupations than with revitalising crofting, and from the report one gathered that there was now no real intention to promote the basic facilities for the Highland crofter who wanted to expand his land and become a small farmer.

The Crofters Commission Report for 1958[15] repeated much that was already known, or believed, about the Highland crofter and his way of life, but went on to reveal a change in Commission policy to revitalise the West Highland economy, and there was evidence of some ideas previously held as all-important now being very considerably modified. One was left with the impression in the summer of 1959 that crofting would remain depressed and economically insignificant despite the good intentions and the vigour of the Commission and its aggressively outspoken chairman.[16]

The fourth and, so far, the most important report of the Crofters Commission was presented to Parliament on 11 May 1960,[17] and again it revealed a definite change of emphasis, if not of thinking, and it was asserted, with considerable emphasis, that more purposeful measures must be taken timeously if economic survival was to be possible in the Western Highlands. An increasing awareness of the sociological problems that would accompany practical action was revealed, but the Commission concluded its report by stating that 'crofters have a sound sense of what is right and of what is necessary to put agriculture on a firmer footing under modern conditions'. If this faith was misplaced, the Commission acknowledged, then there was little hope that they could fulfil the real function for which they had been brought into being by Parliament. At this point it is worth saying that drastic action—which undoubtedly was necessary—would have come better in the Commission's very first year of office rather than later on when a pattern of increased doles and economic reaction had already come to be associated with this new organisation set up with so much publicity to administer the economy of the crofting communities of the Scottish Highlands. I have always believed that the Crofters Commission's faith in the crofters of the 1960s was misplaced. The Commission was—and is—pathetically eager to give grants to crofters. Money is there virtually for the asking, but there is little to show on the investment. Many benefit today from crofting legislation and give little or nothing in return. And this is acceptable to those who give and to those who receive. But in many ways the Commission was the helpless victim of the complicated Act of Parliament which had brought it into being. Economic gain or loss was not required to be assessed as in other projects where public or private money is expended. A detailed balance sheet was not required annually and platitudes were always acceptable as a substitute for harsh economic facts. In the fourth report of the Crofters Commission it was stated that there were 220 known vacant crofts for which apparently there was no demand at all. As this was an increase over the previous year's figure of between 130 and 140, it could hardly be asserted, publicly, that progress and Highland economic revival were at hand.

The continued inability of the Crofters Commission to achieve any real economic progress and the weird ramifications of the Highland mind with which it had to deal and which few sophisticated, non-Highland administrators can hope to understand, were revealed in Appendix IX of the 1959 report,[18] which described an abortive attempt to reorganise the crofting township of Big Sand, in the Parish of Gairloch, in Wester Ross.

At their meeting on 27 August 1956 the Commission decided that Big Sand should be reorganised. On 5 September 1956 the Chairman visited the township and met the Township Clerk and a number of the crofters. They expressed themselves ready to co-operate with the Commission in the reorganising of the township. On 7 September 1956 the Chairman called on the factor of the Gairloch and Conon Estates and put to him the Commission's proposals to reorganise the township. He promised sympathetic consideration of any concrete proposals that the Commission might make.

On 19 November 1956 the Chairman visited the township and held a meeting with the crofters, at which he explained what the object of the reorganisation would be. The meeting agreed that the Commission should proceed with their plans to reorganise the township.

In preparing the list of tenants in the township difficulty was encountered in identifying the tenants of certain crofts. The position was finally clarified and the township list, after approval by the Commission on 17 January 1957, was served and advertised in terms of section 19 (4) of the Crofters (Scotland) Act, 1955. One objection was received to the township list, but was subsequently withdrawn.

At their meeting on 23 April 1957 the Commission formally confirmed the township list as previously prepared. The confirmed list was advertised in terms of Section 19 (5) of the Act and no objections were received.

On 26 April 1957 the Senior Lands Officer was asked to make a survey of the township with a view to the preparation of a draft scheme. After sundry visits to the township and discussions of the draft plans, these were submitted to the Commission, to the landlord and to the crofters, and were accepted by all.

At their meeting on 12 December 1957 the Commission approved the final proposals for the reorganisation of the Big Sand township, and agreed that these should be incorporated in a draft scheme to be submitted to the Secretary of State for Scotland in terms of Section 19 (7) of the Act. At their meeting on 30 December 1957 the Commission formally approved the draft scheme, which was submitted on that date to the Secretary of State.

On 17 July 1958 the draft scheme was served on the landlord, in terms of Section 19 (8) of the Act, by the Secretary of State.

In August 1958, and again in February 1959, objections were received from the landlord and were duly answered.

On 3 April 1959 the Department of Agriculture advised the Commission that the Secretary of State had approved the draft scheme with certain modifications. On 16 April 1959 the Department of Agriculture for Scotland advised the Commission that the modified draft scheme had been submitted to the Scottish Land Court in terms of Section 19 (9) of the Act for fixing of rents and assessment of compensation. The Commission was also requested to obtain the lengths and location of the fences changing hands under the scheme.

On 22 July 1959 the Scottish Land Court held their hearing into the remit by the Secretary of State under Section 19 (9) of the Act in the Territorial Hall, Gairloch, and the report on the hearing was received by the Commission on 8 October 1959. The rents for the new crofts and the compensation payable in respect of permanent improvements changing hands under the scheme were set forth.

On 18 November 1959 the Chairman visited the township to discuss the scheme with the Township Clerk.

On 9 December 1959 notices in terms of Section 19 (10) of the Act were served on the landlords and tenants. The resident tenants were required to vote on the scheme within two months of this date.

By 9 February 1960 all resident tenants had voted on the scheme: the result was thirteen tenants voting against and two in favour of the scheme.

On 11 February 1960 an officer representing the Commission visited the township and called on all those tenants who voted against the scheme to ascertain their reasons for doing so. It was found that seven had voted negatively because of the rise in rent; two were aged crofters not now willing to take a feu; three were not in agreement with the form of reallocation of the land, and one gave no reason at all for his decision. The scheme was accordingly abandoned.

Thus, much work by the Commission achieved absolutely nothing and this particular township, like so many others in my native Wester Ross, remains a monument to stagnation, apathy and economic ignorance. Without reorganisation on a very big scale there can be no future for a crofting economy in the Scottish Highlands. Such was the main message of the 1954 Taylor Committee of Enquiry and the 1884 Napier Commission Report.

The most important part of the 1959 Crofters Commission report dealt with the pressing need for amending legislation [19] to relax the rigid securing of tenure that had sterilised crofting agriculture in an outdated pattern of minute units. The report declared: 'Before allowing ourselves to plead that we are legally underpowered we have searched persistently for any factors which might compensate for our inability to hasten the rehabilitation of crofting agriculture.' The Commission felt, not unnaturally one would have thought, that the essential first step towards rationalisation of crofting agriculture must be the recognition and encouragement of ordinary economic trends. For any crofter or administrator to deny this basic assertion was to believe himself above—or beyond—normal worldly influences. But such crofters and administrators exist in 1967.

The Commission went on to assert, pathetically, that the process of unfreezing the crofting system must be effected gradually, allowing crofters to reside in their crofts and live out their lives undisturbed, even if they were not working their crofts. The drastic measures promised earlier and widely expected were being shelved in advance. 'The main weapon in our armoury, as provided by the Act of 1955, has several defects,' says the Commission. 'It contemplates measures which crofters, in a decayed township, seldom favour and requires old people to face abrupt changes when they want to be left undisturbed. *It empowers an inactive majority to outvote an active minority and so is self-defeating.*' [My italics.]

The Commission suggested strongly, that the present reorganisation procedure must be shortened, simplified and strengthened. After a scheme had been approved, after examination of any objections and after full consultation there must be power to put it speedily into effect, subject to any amendments which may be ordered by the Secretary of State.

In this report, as in its previous ones, the Commission refused to define an economic unit for crofting, but importantly suggested three conditions which might be essential:

'First, such a unit should not fall short either as to size or productive capacity of the type of unit which is regarded as viable in other parts of the country, and eligible, as such, for official assistance; second, it should be capable of carrying sufficient stock to yield an attractive income; and, third, the tenant should be required to devote his whole energy to working it.'

Fresh provision for the reorganisation, development and regulation of crofting in the seven crofting counties of Scotland was made in the Crofters (Scotland) Bill published on 16 January 1961.[20] This was done by way of amendment or replacement of certain of the provisions of the Crofters (Scotland) Act, 1955. The new Bill was hailed (as have so many others in the past) as a new scheme to invigorate the crofting economy. On the other hand, there was talk of 'a crofters' revolt' and letters from crofters and landowners, openly hostile to the Crofters Commission, and to the Bill, began to appear both in the national and in the Highland Press.

Six weeks prior to the publication of the new Bill, the Crofters Commission issued a public statement,[21] an understanding of which is basic to the amending legislation that was envisaged. The Commission admitted that many crofters were perplexed by 'inflammatory comment' on proposals contained in its annual report for 1959. Most of this comment, the Commission maintained, was ill-informed and misleading.

In the statement the Crofters Commission proposed that the tenant who was not working his land should sub-let it with Commission approval on a lease of, say, five years or more to a crofter who needed it and who would work it fully with the aid of Commission grants. The principal tenant would not lose crofter's status. His heir, when he came into occupation, would pay compensation for any substantial improvements carried out by the sub-tenant. Alternatively, the tenant could renounce the land while retaining permanent possession of house and garden ground together with rating and peat-cutting rights. There was to be no question of compulsory dispossession and the Commission alleged that, in this way, their proposals would hurt no one but would help many. It is an economic truism, of course, that if no one is to be hurt there cannot be progress, economic or social, in the Highlands, in Scotland or anywhere else for that matter. But, as a race, Highlanders do not like to talk harshly or bluntly. Euphemism is a way of life in the North and any preoccupation with economics is a dismal prospect. It is more normal to talk of the past or the hereafter than of the present.

'We are not seeking to destroy the law but to fulfil it,' the Commission asserted, defensively. Certain elements in the Highlands and Islands were making a tremendous noise, quite needlessly, about security of tenure. Responsible and thoughtful opinion was alarmed lest this clamour should drown out and exclude the expression of moderate and progressive opinion.

'We all know that amending legislation is under consideration. We all see the danger of giving undue weight to destructive and irrelevant criticism. We give crofters the assurance that we will, so far as is within our power, support the views and wishes of the *moderate and progressive elements*. [My italics.] The extent to which we are successful in doing so may affect powerfully the content and form of the amending Act, and its consequent value to the crofting community.'

Other important amendments, they continued, were required, notably to promote the development and better management of common grazings; and the agitation which had concentrated attention so needlessly on security of tenure and controlled sub-letting, they maintained, had unfortunately tended to obscure matters of real moment for the future efficiency of croft husbandry. The Commission saw a real risk that these matters would now be omitted from the amending Act, and that the crofting community would once more gain the shadow but lose the substance. If so, the prime responsibility must rest on the agitators and those who lead them, declared the Commission.

It was obvious from this statement that the Crofters Commission was embarrassingly aware of an atmosphere hostile to the new thinking that was apparent in the 1959 report. The language of the statement was unusually simple and the Commission repeated its assurance that it would support, so far as it was within its power, the views and wishes of the moderate and progressive elements in the Highlands (whoever they might be). There was no question, at this stage, of compulsory dispossession; and anything less than complete security of tenure, an issue basic to the crofting mentality, was hurriedly relegated to its honoured and historic place in the Napier Commission Report of 1884.

The opening clauses of the Crofting (Scotland) Bill of 1961 dealt with the respective functions of the Secretary of State for Scotland, the Crofters Commission and the Scottish Land Court, with regard to the registration of crofts and related matters. They provided that non-crofting land could be constituted only as a croft or as an enlargement of a croft by direction of the Secretary of State, that the Commission should maintain the register of crofts and that the Land Court should have power to determine matters which might arise in connection with the register.

The provisions in the 1955 Act, with regard to the crofter's right to compensation for permanent improvements, were modified fundamentally. The Bill conferred on the crofter a specific right to erect buildings or execute works on his croft which are reasonably required to enable him to make use of the croft for any subsidiary or auxiliary occupation and will not interfere substantially with the use of the croft as an agricultural subject.

Such buildings or works would rank as permanent improvements for the purposes of compensation. And the basis for valuing permanent improvements was to be altered from value to an incoming tenant to the more realistic one of 'open market' value. This was defined as the amount which, 'having regard to the location of the croft and any other circumstances which might affect the demand for the tenancy thereof, the landlord might reasonably be expected to receive in respect of the improvement from a person who might reasonably be expected to obtain the tenancy of the croft—if the croft were offered on the open market for letting'.

Subject to the crofter satisfying certain qualifications, he could request the Land Court to determine the amount payable before the basis of valuation was changed, and if this proved to be greater than the new assessment the difference between the two amounts should be payable to the crofter by the Secretary of State. The cost of this provision to the Exchequer was estimated to be not more than a mere £5,000 a year, so that obviously very little was expected in this regard. This provision would apply only on the first occasion on which any croft fell vacant after the Bill became law.

The Bill removed a restriction on the right of an absentee crofter whose tenancy was terminated by the Crofters Commission to obtain a feu right on his dwelling house. In future such a crofter would be able to obtain a feu of his house, irrespective of the future occupation of the remainder of the croft.

The Commission might require tenants to sub-let crofts which were not being adequately used, subject to the crofter's right to refer the question of adequate use to the Secretary of State.

Where the crofter failed to sub-let, the Commission itself was empowered to do it. But the tenant was not required to sub-let his house or garden ground, and he was to retain crofter's status and all his rights of tenure. In other words, he was to retain his very special privileges.

Sub-tenants of crofts, approved by the Crofters Commission, would be entitled to the financial assistance which the Secretary of State was empowered to give to crofters under the 1955 Act. This same financial assistance was extended under the Bill to occupiers of holdings other than crofts who were of comparable status to crofters.

The new beneficiaries would be occupiers of holdings, other than crofts, situated in the crofting counties which were either holdings of not more than 50 acres (excluding any common pasture or grazing held along with them) or holdings whose annual rent did not exceed £50, who, in the opinion of the Secretary of State, were of substantially the same economic status as a crofter.

It was estimated that the additional expenditure likely to be incurred as a result of this extension of the Secretary of State's powers would be £200,000 a year. This estimate took account of the savings which would arise in other statutory schemes under which assistance was given to persons who would, in future, benefit from this extension of the powers of the Secretary of State for Scotland.

Under the provisions of the Bill, common grazings regulations could restrict the use of any part of the common grazings on which works of improvement had been carried out to those crofters who contributed towards the expenses incurred by the common grazings committee in carrying out these works.

Where the use of any part of the common grazings was so restricted the regulations could control the number and kinds of stock which each contributing crofter could put on that part, and the number and kinds of stock which each crofter (whether or not he is a contributing crofter) could put on the remainder of the common grazings.

The Bill revised, fundamentally, the procedure for reorganising a crofting township. Under the 1955 Act any scheme for reorganisation, before being confirmed by the Secretary of State, had to be approved by a majority of the crofters ordinarily resident in the township. Under the proposed provisions a majority of crofters would still have to approve any such scheme, but whereas under the 1955 Act the crofters' vote was the last stage in a long procedure, in the new Act it was to be one of the early stages thus reducing the risk of time and money spent on a scheme being completely wasted. If the Crofters Commission, after making such inquiries as it thought fit, was satisfied that any township ought to be reorganised in order to secure its preservation or better development, then it could, after consultation with the landlords and the crofters proposed to be affected, prepare a draft of a scheme for reorganisation of the township. A reorganisation scheme would provide for the re-allocation of the land in the township 'in such manner as is, in the opinion of the Commission, most conducive to the proper and efficient use of the land and to the general benefit of the township'. This was the crux of the Bill.

Among other things a reorganisation scheme could, if the Commission thought fit, provide for the inclusion of land in the vicinity of the township which, in the opinion of the Commission, ought to be used for the enlargement of crofts in the township or of common grazings used exclusively or shared in by the township; for the admission into the township of new crofters and the allocation to them of shares in the common grazings; for the apportionment of all or of a part of the common grazings for the exclusive use of individual crofters in the township; and for the grant to any crofter (not being a person who under the scheme becomes the tenant of a croft), who so wishes, of a conveyance in feu of the dwelling-house which formed part of the croft of which he was tenant immediately before the date on which the scheme was put into effect.

The Commission would submit to the Secretary of State the draft reorganisation scheme, and such maps and plans as would be necessary to indicate the general effect of the scheme, together with such information as it thought necessary, for the purpose of informing him of the general purport of the scheme. It would submit also its views on the prospects of the development of agricultural and other industries in the township, and in the locality in which the township was situated.

The Second Schedule to the Bill provided that before confirming a reorganisation scheme the Secretary of State would serve on every owner and every occupier of land to which the draft scheme applied a copy of the scheme. If no objection was made, he might confirm the draft scheme with or without modifications. If there was an objection, the Secretary of State would cause a public local inquiry to be held, and after considering the objection and the report of the person who held the inquiry he could, if he thought fit, confirm the draft scheme with or without modifications.

The stage then, was set in the Bill for the long-awaited ruthless reappraisal and reorganisation that alone would bring economic progress to crofting in the West Highlands. The provisions of the 1955 Act relating to the dispossession of crofters on the ground of bad husbandry were to be repealed, and the Commission was to be given new powers to compel the bad crofter to sub-let if he was not making adequate use of his croft, it would serve on him a notice stating its opinion, and that the croft would, one month from the date of service of the notice, become subject to a requirement that it be sub-let. This was subject to the qualification that a crofter on whom such notice was served could, within one month of the date of service, refer to the Secretary of State the question whether he was making adequate use of his croft. The Secretary of State, after affording the crofter an opportunity of making representations to him, might annul or confirm the notice. If, after the service of such a notice, the crofter either made no reference to the Secretary of State, or the Secretary of State confirmed the notice on such reference, the Commission might serve on the crofter a further notice requiring him to submit within one month proposals (other than any relating to rent) for sub-letting his croft. The Commission might approve any such proposals, and in giving its approval might impose such conditions (other than any relating to rent) as it saw fit.

The duration of any sub-lease granted by the Commission was to be determined by it, but was not to exceed seven years. It was to be conditional on the tenant's making adequate use of the land comprised in the sub-lease and on his maintaining in a proper state of repair any permanent improvements existing on the land at the beginning of the sub-lease. If he failed to do so he would be required, on the termination of the sub-lease, to pay to the crofter such sum in respect of any depreciation in the value of the improvements resulting from his failure, as the

Land Court, in the absence of agreement between him and the crofter, might determine.

There was provision for the termination of a sub-lease if the Commission was satisfied that the sub-tenant had broken one or more of the terms or conditions of the sub-lease, or where either the crofter or sub-tenant represented that the circumstances of either of them had so materially altered that it was reasonable that the sub-lease be ended.

I have dealt at some length with the Crofters (Scotland) Bill 1961, because I believe it represented the minimum require-ments that the Crofters Commission believed to be necessary for it to fulfil its function. For me the Bill represented the climax of recent economic thinking on the problems of crofting. As such I regard it as much more important than the Act of Parlia-ment which followed it.

On its way through Parliament the Bill was mutilated almost out of recognition, and so it was the Bill, rather than the Act which followed it, that represented the high-water mark of Crofters Commission policy and thinking on Highland Develop-ment. Even their scheme for compulsory sub-letting (Section 12 of the Act) was not brought into operation along with the re-mainder of the Act. It is specifically provided that a resolution of both Houses of Parliament is required before it can be brought into operation. I am sure that those who pressed for and won amendments to the Bill did so, sincerely believing that they were acting in the best interest of the Highland crofter. And it may well be that they were right if one takes the *existing* crofters as those that matter in the legislation. But the new Act seals the doom of crofting as an economic undertaking for future generations.

The Crofters Act was the main item of Scottish legislation in 1961. But in one year it was already a dead letter. It was rendered so by the indifference of crofters to the future and by the timidity of our legislators in Westminster and their ignor-ance of the Highland situation. The Crofters Commission, in its fifth annual report, presented to Parliament on 5 June 1962,[22] had this to say:

'It was evident, at the end of 1961, that the revised formula in the Act of that year had no ready appeal for crofters or landlords.'[23]

The formula in question—basic to success—related to the re-organisation of the crofting township. It was to have been a vital remedial process. On it all else depended. The Napier Commission had said so, as had the Taylor Commission of Enquiry. The Crofters Commission, as soon as possible after the Act had gone through Parliament, held a referendum to assess the re-action of the crofting communities to the new proposals. Their report shows that only 28 townships out of 759 took the trouble to reply. None asked for reorganisation, and only 2 out of 263 landlords expressed any interest in reorganisation. Everything was fine. The Commission, therefore, had now no mandate to proceed further. That left only formal sub-letting to be salvaged from the wreck as a positive possibility and no one with under-standing of the situation really believed that crofters would take advantage of it to any appreciable extent. In any case, sub-letting will not bring economic salvation. It cannot. The Com-mission did not lament for the 1961 Act, for it did not give them the powers they had sought. In these circumstances, they said, crofting must remain much as they found it in 1955 when the Commission was formed to revitalise crofting.

The Commission, however, did not resign, but began to talk and write and broadcast in Gaelic and English about land improvement—'a new element in crofting husbandry'—and to this the Commission now proposed to divert their energies. The techniques of land improvement, by surface treatment, by ploughing and by variants of both, they argued, are being adopted with considerable enthusiasm by crofters. The heather is giving way to grass and for the first time a growing number of crofters are able to feed a sufficiency of it to their animals.

The Colleges of Agriculture are teaching how the new grass should be managed to best advantage. The shortage of winter feed is being tackled. The plough is being used to condition the land, hitherto thought to be fit for rough grazing only, so that hay or silage can be grown and harvested. A few new crofter contractors are setting up business in Lewis, where land im-provement work is said to be proceeding on a large scale. I am not convinced in 1967, that the Lewis experiment has been successful, as the publicity given to it would suggest.

The tenth annual report of the Crofters Commission[24] was published on 14 June 1966 and gives the impression once again of being much more concerned with tourism than with crofting, with holiday homes for visitors rather than with reviving the crofting economy of Gaelic Scotland. The tourist bandwagon is, as always, conveniently at hand when all else seems to have failed.

In fairness, however, it must be stated that the Commission, in 1966, outlined some blunt and some hopeful economic facts. The economic position in general, in the Highlands, is more promising; the prospects for employment are better than they used to be and crofting could continue to exist side by side with new industry if given a proper chance. But the Commission maintain that their ability to help crofters is very largely indirect and negative because the Act of Parliament under which they operate does not give them enough power. So the best hope for the Highlands, they continue to suggest, is tourism and holiday homes, maintaining that these pursuits, if carried out with enterprise could give new life to the Scottish Highlands. I, personally, do not hold to this view for one moment and I do not think that the Highlander, by his very nature, is ever likely to be successful in making much of a living out of tourism. One or two people in a community will make such a living perhaps: but the bulk of them will not unless their whole outlook on life changes very considerably. Tourism and the Highland character clash. And in any case a tourist economy in Gaelic Scotland would require National Assistance to sustain it for nine months of each year. What then of our famous Highland independence? And despite official statements to the contrary our Highland weather is unlikely to have much appeal but to the physically robust. To pretend otherwise is to court financial disaster.

The Commission returns for the tenth time to the need to enlarge crofts. Where small crofts are concerned the first consideration must be to try and get them into the hands of young men with other employment in the district who need a supplement to the family income; or alternatively they could be given to people from outside the district who can bring in new skills, capital and ideas for development which may lead to the creation of even a small amount of employment locally. Like the Commission, I, too, would today gladly welcome incomers. They would upset some people and this, in my opinion, would be no bad thing. But if they come there may well be life and prosperity in the glens in fifty years time, but without new blood there will be a vast army of pious old-age pensioners in strategic control of the Highlands and Islands before very long. The social atmosphere in any community will affect fundamentally the economic development of the area. I have nothing against old-age pensioners—but if you have no youth, no young men or young women living *all the year round* in the Highlands, then as a race we have no future nor do we deserve one. And tourism will not save us. It is not people looking for cheap holiday homes that we want to attract to the North today, but young enterprising Highlanders, and others, who are frequently engaged in unsatisfying work in the industrial cities of Scotland and England.

Some of them understand only too well what is wrong and what is required to put things right in Gaeldom but urbanised Highlanders will want to run their own lives according to their own lights and, above all, they will want steady work and a steady wage—a weekly wage every Friday—not just a lump sum when the wool clip is sold or the subsidy comes in for the cows or the sheep. In other words they want industry offering jobs comparable to that pertaining elsewhere in Scotland. If they get this, they may well return and stay in Gaelic Scotland. If steady employment is not offered to them, they and their like will continue to leave the Highlands in the steady depressing stream with which we are so familiar.

The number of crofts worked, the Commission tells us, in 1966, continues to decline—155 less last year than the previous year. And the old crofter who does not work his land holds on to it selfishly. He doesn't work it. He can't. But he sees to it nevertheless that no one else gets the chance to try and work it either. And nobody can do anything about it. Parliament has so decreed. In some places, says the Commission, the crofters have made some progress—in Shetland, for example, where they are trying hard, and with some success, to make crofting a full-time rather than a part-time occupation. And the Commission feels that such progress could perhaps come elsewhere if only crofters would themselves take the right decisions. But this, let us be quite frank, they do not now do nor is there any evidence of new ideas on crofting being discussed at any level. Crofters lack effective leadership; and as a race they are submissive and apathetic and they continue to quarrel with their neighbours about trivial things, seldom working together for the common good. In the Highlands the really important issues seldom seem to matter nor are they often discussed.

I have very considerable respect for the present Chairman of the Crofters Commission,[25] now incidentally its only full-time member. He knows his Highlands and his Highlanders intimately. He knows what his fellow Gaels can do and what they will refuse to attempt. This man had considerable vision as editor of the *Stornoway Gazette* when he became a part-time member of the Commission in 1955, when it was first formed, but to me his last report suggests failure and it is my considered opinion that the Crofters Commission, after eleven years, has now ceased to be meaningful in its present form. It no longer has any real contribution to make to the economic revival of the Highlands and Islands. The Commission's annual reports after 1959 have increasingly lacked purpose, consisting of little more than pious platitudes and a melancholic undertone of helplessness. The Commission should now be disbanded and its function absorbed by the Highlands and Islands Development Board.

The Labour Party in opposition was much concerned with the Highland economic imbalance and in its election manifesto for the General Election of 1964 there was a pledge that Labour, if elected to form the government, would set up a new authority to accept public responsibility for the economic development of the Highlands and Islands. The Highland Development (Scotland) Bill presented to Parliament on 23 February 1965 by the Labour Secretary of State for Scotland was the outcome of this pledge and was a brave and challenging document representing the culmination of much discussion and work within the Labour Party over many years. It proposed extensive power for a new Highland Development Board that was to be created in the summer and it outlined legislation for the compulsory acquisition and development of land in the Scottish Highlands. The new Board, in addition, was to be empowered to:

(i) erect buildings or other structures and carry out works on land;

(ii) provide equipment and services on or in connection with land;

(iii) hold, manage, maintain, hire, let or otherwise dispose of such works, equipment or services.

Those proposals, on publication, brought an immediate hostile reaction from the Conservative Party and from the former Secretary of State for Scotland,[26] who suggested that they virtually amounted to the nationalisation of almost the whole of the North of Scotland. And, as such, he gave notice that his Party could not support the Bill as presented.

Two previous commentaries on Highland Development are worthy of mention at this point. In a note of dissent[27] to the Taylor Commission of Enquiry in April 1954 Mrs Margaret H. Macpherson maintained that the crofting counties of the Scottish Highlands could not have an economic future until the State owned all crofting land. This, she concluded, was the only way in which control and supervision could be real. Without it, the effect and purpose of the Report would be lost. She argued that the Highland landlord was a curious anomaly in the middle of the twentieth century and greatly regretted that her colleagues on the Commission of Enquiry were prepared to let him continue 'as a figurehead, *un roi fainéant*'. The landlord would not co-operate, she believed, with any new authority nor would he be amenable to the necessary measures of supervision. She thought that his real interest was in his sporting rights, and since 1886—and indeed before that—very few landlords had wished to stimulate in any way the economic development of the crofting counties; their aim had rather been to destroy, systematically, the crofting way of life, and in this they had all but succeeded. As a direct consequence of this complete indifference by landlords, Mrs Macpherson maintained, nearly half the land in the island of Skye was already state-owned and from her personal experience of having lived all her working life on a State-owned holding she maintained that the system was working well and she would like to see it extended to the whole of the crofting area. In Skye, according to her, State land was well worked; private land was not, and she suggested that the Secretary of State should, therefore, acquire all crofting land in the Highlands and landlords should be compensated on whatever terms were considered equitable. The former owners, she conceded, should have a preferential right to rent the shootings from the State.

On 16 December 1964 the Advisory Panel on the Highlands and Islands submitted a rather startling report[28] to the Secretary of State for Scotland. It was signed only by the chairman of the panel, Lord Cameron, although, occasionally, in reading it one feels that Mrs Naomi Mitchison (now Lady Mitchison), a member of the panel, may have had a hand in the compilation of the document. It recommended integrated development in the Highlands in four basic fields and it was asserted that for the plans to succeed sweeping changes must be made in the administration and control of the region. Land is of basic importance to the Highland economy, said the Report, and at present it is under-used and, very frequently, grossly mis-used. It was recommended, therefore, that the Secretary of State take over, by compulsory acquisition, large areas of the Highlands and Islands to be developed for farming and forestry. A great deal more of the land could go under forest without any damage at all to the agricultural potential, and new farming developments could readily be encouraged to produce beef calves, for example. Family holdings, owned by the State, would be let to people prepared to work them diligently.

The thirty government and other agencies wholly or partly at work in the Highlands, it was maintained, represented a multiplicity that was neither necessary nor effective. Considerable administrative rationalisation and streamlining was logical and reasonable, including the allocation of money for Highland affairs. The report maintained that there need be no real conflict in land use and called for an open mind in determining, objectively, what constitutes proper land use. Specific proposals were then made:

1. *Agriculture*

Intensifying of crofter and other co-operative ventures with financial aid to promote developments. Extension of credit facilities, perhaps by the provision of a "land bank". The Crofters Commission to be allowed to give more effective inducement for general development. Government pilot experi-

Economic Life

ments in creating family farms designed to yield a minimum annual income of £750. Government pilot schemes of land reclamation to be introduced.

2. *Tourism*

State deer forests, deriving from land already publicly owned, to be available for tourists desiring deer stalking facilities. Public and private co-operation to develop salmon fisheries, coupled with the extension of Government supervision into trout fishing. Research facilities to be made available for freshwater fisheries potential. Highland areas suitable for major comprehensive development to be identified and studied systematically. Joint groups to plan the opening up of areas of scenic beauty with full oversight of access, publicity and information.

3. *Forestry*

An increased timber planting programme of 20,000 acres annually, over 20 years, to use the one million acres completely suitable for afforestation. The government to make more use of statutory powers of land acquisition for afforestation and more flexible powers to be introduced. Compulsory land acquisition for forestry would be needed and despite the opposition that it would engender should not be shirked.

4. *Industrial*

The new National Resources Council to investigate mineral and other resources with a view to eventual exploitation. A proper survey was long overdue.

Basically, then, the Advisory Panel on the Highlands and Islands, in this, its last, report was recommending, unanimously, that the State should intervene positively and control Highland land use. It recommended, specifically, however, that the whole system should be reviewed within five years and that, at all times, there must be a due balance of economic and social considerations, and it emphasised that its proposals on land use could only be a beginning if real solutions were to be found to the economic malaise of the Highland economy.

The Highland Development (Scotland) Bill,[29] presented to Parliament on 23 February 1965, had eighteen clauses and provided for the creation of a Highland Development Board consisting of a chairman and up to six members. In addition, there was to be a Highland Development Consultative Council drawn from local authorities and other Highland interests to advise the Board, whose general function would be preparing, concerting, promoting, assisting and undertaking measures for the economic and social development of the Highlands and Islands. It would keep under general review all matters relating to the economic and social well-being and development of the area, consult with local authorities and other bodies and submit development proposals to the Secretary of State for Scotland. Where there was no authority to carry out any proposal that had been approved, the Board itself would be empowered to do the job. It would have the power also to request the furnishing of information about any business or undertaking, subject only to specific restrictions on the disclosure of such information.

While the Bill was initially concerned only with the seven crofting counties, provision was made for extension to such other areas of Scotland as, having regard to their character and proximity to the crofting counties, the Secretary of State for Scotland might from time to time designate.

The Board was to be authorised to provide advisory and other services to local industry and business enterprises, and professional assistance could be given with staff training, management, technical advice and accountancy. The Industrial Estates Management Corporation for Scotland was to be empowered to act as the Board's agent for building and other work. Powers of entry to land to survey it were to be given to the Board, and this included power to search and bore for minerals. It could also commission any investigation or research that was deemed necessary to any of its functions and could charge for such services and could accept any gifts which could be applied to its purposes. Except with the express consent of the Secretary of State the Board would not have power to borrow money.

The board would keep proper accounts and other records in

relation to the accounts and would prepare in respect of each of the financial years a statement of account. The Secretary of State would, on or before 30 November in any year, transmit to the Comptroller and Auditor General the accounts prepared by the Board for the financial year last ended.

Any scheme approved under the Act by the Secretary of State for Scotland would carry automatic planning permission after he had consulted the local planning authority, though he might at any time impose conditions upon any approval that he gave.

The Highland Development Board, then, was to have very considerable executive powers, and in the Highlands many people of all political persuasions were impressed by the courage and sweep of the proposals. Even the Scottish Landowners' Federation announced that it would do its best to co-operate with the new body, though it would look closely at the clauses of the bill dealing with the compulsory powers to be given to the Board, to ensure that owners' interests were adequately safeguarded and the merits of development proposals fully considered.

The crux of the matter, it seemed to many observers, at this stage, was no longer political but financial, and it was here that the Bill was most disappointing, providing only for a sum of £150,000 in the financial year 1965–66 to meet the cost of the Board's administration of operations carried out by it. By 1968–69 the expenditure was estimated to rise to about £1 million. This sum was, of course, extra to what was already paid to the crofting counties by government departments and official agencies, but the smallness of the amount was quite startling in the imaginative context of the Bill itself and it was said, unkindly perhaps, that the smallness of the amount of money to be made available explained why even the Scottish Landowners' Federation were not really unenthusiastic about the Bill as a whole. Without adequate money the Board could not succeed in its task.

It is impossible to say just how much money would really be required to be used in the Highlands to boost them economically into a viable region of the British economy, though in the past many suggestions have been made—some carefully calculated —others, no more than reckless guesses. The Labour Party was usually deliberately vague on this point but the Scottish T.U.C. is on record as thinking that £250 million was necessary.[30]

In the 1964–65 financial year Inverness County Council, a typical Highland local authority, had a budget of some £7 million, and Government grants to the seven crofting counties that year were in the region of £30 million and, in these circumstances, the addition of an extra £1 million by 1968–69 was thought unlikely, by critics of the new Bill, to make very much difference economically. But, said the enthusiasts, the personnel of the new Board when elected, will consist of men or women of vision and action who will quickly produce positive plans, for which money will be readily made available by the Treasury and by private enterprise. Money was certainly necessary for success: so were men of personality and vision on the Board.

The Bill was expected to have a stormy passage through Parliament, but the second reading on 16 March 1965 was neither particularly lively nor controversial, for basically this was a sound Bill and on it, it was realised by members on both sides of the House, the future, economic and social, of the Highlands most certainly now depended. This was to be a final exciting experiment and no one seemed anxious to oppose it.

On 5 October 1965 the names of the members of the new Highlands and Islands Development Board, as it was now called, were announced. Five appointments were made with one other place to be filled later by the Secretary of State for Scotland at his discretion. The Board was formally to start its operations in Inverness in November 1965. The Chairman of the Board, previously announced, was Mr Robert Grieve, recently appointed Professor of Town and Regional Planning at the University of Glasgow and who, previous to his professorial appointment, had been Chief Planning Officer for Scotland at St Andrew's House, Edinburgh. His appointment was well received everywhere. It was seen as a highly imaginative appointment for it was well known that Professor Grieve had been deeply involved in the important new-look plan for Central Scotland from which so much was expected. Grieve was an acknowledged planner; he was a Scot who knew his Highlands and he had a reputation for getting things done. The choice of the other members of the Board was very much less imaginative, however, and surprisingly and disappointingly Gaelic Scotland, as such, was not represented at all on the new Board, and it was clear that political considerations rather than professional qualifications had been an important criterion in the selection of some of the members.

Mr John Rollo, a Bonnybridge industrialist, with a small factory employing three men at Inverasdale, was elected as Professor Grieve's full-time deputy chairman and while he had a long record of service to the Highlands as chairman of the Highland Fund Limited, an agency formed after the war, to provide fiscal and other aid for development projects, few had expected him to be chosen as deputy chairman of the new Board.

Two other full-time members were Mr Prophet Smith, a Trade Union official and a former convener of Shetland County Council, and Mr J. C. Robertson, an Easter Ross farmer who, surprisingly, on his appointment, was already a part-time member of the Crofters Commission. One of the two part-time members, very imaginatively, was the late Mr William Logan— the Muir of Ord industrialist whose personal and professional reputation throughout the Highlands, at that time, was second to none. His reputation as a successful civil engineering contractor with extensive experience of private, public, government and NATO contracts meant instant approval in the North of Scotland for his appointment to the Board. This was a businessman whose enterprise and integrity were widely respected throughout the Highlands and Islands of Scotland. The other part-time member was Mr William Scholes, from Motherwell, the Scottish organiser of the Transport and General Workers' Union.

None of the members of the Board was known to be Gaelicspeaking and while Professor Grieve's professional qualifications, as a planner, were highly respected and Mr Logan's enterprise was almost mythical, doubts were immediately and freely expressed about the wisdom, for example, of having no one on the Board who was known to be acquainted with the special problems of the Outer Isles. A national newspaper[31] on 6 October 1965, in a special article, conceded that Professor Grieve's appointment was potentially brilliant but that he was supported by a fairly unimpressive team. This was an opinion frequently stated at the time by responsible supporters of the new Board.

On Mr Logan's untimely death, Mr Frank Thomson was appointed to replace him. He was an Aberdonian by birth and an accountant by profession, enjoying a reputation, at that time, as a Highland entrepreneur, earned in the meteoric development of the massive new grain distillery at Invergordon of which he had been, for a time, managing director.

Professor Grieve inevitably must have influenced some of the Secretary of State for Scotland's appointments to the Board but despite this and because of territorial, political and past commitments and performance—many in the Highlands felt that the newly elected members would be unlikely to coalesce into the effective team for which people had hoped and from which so much was expected in, and for, the region. Apart from Logan the composition of Grieve's team seemed singularly at variance with what many had envisaged as necessary to ensure the co-operation and initial inspiration on which so much would depend.

On 1 November 1965, just one year less two days after the Government had first announced that a Bill would be introduced in Parliament to set up the new authority, the Highlands and Islands Development Board took office in their new headquarters at Inverness. A new phase in regional planning in Britain had begun and Professor Grieve announced that a first concern of the Board would be the provision of financial inducements for the promotion of industrial and other enterprises. His Board, he maintained, was a regional board with genuine executive power and the Highlands and Islands would be developed by special work programmes and the new Board, itself, would inaugurate projects of its own. Grieve was confident of success. Two controversial issues—Highland power—hydro and nuclear—and afforestation were to be considered urgently. It was well known that the Government would have to make an early decision on whether to approve further hydro projects as well as develop a new commercial prototype fast reactor and Grieve, in his first pronouncement, promised to give this his immediate attention. The Secretary of State for Scotland, some weeks later, surprisingly, it seemed to me, rejected the hydro-electric schemes proposed for Fada-Fionn and Laidon and Grieve was thus faced with the challenge of getting the nuclear power station to Dounreay where the Atomic Energy Authority's successful experimental unit was located. Contrary to informed opinion, he succeeded in persuading the Minister of Technology, Mr Frank Cousins, to establish the station in Caithness. He had won his first victory; he had already made a practical positive contribution to the Highland economy. And now he was all set to rehabilitate the area as an integral part of the United Kingdom, over the long term. And in a television interview on 9 September 1966 Professor Grieve repeated his belief in the positive integration of the region into Scotland and the United Kingdom. He believed that the increasing congestion of the industrial conurbations would work in favour of Highland redevelopment and he believed that the Southerners who would go North would be readily accepted and absorbed and would become genuine Highlanders in one generation. But the Gaelic tongue, he believed, had no future.[32]

The Board was invested with powers unequalled by any similar public authority in Great Britain and this uniqueness was widely regarded as a tangible token of the Board's strength and purpose. Its members were specifically permitted, by its charter, to hold financial interests in projects financed or assisted by the Board and by this quite unusual privilege it was argued, entrepreneurs, of proved ability, would be willing to serve on the Board and would thus bring public and private enterprise together to foster economic growth in the area. Operationally, however, the Board began cautiously, supporting, as many expected, a small firm to manufacture fishing flies, building a few fishing boats; encouraging tourism by sponsoring a caravan site in the historic setting of Glencoe; giving £1,000 to a man claiming, that with advanced and really modern scientific equipment, he could, professionally, photograph the Loch Ness monster. On a bigger and more controversial scale the Board announced that it would make £1 million available for the building of a chain of five hotels in the Western Isles and on the west coast mainland. These, it was stated, would cost about £200,000 each, would each accommodate 100 guests and would be leased to tenants at economic rents. And a Board member (Mr J. C.

Robertson) claimed that the hotels could be filled for eight to ten months of the year. A tourist unit, a small expert section, was to be established to deal with problems of accommodation, resort development, servicing, sales and marketing. I, for one, have had considerable reservations on the economic viability of this particular tourist project and I am surprised that the Board was able to persuade the Treasury to invest the comparatively large sum of £1 million in it. Undoubtedly, the Board's powers of persuasion, at high level, are to be acclaimed. This is highly significant in terms of the problems confronting the Board.

In this setting which inspired but few observers in its first year of office the Board's aspirations for the Highlands and Islands suddenly, and apparently without planned publicity, assumed grandiloquent dimensions. They were soon committed to create a petro-chemical complex in the Invergordon area which would produce fertilisers, polythene fibres and ammonia for world markets. To cost £50 million, in its first phase, the Treasury, it was said, was willing to invest, initially, £20 million in this single project whose eventual investment value was said to be £150 million. In the White Paper on the Scottish Economy of January 1966 (Cmd 2864) with which Professor Grieve, as a senior Civil Servant, had been professionally involved, the Government had clearly stated that the environment of the Beauly and Cromarty Firths was likely to become increasingly attractive to industry and commerce, offering special facilities and prospects of development which were unique. In Appendix A of the White Paper a new linear development was envisaged for this area with an increase in the present population of at least 120 per cent.

The Board, in 1966, accepted this suggestion and its strategy for Highland development thus became concentrated on establishing in the Invergordon area a major centre of modern industry developing into a planned, modern city of 300,000 inhabitants. There would be job opportunities not only for those Highlanders who would be willing to move to the area but also for people from all over Britain, who would be offered conditions of work and social and cultural activities comparable with the best pertaining elsewhere in the United Kingdom. The urban and industrial development of Invergordon thus came to be, for the Board, the key to the regeneration of the Highland economy: the petro-chemical complex was to be but the start of the new strategy and the provision of very cheap power was to be a main attraction to other electricity-using industries. Moray Firth Development (MFD), with all its implicities, by the end of 1966, came to be regarded, by the Board, as crucial to their resolve to improve the economic and social conditions of the people who lived in the Highlands and Islands. To many people it seemed that the Board's singleness of purpose was misguided but its very magnitude commanded admiration. To the Board it had become the linchpin of their policy.

Early in March 1967, the national Press began to give considerable publicity to the dismissal by the Board, of Mr Philip Durham, one of its part-time officials who had written a critical memorandum on the Board's activities and had handed this privately to *The Times*. On his dismissal Mr Durham was warned by official letter of his responsibilities under the Official Secrets Act and the British Press, almost unanimously, suspected automatically that the Board had something to hide. From this point on the Highlands and Islands Development Board received much adverse publicity and, unfortunately, it must be stated, at this point, that its public relations, in all its aspects, have at all times since its inception, been incredibly poor, misguided and defensive to a fault. On the eve of the dismissal controversy the Board's Information Officer had an article in the *Glasgow Herald* (4 March 1967) which was a reply to three interesting articles by a special correspondent (John Kerr) which had raised issues basic to the economic revival of the Highland area. Kerr had cast some doubts on the feasibility of the Invergordon project and he was unenthusiastic about the new 100-bedded hotels proposed for the Western Isles. The Board's Information Officer, hypersensitive to Kerr's criticism, attacked him strenuously for his views, his use of language and 'his sour attitude to the Board ... betrayed ... by his use of words'. It seemed to me, then, that Mr Grassie had missed a marvellous opportunity to improve the Board's tarnishing image and, incredibly, he made no attempt to answer those questions on Board policy that he and everyone else concerned with the Highlands, knew were being asked by those most directly concerned with the Invergordon project. The Board was on the defensive: it was making no attempt to cultivate its friends. Its public relations organisation was out of touch with Highland thinking.

The man who had stimulated the Board to concentrate on the Invergordon project was its part-time member, Frank Thomson, and it was over his business interests in the Invergordon area that the controversy broke, publicly, and on 17 March 1967 the Secretary of State for Scotland, in the House of Commons, attempted to reassure the House that the business interests of certain Board members were not in conflict with the aims of the Board; that though certain members had received substantial amounts of monies in grants and in loans for companies with which they were personally associated he was, nevertheless, completely satisfied that this was all in order. He stated, categorically, that it was neither relevant nor proper to detail the names of the members nor the companies concerned without their permission. The statement was ill-received by the British Press in general and by critics of the Board whose identity frequently revealed no common interest whatsoever except a scepticism that the Board was now unlikely to succeed in its aims. Some, undoubtedly, were pleased that this should be the case: others, and they were much more numerous, were depressed in the extreme for the Board had come into existence with much goodwill and hope of success. But now the radicals and the reactionaries were on a common ground: the great Highland experiment was unlikely to succeed. The Board was not equal to its task.

On joining the Highlands and Islands Development Board Thomson had taken with him a report which, later, was to receive much publicity in the press, on ways of utilising surplus chemical compounds which had led to a further major professional study on the economic potential of the Invergordon area costing, it was said, £55,000 to execute. Thomson had created a new company, Invergordon Chemical Enterprises Ltd. which had a total paid up capital of £2 with himself and a Mr C. J. Campbell as co-directors. The Highlands and Islands Development Board were enthusiastic about the petrochemical complex proposal and Prophet Smith's comment later received national publicity. 'It would be daft,' he said, 'to try and catch sprats when they could catch a whale.' Ross and Cromarty County Council, with the exception of its Planning

Staff, who later resigned, obviously shared this point of view. The farmers of the Invergordon area took a very different view, however, and criticism began to mount though the Board continued to discount it until, at last, public pressure forced the Secretary of State for Scotland to make a statement first to the Cabinet and then to the House of Commons.

Accepting Mr Thomson's resignation from the Board the Scottish Secretary did so in a prepared statement which contained little that was not already public knowledge.

Mr Ross said that Mr Thomson was chairman of Invergordon Chemical Enterprises, Ltd., and in that capacity would have an interest in the petro-chemical development at Invergordon should it go ahead. But Mr Thomson had not been able to assure him that he would not accept an appointment in the enterprise, should it materialise. In all the circumstances, Mr Thomson had decided that in order to avoid any possible misunderstanding, he should now resign from the board. The Scottish Secretary had accepted his resignation with regret, knowing the enthusiasm, concern and effort that Mr Thomson had put into the development of the Highlands.

Referring to the Board's examination of the possibilities of petro-chemical and associated development in the Invergordon area, he said that clearly this could be a highly desirable project and could contribute greatly to the economy of the Highlands. But he had to emphasise that a great deal of study and investigation would be required before the technical and commercial feasibility of such a major project could be established, and there would be important issues to be considered by the Government.

Various studies and investigations were proceeding, and whether or not the development would prove feasible could not be decided until these were completed. He must therefore make it clear that there had not been, nor could there be at present, any commitment by the Government in this matter. When he had appointed Mr Thomson to be a part-time member of the board he was aware of his other activities, including his active desire to encourage a major petro-chemical project in the Invergordon area. He accepted that in the Board's study and exploration of the possibilities, Mr Thomson had played his part with genuine regard to the wellbeing of the Highlands. While

Mr Thomson had been a member of a partnership who owned Kincraig Farm and House, in the vicinity of Invergordon, he had sought the agreement of his partners to withdraw from it. But he was also chairman of Invergordon Chemical Enterprises, Ltd., and in that capacity he had an interest in the petrochemical development, should it go ahead. Mr Thomson had told him that, in that event, he would take steps to see that he did not derive any profit from either of these interests, and that he would not take any financial interest in the new enterprise.

Mr Ross had begun his statement by saying that on 17 March he had undertaken to let Mr Gordon Campbell M.P. (Con., Moray and Nairn) have information about the assistance given to businesses in which members of the Board had an interest, if he obtained the consent of the businesses concerned. Having obtained that consent, he could now give the following details:

1. On 24 March 1966 the board had approved a loan of £7,500 to R.T.S. (Potatoes) Ltd., who rented a building from Mr John C. Robertson.

2. On 12 May 1966 the Board had approved a building grant of £1,500 and a loan of £23,500 to Polyscot (Polycast) Ltd., of which Mr Frank Thomson was one of the two principal shareholders.

3. On 23 December 1966 the Board had approved a loan of £4,000 to Shetland Knitters' Association, in which Mr Prophet Smith held ten £1 shares.

4. On 26 January 1967 the Board had approved a building grant of £1,687 10s. to Buchan Meat Producers Ltd., in which Mr Robertson held 100 £1 shares.

In each of these cases the member concerned had declared his interest, and Mr Ross was satisfied that throughout these transactions the Board had not only complied with the statutory requirements governing pecuniary interests, but had also acted fairly and objectively in the discharge of their duties. Having given this information in the very special circumstances created by the recent spate of innuendo and rumour, he hoped he carried both sides of the House with him in emphasising how vital it was to the Board's operations in the field of financial assistance for private industrial and commercial projects, that those who came to the Board for assistance should be able to rely completely on the confidentiality of their dealings with the Board. This was a cardinal principle, and it would be nothing short of a tragedy if the splendid work the Board had done and was doing in this important field were to be impaired or frustrated.

Mr Michael Noble, Opposition spokesman on Scottish affairs, thanking Mr Ross for his statement, said Mr Ross had stated that the Board had approved these various monies to different people, but had the Secretary of State himself approved of proposals which appeared to have given more than 10 per cent of the money paid out by the Board to companies in which Board members were directly involved—and these members had themselves been appointed by the Secretary of State? Had the Secretary of State satisfied himself that there had been no private commercial benefit to accrue to members of the board as a result of the board's policy to develop, if possible, a big chemical complex at Invergordon? Mr Ross's statement seemed to make it clear that Mr Thomson had considerable interest in this development and that it was his intention to develop his own personal interest as well as that of the Highlands and the Board. Mr Thomson had now resigned, but had his resignation removed, in the Secretary of State's view, the very difficult position—that he had been using to some extent taxpayers' money and his position on the Board to develop an interest in which he had, in the past at least, an intention of taking a considerable part? Did the Secretary of State not think the delay in making this full and frank statement had done serious damage to the Board's reputation, and was it not the Secretary of State himself who, through his own office, had taken so long to clear up the whole of this position? Did Mr Ross not think, therefore, that in view of the very complex nature of many of these things, it would be wise to publish in a White Paper a full statement of all the documents in this case?

Mr Ross said he did not think a White Paper was essential; there had been far too much paper about this.

It would be interesting to ask everyone in the House if they could swear to the fact that they had not themselves seen confidential and private documents which were really the Board's property. The answers would be surprising.

The Secretary of State's approval was not required for proposals for financial assistance considered by the Board. He recalled that during the committee stage of the Bill, Mr Noble himself had suggested that the ceiling under which the Board could operate without the Secretary of State's approval should be £50,000—twice the present sum; Mr Noble had put this forward in order to give the board freedom, prestige and the like.

Mr Ross emphasised that the Board had been set up to be able to assist in the exploitation of the resources of the Highlands. Mr Noble should appreciate that the Board themselves were not developing in the case of the petro-chemical project; it was a private investor who might or might not do so. In relation to the suggestion that the taxpayers' money had been used for a private purpose, he thought Mr Noble was really quite wrong in this. Indeed, he could tell him that there must be few members of the Board who had sent in fewer expense accounts than Mr Frank Thomson. There had been no delay in making a statement, he declared. It would have been quite wrong for him to have made any announcements about this last week without the consent of the businesses concerned.

Mr George Willis (Lab., Edinburgh E.), former Minister of State for Scotland with special responsibility for the Highlands, said that some M.P.s were very seriously concerned at the manner in which certain persons and certain interests, in their very vicious pursuit of Mr Thomson, had impugned the integrity of the Board and their very good public service. They had been very seriously concerned at the apparent willingness to sabotage the whole conception of the Highlands Development Board in carrying out this vendetta against Mr Thomson.

Mr Ross said there could be no doubt of the effect on the future work of the Board if the attacks went on. Everyone knew how it had started; surely no one in the House could justify the leakage of information from someone who had been employed and paid by the Board and did not give them the loyalty they merited. The Board were the first instrument to have shown themselves prepared to do the kind of thing the Highlands wanted. He asked the House to give its support to the Board to ensure that their work went on.

Mr Anthony Stodart (Con., Edinburgh W.) asked whether

Mr Thomson had had a controlling interest in a travel agency who handled the Board's account, and could Mr Ross explain why the firm, Timber Systems, Ltd., which was one of Mr Frank Thomson's, was the only company who was given a commission by the Board to prepare a possible hotel project without any other company being allowed to quote.

Mr Ross said Mr Thomson had not got a personal interest in the travel agency other than that this travel agency was owned, he thought, by a trust. They were the only travel agency in Inverness ... the Board had been using this travel agency before Mr Thomson had become a member.

Regarding the contract for timber houses, he assured Mr Stodart that the Board's idea was to support industries and firms in the Highlands. This firm was in the Highlands, and he thought Mr Stodart should not read too much into this; this had been a perfectly suitable and reasonable way of doing this particular job. The cost in respect of this had been somewhere around £300.

Mr Russell Johnston (Lib., Inverness) said everyone welcomed the Secretary of State's unequivocal statement; there had been no improper activity by any member of the Board. The lesson to be drawn from the whole of this very sorry story was that no Board member should be in a position where he might be suspected by the public of having private gain out of public activity; this was particularly true where there was a board involved in risk enterprises. Would Mr Ross agree that the lesson was that all board members henceforth should be full-time and should be asked to sever all business connections whatsoever?

Mr Ross said he would not accept that; this had been debated very fully when the Bill went through. M.P.s then and himself now still thought the position was properly covered by the part of the Act relating to declarations of interests by members of the board.

Mr Robert Maclennan (Lab., Caithness and Sutherland) said Mr Ross's statement had cleared the air. It had been of great service to the future of the Highlands that the resignation of Mr Thomson was nothing more than to protect the future good name of the Board; there was no imputation of impropriety which the House could draw from it.

Mr Ross said he hoped his statement would clear the air, but he stressed how the air had been muddied. This, to his mind, was one of the most disgraceful episodes in the Highlands in relation to how information, according to reports he had read, had been deliberately passed on to everyone except to Ministers. [Public statements by Mr Robert Maclennan, and by Dr Ian Grimble, chairman of the Caithness and Sutherland constituency Labour Party, have made it clear that Mr Durham had placed his information exclusively at the disposal of Ministers several months before he told the Press.]

Mr Alasdair Mackenzie (Lib., Ross and Cromarty) assured Mr Ross that his statement putting the position of the petro-chemical project at Invergordon into perspective would cause great satisfaction in that area. He asked the Minister to ensure that in future the people intimately concerned in that parti-cular area would be adequately informed; this would help pre-vent rumour and speculation.

Mr Ross said he took the point. The source of the information in respect of this had been far from accurate; that was why he had gone out of his way to stress that there had been and, at this stage, could be no government commitment in respect of this.

Mr Donald Dewar (Lab., Aberdeen S.) said the most useful contribution that could now be made to the work of the Board and the future of the Highlands would be the co-operation of both sides of the House to see that no encouragement was given to interests outside the House in their attempt at a stupid and useless witch-hunt of a man who had now been completely exonerated.

Mr Gordon Campbell (Con., Moray and Nairn) said his criticism was of Mr Ross, not of the Board. Had this not been an unwise appointment, an error of judgment on Mr Ross's part, not only because of the known commercial entanglements but also because Mr Frank Thomson had publicly declared his full support for the Labour Party, which had caused a great deal of criticism in the area?

Mr Ross said he had not been aware of Mr Thomson's full support for the Labour Party when he had made him a member of the Board; there had been no indication of that in relation to the 'Macpuff' campaign. It was open to everyone to say this had been an unwise appointment; there were very few appointments that were recognised by everyone as wise—but this particular appointment had been praised by the very people who were now participating in this vendetta.

Mr Tam Dalyell (Lab., W. Lothian) asked when the feasibility studies at Invergordon would be finished, and demanded that Mr Noble should explain precisely what he had meant by his reference to the appointments.

Mr Ross said he could not give accurate information about the feasibility studies.

Mr Ian MacArthur (Con., Perth and E. Perthshire) said that in view of the interest of certain Board members, had the Secretary of State approved these loan-and-grant arrangements under Section 8 of the Act? If he had not, should he not have done so? If he had done so, had his judgment not been wholly wrong? In either case, was not the best protection he could give the board to resign himself?

Mr Ross declared that this was quite wrong. Part of the criticism made of the Act when it had been going through committee was that he was to give the Board as much freedom as possible in respect of this. He thought he had been able to exercise the right kind of judgments in relation to how they had been conducting their business. There had been a searchlight on a very small part of the Board's work; he hoped when they received the Board's report next month—and he hoped, debated it—they would get properly into perspective the wonderful work that the Board were doing which was fully appreciated in all parts of the Highlands.

Mr John Rankin (Lab., Govan) said that if the Highlands were to be properly and fully developed, they could no longer rely merely on supply industries like hydro-electricity and afforestation; developments like the petro-chemical complex at Invergordon were absolutely necessary if the Highlands were to be modernised.

Mr Ross pointed out that if the Board had ignored the possibilities at Invergordon, they would have been under even more severe criticism from other M.P.s. What had to be realised was that there were many people in the Highlands who did not want anything done.

Mr Noble said that when it was a question of people that

Mr Ross himself had appointed to the Board, ought not allocations of money to come to the Secretary of State for his personal approval.

In the particular circumstances of Invergordon Chemical Enterprises, there was a good deal of information which the Secretary of State possessed, and which might have come from a 'leak' to the Press and to the Scottish Office. He suggested that the wisest thing the Government could do now, as Board documents appeared to have been involved, was to publish the documents in the form of a White Paper.

Mr Ross said it was quite wrong of Mr Noble to assume that the documents that had been pirated around the Highlands had been sent to himself or other Ministers. He would like to know from whom or from where Mr Noble had received his information; was it from the sender? The honourable gentleman should really watch his words very carefully, he added. Mr Noble should appreciate that the difficulties which had arisen would arise with anybody in the area who was actively engaged in business and who was the kind of person wanted. They might well have arisen when appointments were being made in relation to the man who went before Mr Thomson (the late Mr William Logan).

The Scottish Secretary did not improve his parliamentary standing with this statement but at least the air was cleared and Professor Grieve was, again, in a position to assert himself and his Board. The future of the Board, and the Highlands, had been put in jeopardy and the judgment of Professor Grieve and Mr Ross had been shown to be less sound than most observers had assumed. A warning note had been sounded, however, and future developments will show whether the Board has taken fright or will recover its prestige by its enterprise and dedication to the massive task for which it was created.

On 31 May 1967 the first annual report of the Highlands and Islands Development Board was published.[34] It was out of date on publication and a Press conference was called at Inverness that day to reveal board policy and action in 1967.

A total of £1,688,112 was invested in development in the Highlands and Islands during 1966 creating an estimated 1,024 new jobs, maintains the report. The Board's share of this in grants and loans was £838,292. Private investors who obtained grants or loans from the Board put up the remainder of the money, £849,820.

The report reveals that the Board are seeking a meeting with the general managers of the joint stock banks so that their combined efforts to promote development in the Highlands and Islands could reinforce each other. Tribute is paid to bank managers who 'have helped in a practical way by providing bridging finance while we were processing applications for financial aid'.

In a foreword to the report, Professor Grieve likens their purpose to that of agencies such as the Tennessee Valley Authority, and states: 'It is . . . no exaggeration to claim that the efforts of this Board will have world significance.' The main challenge facing the Board is described thus:

'It is significant that most opinions . . . accept that depopulation of the area is the central problem. The only exception to that is a curiously diverse group of attitudes, almost wholly urban in origin, which sees the Highlands as the natural relief valve for an over-urbanised country—a kind of "national wilderness". We have heard this opinion expressed frequently, although not often publicly, by influential and responsible people . . .'

The report refers to the range of solutions suggested for Highland problems, including the extreme 'Highland way of life' concept. It continues:

'The Board can see and appreciate all the historic, romantic, economic, preservationist, social and even music-hall influences that have produced this confusion of ideals and attitudes—but is aware of the vested interests, cultural, economic and sporting, that use the various elements of them as they suit their arguments . . . We see . . . relevant weights and priorities something as follows: Agriculture, which . . . so often simply has meant sheep-rearing in the Highlands, will, as it is practised at present, worsen the depopulation problem and also the problem of greater production. It must remain, however, an important part of the Highland economy. The Board believes that much more can be produced from the Highlands, but this is highly unlikely to be accompanied by an increasing population in these activities.

'Forestry is of great importance. Its acreage in the Highlands must be extended, but more and more purposefully in its location relative to transport and utilisation of the timber. . . . We are a grossly under-forested country relative to most other comparable countries in the world.

'Tourism . . . can make a rapid impact on the economy of the Highlands; its potential is great but it must: (*a*) be more selective in its planning and publicity for specialised markets offering facilities from the sophisticated sports centre to various kinds of accommodation for city dwellers who search for peace and relaxation in an atmosphere of great natural beauty; (*b*) search constantly for ways of extending the season; (*c*) be capable of development without spoiling one of the last great, unspoiled, beautiful landscapes of Europe.

'Fishing . . . is very important in certain island and other communities . . . where processing of the fish can be the basis of a land-rooted industry. The Board's plans take special account of this geographical significance.

'Manufacturing industry . . . we increasingly regard as the most urgent of all relative to the immediate need to stem a substantial proportion of the emigration from the Highlands and Islands. Industrialists unlike tourists, do not flood in voluntarily, or even through general publicity drives. It is our clear duty to see that this most important and most deficient element in the Highland economy is furnished.

'Our policy in this field is threefold; we encourage growth of industrial enterprise wherever a developer shows a personal and specific desire to settle or expand his enterprise; we will pursue, however, a more methodical programme of building small industrial growth points in scale with the possibilities of the west and islands; we will do our utmost to generate major growth points . . . the Moray Firth is unquestionably the most important of these areas.

'Crofting . . . if one had to look now for a way of life which would keep that number of people in relatively intractable territory, it would be difficult to contrive a better system. But its future depends on other employment support. This the Board accepts as a clear challenge and duty.'

In a comment on this statement of aims, the report emphasises that the Board are well aware that 'no matter what success is achieved in the eastern or central Highlands . . .' the Board will be judged by their ability to hold population in the true crofting areas.

The report reveals that at the end of 1966 the Board had forty-two employees. It states:

'This Board has at present a temporary lease of premises at 6 Castle Wynd, Inverness. By the autumn of 1966 expansion of staff made it necessary to acquire additional premises and a house . . . was purchased and occupied in November. Clearly arrangements to provide permanent headquarters for the Board must be made as soon as possible and we were urgently trying to find a solution to this problem at the end of 1966.'

Analyses of the £838,292 grants and loans given by the Board for business projects during the year disclose that loans totalled £708,635 and grants £129,657. A total of 176 applications for grants or loans were approved, most of them from Inverness-shire and Ross and Cromarty. Approving 61 applications from Inverness-shire, the Board gave £276,892 loans and £44,840 grants. From Ross and Cromarty 42 applications were approved and £172,450 loans and £31,527 grants given. Of the total grants and loans £193,963 was given to projects in manufacturing with 303 jobs prospects; £295,279 to tourism with 280 jobs prospects; and £349,050 for projects in other fields with 441 jobs prospects.

Commenting on the Board's powers not only to assist the creation of fresh jobs in the Highlands and Islands but also to prevent loss of employment by contraction or closure of existing business, the report states:

'While we recognise that there may well be times in future when we shall be called upon to perform an emergency financial operation to save a business from failure, we hope that this will gradually become a less common feature of our grants and loans function. It would be helpful if, when assistance is sought from the Board, we could be given sufficient time to carry out a careful study of the capital and other requirements. Quick decisions to meet emergencies carry with them obvious dangers.'

The report describes 'other ways' in which the Board undertake industrial promotion. On attraction of industry it admits:

'While we cannot claim any dramatic success, our efforts have not been without achievement: this includes establishment of an angling fly-dressing enterprise, an electronic components venture, a precision engraving firm, two textile manufacturing companies and a pottery. As the year ended there was heartening evidence that other entrepreneurs in the south were taking a practical interest in the Highlands and Islands.

'Our experience is that businessmen look for the following main factors when considering setting up business in a new location: the ready availability and assured future supply of labour with the skills needed (or at least the ability to acquire these skills): accessible, attractive, reasonably priced sites preferably already serviced: access to the main routes to markets and sources of raw materials; nearness to airports and direct rail services; good amenities; co-operation from central and local government agencies; and reasonable financial facilities.'

A hint of Board action to provide advance sites and factories in more difficult parts of their area emerges from the report's comment on the importance of these:

'Industrialists rapidly lose interest if there are long delays while sites are being acquired and services installed. This raises the question of prepared factory sites and advance factories to which we were giving consideration at the end of 1966. In considering this, the Board has in mind to take into account the needs of viable communities in the islands and more difficult parts of the mainland area.'

The report outlines the background to the Board's key Moray Firth Development plan:

'In March 1966 we commissioned Product Planning, Ltd., to carry out a study of the credibility of major industrial development in the area between Nairn to the south and Tain to the north. Their report, in August 1966, confirmed us in our thinking that major growth should be pursued as a key element in our longer-term strategy. We accepted Proplan's conclusion that a substantial growth of population was possible in this area over the next twenty years or so. We were convinced that Moray Firth Development would make real development and growth in other Highland centres more practicable and more probable and that it would promote confidence in the future, the lack of which had been a very real hindrance.

'Within this broad field the first project to be considered related to the possibility of establishing a petro-chemical complex at Invergordon, a possible major step towards the development of the Moray Firth area. This area, in the Board's view, has great potential because it possesses resources that are highly attractive to modern industry. The most important are: a sheltered deep water harbour capable of taking very large tankers up to 200,000 tons and all the biggest bulk cargo carriers likely to be built; ample supplies of fresh water; and the very unusual situation where suitable areas of flat land lie adjacent to the deep water. It also enjoys a good climate. Quite clearly, these are of crucial importance to the proposed complex.'

After referring to discussions with Occidental Petroleum of Los Angeles about the proposed Invergordon complex, and to other possibilities which the Board have in mind for the Moray Firth area, including mineral processing industries, the report continues:

'On 28 December 1966 the Board made a formal submission to the Secretary of State about their ideas for the urban-industrial development of the Moray Firth area. This proposal sought the Secretary of State's support for initiation of necessary studies and consultations in preparation for consideration and decisions that would arise if any specific project or prospects should materialise. These would include questions of infrastructure such as dock facilities and the question of competitive power generation.'

At the time of preparation of the Board's annual report the Scottish Secretary's decision on this submission was still awaited.

Recalling that the siting of the experimental fast reactor at Dounreay had brought 'vigorous new life, thought, and hope to the area' and that, accordingly, the Board had urged successfully that the prototype fast reactor should be sited there, the report declares: 'But this is only the first step in the process of developing the area, and we mean to examine all the possibilities of bringing industry to the Thurso–Wick area.'

Turning to the fishing industry, the report points out that while it is generally correct that fishing cannot be looked to as a significantly expanding sector of the Highland economy, there are specific areas where fishing is of prime importance.

'We are convinced that an increase in the numbers of locally-based fishing vessels is possible. Firstly, the agreement concluded by the Government on fishery limits in 1964 has restricted the number of foreign boats fishing in Highland inshore waters. Secondly, we are satisfied, following discussions that the resources of Highland waters can stand more intensive fishing without imperilling future stocks. Finally, we were encouraged by the success of the Outer Hebrides Fisheries Training Scheme operated in 1959–61 to introduce the nucleus of a locally based fishing fleet in the Outer Hebrides.

Farquhar Gillanders

'Accordingly, the Board submitted to the Secretary of State a formal proposal for development of the Highland fishing fleet. Under the proposed scheme, estimated to cost £750,000, twenty-five fishing boats would be built for new entrants to the industry over the next five years. These would be additional to the fishery authorities' normal programme of loan and grant aid for construction of new boats.

'The Secretary of State approved the proposal in principle. By the end of 1966 twenty-six applications had been received and nine applicants had been selected for boats. It is expected that eight new boats will be in the water by the end of 1967. In order to provide successful applicants under this scheme with the most modern design of fishing vessel, we commissioned a team of naval architects to design a 54-foot stern trawler suitable for dual-purpose fishing in Scottish waters. Our fisheries development scheme will result in additions in 1967 to the fleet fishing out of Stornoway, and we are accordingly assessing processing prospects at that port. We are considering, in consultation with the Herring Industry Board, the future utilisation of that body's quick freezing factory and cold store at Stornoway.

'We have also given financial assistance to the fish processing industry in Shetland and further proposals for the expansion of that industry's possibilities were under consideration by the Board at the end of the year. Late in 1965 the Board were approached by Mallaig and North-west Fishermen's Association regarding the redevelopment of the Point area and setting up a harbour trust for Mallaig. Since February 1966, negotiations have been carried out with British Railways, the Department of Agricultural and Fisheries for Scotland, the local landowner and Inverness County Council and we hope they can be concluded successfully as soon as possible.'

The Board are keeping under review, states the report, the potential of their area to sustain fish farming enterprises.

Describing the Board's efforts in tourism, the report recalls that the Scottish Secretary approved their first major tourism proposal, which enabled them to begin a feasibility study of a £1,000,000 project to provide five new hotels in the islands and west mainland. Accommodation would be for about a hundred guests at each hotel.

'We pursued this scheme early in our life because of the great tourism potential of the islands and west mainland. But we realised this potential could never be realised until we broke the vicious circle—no accommodation, few visitors; few visitors, little inducement to anyone to provide accommodation. At the end of 1966 we still had a great deal of investigation to do on the design and costing of the hotels, selection of the best sites and evaluation of the economics of running such hotels.

'We are also concerned to support provision of caravan and camping sites. At the end of the year the Architectural Research Unit, under Sir Robert Matthew, had produced a plan which aimed to provide on a site of 16–17 acres at the northern entrance to Glencoe a fully developed and properly serviced caravan-camping park.

'We undertook this, mainly because of the eyesore that was being made of one of Scotland's most dramatic and best-known glens by indiscriminate camping and caravanning.

'We assured those interests who expressed concern about this project that the site would be landscaped and screened by the planting of additional trees; there would be no pollution of the river; and drinking and dancing facilities would not be provided.'

Commenting on the need for extension of recreational and entertainment opportunities to realise the tourist potential of the Highlands, the report describes support given by the Board to local associations and clubs within the area. Recreations thus encouraged included sand and land yachting in Caithness and South Uist, sea angling, and the possibilities of development of a long-distance walking route on the lines of the Pennine Way in England. The report continues: 'We are, however, satisfied that individual initiatives alone will not suffice to answer the problem. Fairly substantial investments may be necessary and we shall be considering in 1967 how far it will be necessary for us to formulate schemes of a special kind to accelerate recreational development.'

The Highland transport problem, according to the report, 'is more one of small lots than one of long distances'. It states:

'During 1967 we expect in consultation with the Scottish Economic Planning Council to assume many of the responsibilities of the Highland Transport Board and to be involved in consideration of that Board's various recommendations. Potential industrialists always ask about air services and we were pleased when British European Airways announced their intention to double, from November 1966, the frequency of flights to Inverness and substantially increase the number of flights to Wick. When BEA's plans were delayed we received an assurance that the improved service would begin in April 1967. These services will be of great value to the districts served, and we attach considerable importance to the further development of air transport in the Highlands and Islands. By the end of the year arrangements had been made to meet the chairman, Sir Anthony Milward, and chief executive, Mr H. E. Marking, of BEA in London for discussions on development possibilities for the air network.

'The cost of transport of raw materials and produced goods is one of the reasons most frequently given by industrialists for not locating in the Highlands and Islands. Often this is based on supposition, and preliminary studies by the Board suggest that in areas such as the Moray Firth the same factors as elsewhere in Britain influence transport costs. If consignments are large and flow regularly rates are reasonable, but if consignments are small and *ad hoc*, then rates are high. It might be said that the Highland transport problem is more one of small lots than one of long distances.'

Commenting on the idea of a Highland university the report states that the Board accept that the time has not yet come for renewing strong pressure for such a university. They have, however, 'every intention of pursuing the idea of an initial Highland Research Institute, no matter how small its beginnings—although it would be desirable to have a sizeable foundation from the beginning'.

The report concludes with references to social aspects of the Board's work. These include submission of views to the Birsay Committee on medical services in the Highlands and Islands; consideration of comprehensive secondary education in the area; and an examination of youth activities in the area.

At his Press conference to launch the Board's first report Professor Grieve stated that in terms of loans and grants they had spent almost £1,000 on each new job created in the area in the past eighteen months.

Within the past five months the amount of loans and grants issued was almost double the total during the fourteen months covered by the report, he said. During the report period £840,000 had been issued, while during the past five months a further £620,000 had been authorised, making a total of about £1·5m. Added to the amount of private capital involved this came to a total of almost £3m. The total sum involved during the report period was apportioned as follows: manufacturing £193,963; tourism £295,279, and other recipients £349,050.

From the end of the report period, when the total of new jobs was 1,024, the number had increased to just over 1,500.

Professor Grieve said the Board had done a lot considering that they were an entirely new administrative body in Britain. He emphasised that they were anxious that people reading the report would either assure them that they were being supported in their priorities or that they had reservations which ought to be looked at during the next year.

Regarding the proposed Invergordon development he said the feasibility study being carried out on behalf of the Occidental Oil Company of California was a private survey to see if the area was suitable as the site for the proposed £50m. petrochemical complex. The Board would not necessarily see the report and the best they could hope to know was whether the project was feasible or not.

The Board chairman conceded that the resignation of Mr Frank Thomson as a part-time member of the Board in March had done damage, but not fundamental damage.

Mr John Rollo, deputy chairman of the Board, said they were awaiting the approval of the Secretary of State for Scotland for a ship-building venture at Campbeltown because the amount of capital needed was beyond the Board's permitted maximum. He said the firms involved were a Thames concern and Lithgows, Ltd., Port Glasgow. To start with, about forty persons would be employed, but that number would be almost doubled in three years. The second project, he said, was at Kingussie, Inverness-shire, where it was proposed to set up a factory to produce precision parts for computers and the aircraft industry.

The Board's first report is not what I expected. It is an unremarkable document, an anti-climax to the earlier controversy which had received so much unfavourable publicity. The Board's three hopes for the Highlands—forestry, tourism and general manufacturing are discussed intelligently and hopefully but nothing new is stated.

On 29 June 1967 an exclusive Press report,[35] summarised here, stated that the Scottish Office has decided to disallow for at least two years the Highland Development Board's controversial £50m. plan for an American petro-chemical complex at Invergordon. The reason given is that the Board wanted to invest too much public money in the project, which would have been designed, in any case, to make profits for an American firm, Occidental Petroleum of California. The Board has been proposing that the Government should invest in grants and interest-free loans 72 per cent of the capital required for machinery, and 67 per cent of the capital required for buildings.

Occidental has been considering since March a report by the Kellog Corporation, industrial consultants of New York, for which it paid £120,000. The report says that the project is technically possible, and would be financially worth while given a generous level of support by the British Government. The original understanding between Occidental and the Highland Development Board—which was reached in October— foresees Occidental getting investment and building grants at the standard rates (then 40 per cent, now 45 per cent for investment and 35 per cent for building), and foresees further that it would be 'reasonable for the Government to lend Occidental half the rest of the money required'.

The Board undertook to seek to persuade the Government to forgo interest on what would have been a loan, at least for a time, and to postpone demands for the repayment of capital. The terms of this proposal were not known to the Scottish Office at the time, but they have since been communicated to officials at St Andrew's House, Edinburgh.

Mr Frank Thomson, the Highland industrialist and the former part-time member of the Board complained at Inverness (in the same week as *The Guardian* report) that the Scottish Office ('the loving Victorian parents in St Andrew's House who insist on knowing what is best') was letting the Board down. Mr Thomson also criticised the Secretary of State for Scotland, Mr Ross, for failing to protect the Highland Development Board. Mr Thomson urged Mr Ross to 'be the Scottish statesman and not merely the London politician'.

If the Invergordon project is cancelled or delayed the Board and its chairman, Professor Robert Grieve, will have to reassess the main pattern of their future spending. The possibility that Occidental would come to Invergordon was first mentioned officially by the Board in a statement after a meeting at Dingwall, Ross-shire, on 18 January. It was then said that the capital required to build the plant would be £50m. and that—government grants apart—it was hoped that half the private capital would be subscribed in Scotland and half by Occidental. The plant would cover 300 acres and employ 2,000 work-people and would be built in three years. The Government, the Board said at Dingwall, would also have to spend £20m. on infra-structure—docks, roads, drains and housing.

Professor Grieve said that the Invergordon project held 'very great promise'. 'Our American friends,' he said, 'would not be venturing such substantial sums of their money on the study if they did not have considerable faith in a satisfactory outcome.'

The Board had come to an understanding with Occidental at a meeting in London three months earlier. It is the details of this understanding which now seem to have convinced the Scottish Office that the project cannot go ahead for the time being.

On 29 June 1967 the Scottish Office dissociated themselves from *The Guardian* report that they had vetoed the Invergordon development as envisaged by Occidental Petroleum of California. In an approved statement the Scottish Office stated: 'Occidental Petroleum have not submitted any proposition, and consequently we are not in a position to accept or refuse.'

The first phase of the feasibility study is complete: the project has run into difficulties over the financing arrangements and a senior civil servant is now said to sit in at all meetings of the Highlands and Islands Development Board.

The prospects for the Board, and for the Highlands, are again dimming and if the Treasury is to determine the behaviour and policies of the Board from now on its prospects of success are small and the resignations of key personnel seem inevitable.

It is too early yet to say how the Highlands and Islands Development Board will progress. To succeed they must have more money at their disposal: and to make positive gains they must have a Grieve, at least, in control. But Professor Grieve has been released from Glasgow University for only five years and his new Chair of Town and Regional Planning is an exciting one, from which much is expected not only academically but in terms of positive Scottish economic and social development as well. It must, today, seem very attractive to him.

I, certainly, believe that the Highlands and Islands Development Board, if given adequate funds, leadership and team work, could still transform the economic chaos of the area into a thriving, living part of the Scottish and British economies.

The real hope for the Highlands today—as I see it—cannot be in tourism but in the simple courage to implement proved economic principles. The Highlander must cease to regard himself as a member of a chosen race to whom normal economic laws do not apply. If he—and Highland administrators—accept this reorientation, then industrialists and others may yet, with subtle encouragement, become interested, positively, in the Highland economy and its problems. Neither cultural nor spiritual distinctiveness can be maintained much longer unless a sounder economic basis to the community is devised. It is not enough for the Highlander to look back and bemoan his lot. He must assert himself and there must be outward signs of achievement and there must be a belief in progress throughout the community. It is not enough to receive long-term financial support from the rest of the community while stubbornly refusing to consider non-viable holdings as other than a sacred heritage that must not suffer change at any price. It is not the possession of land that is important; it is how the land is being used. And, so far, no one in authority has even initiated a responsible survey on land use in the Highlands without which real economic progress cannot be achieved or even planned.

The shadows in the West Highlands are long and numerous. The landlord, for one reason, and the ageing crofter for another, will continue to oppose change. And elsewhere sentiment and emotion persistently bedevil Highland economic analysis.

Land must be taken away from those who cannot, or will not, use it and it must be given to the young, the enterprising and the farseeing, if such can still be found in the Highlands. Our main export from the Highlands and Islands is not whisky, as we are so frequently told, but young men and young women who possess these essential qualities. It is to them and not to the aged, the infirm and the apathetic, that the Highlands and Islands Development Board must turn. It is not to their sentiments that they must appeal but to their sense of economic reality. And it is they, the young, and not their elders, who must devise a way of life in which economic progress and social enlightenment may yet take root in Gaeldom.

In Gaelic Scotland—even in the smallest village—there is too often an inability to act in unison and the attitude of mind of any community is difficult to define. But to succeed we must understand the Highland mentality and the events of the last few months suggest that present Highland administrators have failed to do this.

Crofting is no longer a way of life in the Scottish Highlands and if we persist in maintaining that it is, then Highland depopulation will continue at an increasing rate. In my opinion, industry alone—no matter how small—will reverse the mass exodus to the South, of the young in mind and in body. Fort William and Thurso (where the Atomic Energy's enterprise has increased the population from some 3,000 to 10,000 in ten years) shows what can be done. But progress—real progress—will also be achieved if new skills can be transplanted to parishes like my native Applecross where a small industry, like boat-building, for example, employing only ten to twelve men would make the difference between a decadent community, without hope, and a human growth point.

Professor Grieve and his new Board have a colossal task in front of them and my hope is that they will be able to face up to it and that the Highland people will give them the chance to succeed.

NOTES

[1] I am grateful to the Gaelic Society of Inverness for granting me permission to quote from a paper *The West Highland Economy*, which I read to them on 14 December 1962, and which they later published in Vol. XLIII of their transactions.

[2] *A Programme of Highland Development* (Cmd. 7976), H.M.S.O., 1s. net.

[3] Caithness, Sutherland, Ross and Cromarty, Inverness, Argyll, Orkney and Zetland.

[4] The restricted census for 1966 estimates the population of the seven crofting counties to be 274,170 against 277,948 at the 1961 census. The population of Renfrewshire in 1961 was 338,815.

[5] Earl of Home, Minister of State, Scottish Office, speaking at Inverness on 28 May 1954.

[6] Dr Frank Fraser Darling's *West Highland Survey* had been available in typescript for several years to a favoured few, but was published in book form by Oxford University Press in 1955 (30s. net).

[7] *West Highland Survey*, p. 13.

[8] *The Crofting Problem*, by the late Adam Collier, with a Foreword by A. K. Cairncross, Cambridge University Press (1953), 25s. net.

[9] *Report of the Commission of Enquiry into Crofting Conditions*, Cmd. 9091, 3s. 6d. net.

[10] Ibid., para. 12.

[11] Ibid., para. 281.

[12] Crofters (Scotland) Act 1953 3 & 4 Eliz. 2. CH. 21.

[13] *The Crofters Commission Annual Report for 1956*, H.M.S.O., 1s. 4d. net.

[14] *The Crofters Commission Annual Report for 1957*, H.M.S.O., 1s. 3d. net.

[15] *The Crofters Commission Annual Report for 1958*, H.M.S.O., 1s. 3d. net.

[16] Sir Robert Urquhart, K.B.E., C.M.G., LL.D.

[17] *The Crofters Commission Annual Report for 1959*, H.M.S.O., 2s. net.

[18] Ibid., p. 35.

[19] Ibid, see pp. 16–24.

[20] [Bill 59].

[21] *Crofters Commission Bulletin*.

[22] *The Crofters Commission Annual Report for 1961*, H.M.S.O., 2s. 3d. net.

[23] Ibid., para. 93.

[24] *The Crofters Commission Annual Report for 1965*, H.M.S.O., 4s. net.

[25] Mr James Shaw Grant, O.B.E.

[26] The Rt. Hon. Michael Noble, M.P.

[27] Ibid., pp. 89–93.

[28] *Land Use in the Highlands and Islands*, H.M.S.O., 10s. net.

[29] [Bill 86].

[30] See Naomi Mitchison *Highlands and Islands* (Unity Publishing Company).

[31] *The Guardian*.

[32] This chapter was originally written in 1966 and was in the Editors' hands before the end of that year. It has been rewritten from this point in the light of the recent controversy involving the Board, its policy and its members and the publication, on 31 May 1967, of its first annual report.

[33] H.M.S.O., 7s. 6d. net.

[34] *The Guardian*, 29 June 1967.

Unsceptred Isles

Ian Grimble

Unsceptred Isles

Europe north of the 55th parallel of latitude consists of Scotland and Scandinavia, and the satellite islands that are scattered throughout the North Atlantic and the Baltic Sea. Among these islands—which range from Greenland, the world's largest, to the myriad skerries of the northern Baltic—are the three archipelagos which belong to Scotland. Those of Orkney and Shetland extend to the north of the mainland, the Hebrides to the west. The Orkney and Shetland groups are each a separate county, but they share a Member of Parliament between them. The Hebrides are divided between the mainland counties of Ross-shire and Inverness-shire, and the outer isles possess a Member of Parliament of their own, while the inner isles (including Skye, the largest) are represented by the Member for Inverness-shire. Not only does the structure of local government vary as curiously as the Parliamentary representation of these three archipelagos, but their status also contrasts most oddly with that of other satellite islands of the British galaxy. For the Channel Islands to the south are represented by no Member of Parliament at Westminster; its two principal islands of Guernsey and Jersey flourish in virtual autonomy, each with its own Parliament. The Isle of Man is equally favoured.

Shetland, Orkney and the Hebrides are the most distant of all the lesser British isles from Westminster; depopulation is probably a more serious problem in them than anywhere else; economic depression is a more constant menace; unemployment in these isles often soars high above the national average. All three island groups are included within the seven 'crofter' counties for whose welfare the Highlands and Islands Development Board was given responsibility. One Shetlander, Mr

Prophet Smith, was appointed a member of the Board. Apart from him, the islanders were not represented on it, an omission which Lewis in the Hebrides has been particularly active (though without success) in attempting to rectify.

It can be seen that the solution to the acute and highly specialised problems of these islands was designed to reach them through the traditional mechanism of remote paternalism. The planners and administrators might plan and administer in Inverness rather than in Edinburgh or London, but the islanders themselves were to have no hand in it, neither was the centre of decision making to lie within the islands. It is possible that the choice between the alternatives of autonomy and paternalism was made after careful deliberation, rather than adopted by force of habit. But it remains a fact that the islanders themselves were never consulted. Although they have made their attitude as clear over the years as the limited means of expression open to them permit, it has been, as usual, ignored. Nobody has ever thought it necessary to explain why the present structure of the Board in its relation to the islands was adopted, although it would have appeared out of date in other parts of Europe in the nineteenth century. The matter of our remoter islands does not appear to interest this highly urbanised and industrialised nation sufficiently to compel Ministers to explain their policies on the subject properly, or even to inform themselves upon its essential features.

This state of affairs accounts for the tone in which the subject is apt to be discussed, on those occasions when it succeeds in finding a forum at all in metropolitan Britain. A letter that was published in *The Times* on 6 July 1967 exemplifies this, quite apart from its subject-matter. The letter was signed by the Liberal Member of Parliament for Orkney and Shetland, Mr Jo Grimond, by the Conservative Member for Moray and Nairn, Mr Gordon Campbell, by Lord Strathclyde, chairman of the North of Scotland Hydro-Electric Board, and by Lord Ritchie-Calder of Edinburgh University, a member of the Labour Party. There were twelve signatories in all, and this is what they wrote:

'Where there is controversy such as that over Stansted aerodrome, where large sums of money and many people are concerned, it is, as has been shown, possible to generate widespread opposition. But where smaller communities are concerned the unanimous views of those most intimately affected seem powerless against decisions based apparently on undiscriminating love of centralisation and administrative convenience.

'Such a case is the proposal of the Government to include the counties of Orkney and Shetland in a water authority—which will be administered from Wick and embrace Caithness and Sutherland. This would be less sensible than setting up a water authority to combine Cumberland and Cornwall. To attend a meeting in Wick means being away from the islands for three days. You can hardly pipe water across the sea and there will be a large increase in administrative work. Aberdeen, not Wick, is the mainland link with the islands—indeed to Caithness there are no direct sea services from Shetland.

'The Government, recognising common sense and the unanimous wishes of the island local authorities, at a meeting on 31 March agreed to consider a separate water board for Orkney and Shetland, if Ross and Cromarty would join Caithness and Sutherland. This, however, Ross and Cromarty refused to do. The Government then insisted that Orkney and Shetland must join Caithness and Sutherland. Why, because a county which is contiguous to Caithness and Sutherland will not join them, should two counties separated from the mainland by many miles of sea be compelled to do so?

'As a consequence of strong local representations an amendment was moved and carried in the House of Lords setting up a separate water authority for Orkney and Shetland. There will be an equally strong demand from the Islands that the Lords should insist on this amendment. But even if this is done the Government could reverse the Lords' decision in a few months. We would appeal to reason and good sense. We accordingly hope that Ministers will accept the solution which they appeared to favour on 31 March and which will give the islands a separate water board.'

The argument for controlling this department of island life through a distant mainland authority does not lack plausibility. The larger the authority, and the nearer to the centres of government, the greater the resources in money, planners and technicians. On the debit side must be weighed the loss to island pride and sense of local responsibility, loss of jobs carrying such responsibility within the island world, loss of proper scope for local knowledge. But however these considerations might affect the particular question of the water board, they do not appear to have had anything more to do with the solution of the issue than the expressed wishes of the islanders themselves. Distant islands are to be attached to a mainland authority because it has been found convenient in mainland interests. They are even to be attached to the portion of the mainland whose convenience is thus satisfied, rather than the portion with which the islands are linked by sentiment, trade and transport services. For everyone who knows Orkney and Shetland is aware that Aberdeen is the mainland city belonging to the nexus of their island life.

The benefits of mainland control nowhere lack plausibility more obviously than in the sphere of transport. Island life could once flourish in isolation, but today it depends entirely upon satisfactory communications, and Britain has demonstrated once and for all that the infallible way to destroy islands is to hand the control of their communications to a mainland authority.

The world-famous kippering industry of Lewis was destroyed by this remote control, and when Lord Leverhulme bought the island, he wrote to the Postmaster-General in 1920: 'Anything more callously indifferent to the interests of a section of the community I have never experienced.' Nigel Nicolson quoted these surprisingly forceful words in *Lord of the Isles* and wrote in explanation:

'The passenger, mail and freight services to the Hebrides is still a subject of frequent parliamentary controversy. At the end of the first World War, it was a grievance that tended to dominate all others. At one stage, all members of public bodies in the island threatened to resign *en bloc*, and refuse to stand at the subsequent elections, unless something were done to improve the service. Leverhulme himself bought a £10,000 share in MacBrayne's in order to influence their policy, and addressed to one government department after another letters of complaint which were worded with exceptional anger.'

Lewis is the most viable island in the Hebrides, with a population of over 23,000 and over 6,000 living in its port of Stornoway. The vitality of the islanders overflows in the brain-drain that once gave Lord Macaulay to English letters, and still ensures that modern Scottish poetry is of equal quality in both Gaelic and English. Lewismen display as much enterprise and powers of organisation in their unsceptred isle as if they were in control of their own destinies like the Faroes or the Channel islanders. If they could not influence MacBrayne's shipping service to supply island needs adequately, no islanders could. And the reason they could not is that MacBrayne's schedules are designed to serve the interests of mainland visitors to the islands, which are different from those of the islanders themselves.

The predicament of the smaller Hebridean isles is correspondingly more serious. For instance, Inverness-shire contains the parish of the Small Isles, which are Eigg, Rum, Muck and Canna. Of these, Muck and Canna are two of the best grazing and stock-rearing farms to be found anywhere in the Highlands and Islands. Rum is an important nature reserve, popular with visiting scientists and mountaineers. It is the property of the Nature Conservancy, whose headquarters are in London, and on this island experiments are carried out in growing native trees in exposed places. This research could assist in the propagation of shelter belts throughout the Hebrides. Eigg, the fourth island, is another livestock-rearing island, and its natural beauty and comparative accessibility have made it popular with tourists. Dr John Lorne Campbell of Canna describes the present access to the Small Isles.

'The visitor who approaches these islands from the south, if he travels by rail, will come on the Fort William line, which is said to have been saved from closure by the opening of a pulp mill at Corpach. Beyond Corpach he will travel by the Mallaig branch railway line, the only alternative to a road which for two thirds of its length is a single line one with passing places, having innumerable dangerous blind corners.'

The force of these words will be appreciated best by those who can compare the roads of Norway's fjord country with those of the Western Highlands, especially during the holiday season. Dr Campbell continues:

'This branch railway line has been repeatedly and strongly rumoured as being marked down for certain closure, and on the 15th June 1967 the Minister of State, Dr J. Dickson Mabon, was reported as stating that it was "not being proposed for future development." This is taken locally to mean that the line is to be run down and the public discouraged from using it as much as possible, so that justification can be found for abolishing it. It is some time since this line ceased to handle parcels or livestock, greatly to the inconvenience of the local people. In the words of Professor Alex Nove, "It has been decided to concentrate such traffic via Kyle of Lochalsh. The result is that packages handed in at Fort William, which could have been sent in half a day via Mallaig, are routed via Glasgow and Inverness. They take four days, and earn adverse publicity for the railways." '

Dr Campbell continues the itinerary to his island home:

'Having arrived at Mallaig, the traveller must now continue his journey to the Small Isles by means of a converted wooden mine-sweeper, the *Loch Arkaig*. This ship has no first-class accommodation, indeed no cabins of any kind, and offers no proper meals and no refreshments apart from cups of tea or coffee; seating is on benches, too narrow to lie down on, and passengers must share their accommodation with mail bags and perishables destined for the islands, for there is no hold, and therefore no covered accommodation on the ship for mails or livestock. This vessel was substituted in 1964 for the *Lochmor*, a ship which possessed all the facilities referred to, and which linked all the islands of the northern Inner and Outer Hebrides on a run which, starting at Mallaig, included calls at the Small Isles, South and North Uist, Harris and Kyle of Lochalsh. The *Loch Arkaig*'s run links the Small Isles with Mallaig on the mainland and Portree in Skye only.

'On reaching the Small Isles, the traveller will find that the only one of them that has a pier, or is ever likely to have a pier, is Canna, where one was built by private enterprise about 75 years ago. In so far as the inhabitants of the four islands in question enjoy water supplies or electric light, these too have been provided by the proprietors. All four islands have now been provided by the Post Office with radio telephone links with the mainland; the apparatus appears to be still in the experimental stage, breaking down frequently; in spite of this, and of the fact that all these radio links ring in the Mallaig exchange, the Post Office, with the approval of several successive Postmasters General, charges trunk rates for calls from the islands to Mallaig, their principal shopping centre.'

Now a responsibility for island communications is being transferred from one mainland authority to another. The Highland Transport Board has presented its final report before handing its functions to the Highlands and Islands Development Board. The Labour Member of Parliament for the

Western Isles, Mr Malcolm Macmillan, referred extremely unfavourably to this report of the Highland Transport Board, in
the Scottish Grand Committee on 13 July 1967:

'Another example of that Report's unhelpfulness is in its rejection
of the case for a vehicle-ferry, fast, direct sea-link, Stornoway to
Kyle. Merely because there is a period of useful life in the old
steamer, now on that run, the Board objects to putting on a new
modern vehicle-ferry service. It states that it would require a fairly
large vessel. Why not? Of all the reasons for not doing something
this was the most feeble. A lot of other reasons are given for negative
recommendations; and they were very poor.'

Mr Macmillan welcomed the demise of the Transport Board,
but its functions have merely been passed to another mainland
Board over which the islanders exercise no control whatever.

Of all the economic activities of North Atlantic islanders,
there is one in which the exercise of this control operates as
decisively as it does in the field of communications. This is the
fishing industry: and as in the case of transport, the problem is
a comparatively modern one, stimulated by technical advance
and the altered patterns of life that have followed in its wake.

In the days of oar and sail outlying islands possessed the
advantage that they lay near to the fishing grounds. Strindberg's
masterpiece *The Inhabitants of Hemsö* depicts a way of life in the
outer skerries of the northern Baltic which was beginning to
recede as he wrote. Today those Swedish islands have become
increasingly the summer resort of townspeople from Stockholm
and elsewhere. Roland Svensson has witnessed the change
during the past thirty-five years, and has brought this experience to his investigations in Shetland and the Hebrides, which
will be noted presently.

Beyond the 10,000 satellite islands of the Swedish archipelago
lie the Åland Islands, which belong to Finland but are self-
governing, with their own national flag and their Swedish
language fully protected. Here, too, the small communities of
the outer skerries are receding: in fact, Mariehamn the island
capital has a population of 8,000 out of a total island population
of 22,000, which is a higher urban ratio than that of Stornoway
to the island of Lewis. The same tendency is to be found in the
Finnish Åboland archipelago to the east, which completes this

milky way of rocks and islands across the entrance to the Gulf of Bothnia. But here the mainland town of Åbo, which stands in roughly the same relation to its islands as Aberdeen does to Orkney and Shetland, has its magnetism arrested by the growth-point of Pargas within the islands themselves. The trend is there, due to the rising standard of living and the industrial revolution at sea. It is accompanied by a gradual transition in the remoter islands from the Hemsö pattern of life to that of the summer-house migrants. But the process is not nearly so advanced as in the Swedish archipelago, and it is countered by the same means as the Åland islanders possess—an urban magnet within the ambience of the island world. There is this difference, however, that Pargas is built upon land industries, while Mariehamn has succeeded in surviving the passing of the sailing ships and possesses a registered tonnage second in volume only to that of the Finnish capital.

But it is in the islands of the North Atlantic that the most interesting developments have taken place during this century. The only possible excuse for the contrast between those of Norway and the British Isles is that nearly half of Norway's population lives in her islands. Their interests are of political importance, and people who are properly informed about these interests occupy places of authority. There is no powerful mainland lobby as in highly urbanised Britain, impatient of islands unless they can serve some industrial purpose beyond their shores, or remain as an 'unspoilt' region for city holiday-makers. The capital city of Norway contains only about half a million people, while her second city is not so large as Aberdeen.

Thus, even Arctic Norway abounds in islands which, had they been administered by Britain, would almost certainly be deserted by now, or at least in worse economic plight than the far more favoured islands which surround Scotland. A typical example of these is Meløy, an island forty miles north of the Arctic circle, about half of it agricultural, the other half mountainous. It is 15 miles long and 8 to 10 miles broad. For centuries it was the home of subsistence farmer–fishermen who spent eighteen hours rowing into the hazardous northern ocean for their catches. Modern techniques enable the same size of catches to be landed today by a tenth of the number of men.

Hydro-electric power is generated on the island to supply the nitrogen factories that have been planted there, in addition to the domestic and agricultural needs of the islanders. Squid and prawn fisheries have been developed, while some of the outlying islands on which animals were once pastured or hay was harvested are now neglected. Administration has been centralised, but not at a great distance, while a new university has been planted at Tromsø, far deeper in the Arctic, to attract the brain drain north as well as south. Meløy's population of about 5,000 is rising. The situation here is typical of Arctic Norway, in which the population is roughly double that of the Scottish Highlands, though far more remotely scattered throughout a generally less habitable region. And by means of the magnificent steamer service which runs round the North Cape to Kirkines throughout the week, the visitor who sails past Meløy can see this island as merely one iota of the total achievement.

The island of Vågsøy provokes a more direct comparison with one of our British islands. It lies south of Arctic Norway, though in a more northern latitude than Shetland's northernmost island of Unst. Dr Philip Wheeler, who has published a study of Unst, suggested this comparison during a programme broadcast by the Third Programme of the B.B.C. in 1965. He was describing the boom in the herring industry at the end of the nineteenth century which brought 9,000 people to Unst as late as 1906, at the height of the herring fishery. By the 1930s the herring had departed, the last of the herring stations had been closed on Unst, and the island's prosperity as a fisheries centre was over. Its prosperity now rests largely upon the presence of an R.A.F. station.

The Norwegian island of Vågsøy shared the herring boom and suffered the slump that followed it. But a dog-fish industry was planted in Vågsøy to rescue the island's economy. The steamer which passes Meløy on its way round the North Cape each day calls at Vågsøy's flourishing modern port of Måløy, the tiny dog-fish capital of Europe, purveyor of 70 per cent of the total Norwegian catch. 'The town itself has grown,' Dr Wheeler said on the B.B.C., 'both by the accretion of canning factories and so forth, and by people coming in from the surrounding countryside; people who have stopped being part-time fishers and farmers and have become full-time fishermen.'

So the result is, you tend to be either a full-time fisherman or you are a farmer who has employment in the canning factories. And this is irregular throughout the year, and when a load is coming into any one particular factory, the merchant rapidly telephones to his different workers and they come in.' Thus Norway maintains her scattered units of agriculture in a hostile climate and a meagre soil, as Wheeler explained.

'If you take the example of the township of Reifvik, which is on the other side of the island from Måløy, you find that it is fairly efficient agriculturally. It has fairly good land; but the fact does remain that in terms of modern mechanised farming the farms are small and difficult. However, there you have an agricultural township whose prosperity is bound up to a large extent with the fishing industry. Now what is going to happen to that island if anything happens to the dog-fish? They will have to look round very rapidly for some other type of fishing.' This was what they did when the herring departed. They found the dog-fish which they catch today off Shetland, carry all the way back to Norway, and sell as rock salmon on the Billingsgate counters four days after it has been landed at Måløy.

Uttar Brox of Tromsø, author of the recent and controversial book *Hva skjaer i Nord-Norge*, has visited and studied the Hebrides, and in 1965 he also broadcast his observations on this subject in the Third Programme. 'The most striking comparison,' he said, 'is that in natural conditions that a north Norwegian would consider close to paradise, people seem to have to leave the crofts and villages. Take the island of Vatersay, the southernmost populated island in the Hebrides. This island is green all the year, and they don't have to build houses for their animals, and the sheep can be left out all the year. This would seem just like paradise to a Finnmark farmer who has to feed his animals indoors, perhaps seven or eight months a year. And there are lots of fish around as well.'

Uttar Brox dismissed one frequently heard explanation and was confident of the true cause. 'Close to the North Pole people have a remarkably good economy, and they do not feel any urge to leave their locality, and this is being commented upon by foreign observers—by British observers sometimes. And they invent reasons like the hardy nature or the special mentality of the Finnmark population. But it is very hard to prove any difference in mentality. An easily visible difference is the very strong political influence that the rural population of North Norway has had up till now, whereas the crofting population of Scotland has been politically powerless.'

But there is one comparison above all others to shame British complacency. The Faroe Islands which lie 250 miles north of the Scottish mainland share the ethnic identity and some of the early history of neighbouring Shetland. By historical accident Shetland passed with Orkney to the Scottish crown, while Faroe remained the property of the royal house of Denmark–Norway. There is hardly any need to compare the degrees of misgovernment which both groups of islands suffered under the remote control of the absolutist period. Suffice to say, the benefits of neglect and the privilege of being left in isolation were the best that Faroe or Shetland could then hope for. It is the present fortunes of these two neighbouring islands that present such a startling contrast.

In 1800 Faroe contained only 5,000 islanders, speaking a language whose dialect varied from island to island, unstandardised by an orthography of its own, unrecognised by the distant Government. The people reared sheep and lived by a precarious subsistence agriculture supplemented by fishing, in the pattern that was common to the North Atlantic and Baltic islands at this time. Families loyal to the Danish crown had been leased 'royal farms' in perpetuity. This tenure contrasted with the peasant proprietorship which was by this time well established throughout much of Scandinavia: and contrasted more starkly with the feudal serfdom in which most of the peasants lived in the Highlands and islands of Scotland.

By 1900 the Faroese population had risen to over 15,000, the language had been standardised and its traditional literature collected. If this appears to be an irrelevant detail, it did not appear so to the Faroese or to the Danes. The brochure on the islands published by the Danish Ministry of Foreign Affairs explains: 'The remote situation, 828 miles from metropolitan Denmark, the distinctive life of the island population, and the fact that Faroese, though a Scandinavian language, differs widely from Danish were bound to raise the question of some form of self-government at a very early date.' In 1948 Faroe was granted a constitution under which her own Parliament assumed control of her economy and appointed its own executive council to govern the islands. The Danish Parliament, in which a Faroese representative continues to sit, retains a joint interest in foreign affairs, law, the police, the social services and education. Faroese is recognised as the official language, though Danish is permissible in public affairs, and is taught in the schools. Faroe, like the Åland Islands in the Baltic, possesses her national flag as well as her own official language and seat of government.

Her population has now risen to over 36,000 and continues to rise in booming prosperity. Only about 200 people live exclusively by farming in Faroe today, which is less than the number of people employed in one single fish factory in the capital town of Torshavn: and this town now contains over 10,000 people. But agriculture is not neglected, particularly in the relatively fertile islands like Sandøy, where the same family still works one of the former royal farms, using modern machinery. And the Norwegian author Nils Brantzeg has recently written a book about a family that has chosen farm life in far more difficult terrain, connected with the outside world and its markets only by a mountain pass (*Bland Frender På Faerøyene*). But the Faroese economy has been transformed fundamentally from inshore fishing in open boats to deep-sea fishing in ocean-going vessels. Sixty per cent of all Faroese exports consist of salted and dried cod. Quick-frozen fish fillets are a new Faroese product; salted herring a windfall that follows the periodic appearance of herring in Faroese waters. These waters are carefully protected by international agreement and supervision that occasionally results in international incidents.

'In 1839 [writes Eric Linklater in his recent book on *Orkney and Shetland*] a Faroe man had come to Shetland to learn the art of fish-curing, and Shetlanders had taught the Faroese the craft of deep-line fishing for cod. Since then the Faroese had come up in the world, their population had shown a prodigious increase, and the more northerly archipelago was alive with enterprise and manifestly prosperous, though nature had given it a harsh and stormy environment, a sterile soil. What was the reason for so large a disparity between Torshavn and Lerwick, between Suderøy and Yell?'

The Shetlanders have not been backward in studying the lessons of the Faroese comparison, and of the Norwegian one also, as the columns of the *Shetland Times* demonstrate. But the remedies that these lessons suggest lie in the hands of a government as distant from Shetland as Copenhagen is from the Faroe Islands, and as indifferent as such governments used to be to the interests of their remote islands two centuries ago. As Eric Linklater observes in his book:

'Indifference to the wealth of its own waters, and equal indifference to the claims of coastwise fishermen—indifference or invincible ignorance—have long characterized British governments; and only now, after every other European government has protected its own shores, is the insular Parliament at Westminster paying some attention to the riches spawned in its domestic sea.'

The most dramatic attempt to overcome this inertia, and bring a Faroese prosperity to the Scottish islands, was made by Lord Leverhulme when he bought the long island of Lewis and Harris at the end of the First World War. His position was complicated by the fact that he had acquired the title of a feudal superior in a country with a bitter history of landlordism. His aims were jeopardised further by his wish to abolish by degrees the subsistence farming of the small crofts, concentrate agriculture in farm units of the most efficient possible size, and provide an income for the majority of islanders through developing the fishing industry. This is precisely the course which the Faroese have followed with such success. But the Hebridean crofters had only just been released from centuries of insecurity by the passing of the Crofters' Acts, and it was much to ask them to relinquish their hard won rights. What is most surprising is the high proportion of Lewismen who actively supported Leverhulme's venture. The causes of its failure are examined brilliantly by Nigel Nicolson in *Lord of The Isles*. And people still ponder the ultimate cause; whether it was the state of the fishing industry and markets at that time, or the obstruction of a few Hebridean crofters, or the impatience of an old man in a hurry, or the ignorance and indifference of distant politicians and civil servants, actuated by motives that had no relevance whatever to the Hebrides.

It was during the economic stagnation of the inter-war years that Dr John Lorne Campbell and Dr Frank Fraser Darling laid the foundations, in their different spheres, of the knowledge

which, had it been solicited by the Highland Development
Board immediately it was set up, could hardly have failed to
give the Board's activities a more appropriate direction.
Campbell also aided Sir Compton Mackenzie in running the
Sea League from the island of Barra, which campaigned for
the creation of a 13-mile fishery limit on the north-west coast of
Scotland and the Hebrides under the 1895 Sea Fisheries Act.
This would have closed the Minch to trawlers. In 1958 the
Icelanders halted the drastic decline in cod stocks off her coasts
by extending her fishing limits: but it was not until nearly
thirty years after Campbell and Mackenzie conducted their
campaign that a comparable protection was extended to the
Scottish islanders in what concerned their very survival.

However, when Iceland took steps to arrest the decline in cod
stocks in 1958, the British Government attempted to prevent
the extension of Icelandic fishing limits by force. The British
were the most intensive fishermen in those waters after the
Icelanders themselves, and the British Navy was sent in an un-
successful attempt to protect their livelihood before the limit
was accepted. It cannot be said that Britain is especially cul-
pable in the over-fishing which menaces the essential food supplies of the future, and which is such an anxious subject of research and negotiation among maritime nations. But Britain
has moved farther than the countries of Scandinavia in con-
centrating her fishing industry in large ocean-going vessels,
operating at great distances from a few large ports. Several
contributory causes, including the exhaustion of stock in nearby
fishing grounds, are compelling the Scandinavian countries to
follow the same trend. But none of them has accepted this trend
as an excuse to penalise the small societies of outlying islands,
while protecting the interests of the industry when it is operated
on a large scale from centres distant from them. The autonomy
granted by Denmark to Iceland and Faroe would make this
impossible, while the political strength of Norway's islanders
would make it unthinkable.

In the circumstances, the resilience and vitality of some of
Scotland's remote islanders is very remarkable. The population
of Shetland, which was considerably larger than that of Faroe
at the beginning of this century, has sunk to 18,000 while Faroe's
has risen to 36,000. Islands that would certainly flourish if they

were in Scandinavia are dead or dying. But in others an un-
quenchable spirit lives on.

Among these are the Out Skerries east of Shetland, which
Roland Svensson described in 1955 in *Lonely Isles*. 'Out Skerries
is one of the few islands whose population has remained more or
less constant for the past hundred years. One hundred and
twenty-two people are living there, distributed in twenty-eight
families. About half of the inhabitants are under forty, and there
are twenty-four children attending the school.' Svensson
describes the good life that people are able to lead in these
numbers, in such an environment, and he observes: 'Strangers
seldom visit Skerries. There is neither hotel nor boarding house
there—which is perhaps just as well. Tourist traffic may make a
place rich, but it often has a detrimental effect on a community
leading a simple and sound life.' Here is a small island of crofter-
fishermen nearer to Norway than to Britain ethnically, geographically, and (through a mysterious determination to survive) in prosperity. Eric Linklater described its amenities ten
years after Svensson wrote, in *Orkney and Shetland*:

'I went into a doll's-house supermarket—a miniature but most
compendious shop—the most brightly clean, scrupulously ordered
small shop I have ever seen . . . and through a window a sheltered
bay shone like a pool of sapphires in the sun. "But come here in
January, in a January gale," said the girl in the shop—and a very
attractive girl she was—"and you'll see nothing but spray lashing
over us, as if you were on the under-side of a wave, and it breaking
over you." '

Whalsay is another Shetland isle which shows no instinct to
lie down and die.

'What characterises it [writes Eric Linklater in *Orkney and Shetland*]
is the redoubtable character of its inhabitants. A passenger in the
little inter-island ship, the *Earl of Zetland*, may well be surprised to
watch the unloading there of milk from Lerwick. Most manifestly
there is on the island abundant pasture for cows, but no cows are
kept, and milk is imported, "But why?" asks the inquiring passenger. "It takes a great deal of work, and a great deal of care and
trouble, to keep a couple of cows," is the reply, "and for a few quarts
of milk it isn't worth the effort. It's easier, and cheaper in the long
run, to buy milk in Lerwick, for our business isn't farming, it's

fishing. It's fishing that's our interest, and there's not a boy on the island that wants to be a farmer. They want to go to sea." '

Here is the Faroese practice, adopted by islanders whose fore-bears spoke the Faroese language until the eighteenth century. Roland Svensson has observed that they possess the benefit of good natural harbours, and this essential asset must contribute to a confidence found nowhere else in Shetland save in Out Skerries. 'The population is maintaining itself and everyone seems to be working joyfully, and there's a wonderful spirit of future in that place' Svensson found.

The same spirit remains unextinguished in some smaller Hebridean islands, of which Scalpay off the coast of Harris is a striking example. Murdo MacSween, a native of this island, remarked in 1965:

'You find that islanders as a whole have very deep roots in their native village, and most of them would be very reluctant to leave if there were suitable employment. I should think that in my own island, in Scalpay, about eight out of ten of the young men are sea-faring, in the Merchant Navy. If they could fish from their own island and be home every night, I'm quite sure they would prefer that.'

Such was the reputation of this little island that seamen from the west used to pretend they came from Scalpay in order to secure jobs in the east coast ports. And their skill is still one of the needless forms of waste suffered by this country as a whole, as well as suffered with infinitely greater harm by the Hebrides themselves.

Thirty years ago the population of Scalpay was about 950, with 150 children in the school: the population is now about 650, with about 90 schoolchildren. As the island is exceedingly barren, it depends entirely on fishing for its livelihood, and it must be singularly exasperating to the inhabitants to see the fishing boats of so many other nations making a living in their home waters. There are the Norwegian shark fishers who come in the spring, French lobster boats, factory ships such as the German one that Kenneth Smith described enviously in Stornoway.

'From stem to stern the ship was expertly devised to carry out the functions of fishing. As the catch came in over the stern, it was graded and passed on to conveyer-belt lines for processing. At stations along the line, machines which only required supervision carried out the drudgery of gutting and cleaning, until finally the product was boxed, labelled and stored under refrigeration ready for market.'

Yet in 1959 there were no more than twenty-five boats fishing from Hebridean ports of 40 feet or more in length. This was the year in which the MacAulay Trust came to the rescue. It had been set up to employ the fortune made by a Lewisman in Rhodesia for the benefit of his native island, and it set out to increase the number of boats operating from Lewis. In the following year the Government set up the Outer Hebrides Fisheries Training Scheme for those willing to make fishing their career, and provided the financial assistance that launched twelve further boats.

But £6,000 was supplied by the Government as a grant, and £11,000 as a loan for each boat, leaving the fishermen to provide 15 per cent of the cost, which amounted to £3,000. This could be a fatal stumbling-block to the career of a young Hebridean fisherman. The MacAulay Trust assisted until financial difficulties beyond its control forced it to stop. The business community of Stornoway responded to an appeal to help. But by 1965 there were still over fifty young men waiting in idleness with their names down for boats in Stornoway alone, and at least thirty more boats were required. In addition to the wastage in seamanship—which might never be repaired if these young men joined the stream of emigration from the Scottish islands—there was the wastage that resulted ashore. To maintain a local freezing plant in full production would require something approaching sixty seine-netters catching white fish out of Stornoway. Without such employment ashore it is the girls who must leave in search of work: and it has been found invariably that once the girls leave, an island society begins to die.

Various people working in Lewis and devoted to the promotion of the island's welfare deserve the credit for urging the Government to intervene and provide a larger Hebridean fishing fleet. It seems a little odd that the newly appointed Highland Development Board (which contained nobody expert in this field) should have been handed the credit for a result which in any case it required neither the Board nor its new powers to achieve. But it was a gratifying reward for years of patient endeavour when, in March 1966, the Secretary of State for Scotland approved the building of twenty-five new boats during the next five years, in addition to the normal programme of the fishery authorities. And as it is the sole significant achievement that can be credited to the Highland Development Board during its first eighteen months of office (apart from those that might otherwise have been attributable to the Highland Fund) it is perhaps not surprising that the Board should be offered such credit for it.

Perhaps Lord Leverhulme attached too much importance to solving the agricultural problem, bedevilled by the Highland system of land tenure, at the very same time as he sought to develop the Hebridean fisheries. But the Development Board is the first body ever to have been invested by Parliament with the necessary powers to do this; and it caused general astonishment in the Highlands and Islands when no priority was given to this problem and none of the recognised specialists in this field were consulted.

Two of the seven counties that belong to the Board's province, however, have rather different characters from the others. One of these is Orkney, whose prosperous farms, owned by those who work them, are comparable with those of Caithness and Easter Ross. Here is a long fertile corridor, from Orkney's old red sandstone to the first-class agricultural land that faces the Cromarty Firth, where the Scandinavian pattern of peasant proprietorship has taken vigorous root. Here the obstacles to efficient development inherent in a system of landlordism and crofting tenure are absent.

Orkney is an archipelago whose inhabitants find their greatest prosperity in the land, in contrast to Shetland, whose most prosperous islanders are fishermen. The population figures are similar: Orkney now contains no more than 18,000 people today. In 1900 she had double the population of Faroe: today she has half. On the other hand, this is to be expected in an agricultural milieu. The output of Orcadian agriculture has risen impressively as the numbers engaged in it have declined.

There are, however, the same deplorable influences at work here as in other Scottish islands. In the island of Egilsay, which possesses fourteen farms ranging in size from 50 to 300 acres, there is no public water or electricity supply. Communications often impose needless inconvenience as well as a severe tax on the farmer. They are blamed in particular for the decline of Stronsay, an island with a long and vigorous agricultural history.

It is in Orkney that one may assess the benefits brought to small islands when miniature Adens are planted among them. There is the sudden flow of cash, the scope for local labour, especially unskilled labour. The young people enjoy the stimulus of an alien social element in their midst. A golden haze of prosperity hangs over the neighbourhood until remote policy decisions, having no connection with island life, dictate that the bonanza is over. The islands are then left with a disrupted economy, some shabby and dilapidated buildings, and a social atmosphere nostalgic and disturbed. This was what happened in Scapa Flow. But in the northernmost Shetland island of Unst they are only now living in a period of prosperity, and the young Gaelic-speaking people of Uist in the outer Hebrides are tasting the honey of the English way of life, brought to their very hearths by the military authorities. This injection of prosperity into Uist and Unst must be compared to the prosperity that the dog-fish industry has brought to Vågsøy in Norway. Perhaps the dog-fish will fail, as the military requirements of Britain in Unst and Uist will surely end one day, just as they did in Scapa Flow. But Vågsøy will turn then to some other activity related to her pattern of life and surrounding resources. Where will Unst find new R.A.F. personnel to serve, or Uist some new rocket venture?

In the course of the B.B.C. programme of 1965 about North Atlantic islands, Roland Svensson spoke with particular severity of these policies and priorities:

'The assistance given to outlying islands and isolated communities should be far bigger and more far-sighted. Take Britain for example. The population rises yearly. The need for arable land, canning factories, freezing plants and fishing vessels will be of paramount importance. People ask: "Who will pay?" Well, I will give you a drastic example. Look at St Kilda, lying about fifty miles west of the outer Hebrides. The people were evacuated in 1930, partly because the people were unable to maintain communications with the mainland. About eight years ago I saw the Forces move into that island.

171

They brought bulldozers, tractors, big lorries, diesel generators, helicopters and so on, and regular communications were established with the mainland. And if a soldier cut his finger he was brought to hospital on the mainland. But if an island woman of Foula in Shetland, or Fair Isle, or Canna in the inner Hebrides is to give birth to a child, there will be no helicopter to bring her to a mainland hospital. Who paid for all these wonderful modern implements, tractors and lorries? The British paid for them, And we ought to be able to invest the far smaller sum necessary to assist island populations, building what would be of lasting importance.'

In Faroe, whose inhabitants are able to regulate such matters for themselves, special tax concessions are offered to people who live in the island of Nolsøy across the water from Torshavn, in order to inhibit congestion in the capital. And in the southern island of Sudurøy the Faroese tunnelled through a mountain in order to provide a winter link to a village of no more than 700 people, lest they should feel cut off, and encouraged to emigrate to a town.

Islands that live under the direct authority of the Danish Government, without benefit of self-government, provide similar lessons. The twenty skerries of Christiansø are the most distant islands from metropolitan Denmark lying in the Baltic. Under 200 people live in them, and are encouraged to do so by exemption from rates. Denmark's most distant island to the west is Greenland, the largest in the world. It contains little more than 35,000 people and perhaps it will never be able to support more than 100,000. Its climate is too severe for agriculture, and its economy is not self-supporting. But the Danes do not wash their hands of responsibility to its inhabitants on that account, or treat Greenland as a mere military asset or as a tourist attraction for foreigners. They subsidise the building of Greenland's economy, and the planting of hospitals and schools. They take no taxes from Greenland. In particular, they respect and nourish the Greenlandic language and cultural tradition. This investment will be yielding its harvest when Britain's investment in Unst, Uist and St Kilda resembles the ghost town of Lyness by the waters of Scapa.

At every point of examination, the mainland control of Scotland's islands can be seen to be a failure. At every available point of comparison the alternative of island control and responsibility can be demonstrated to be the sensible solution. But beyond the practical advantages of island autonomy, it exercises an influence that Jo Grimond touched upon in July 1967, in an article in *Scotland*:

'By maintaining the power of choice in their own affairs, the Faroese have added immensely to the attraction of living in Faroe. Man is in a broad sense a political animal. A community means among other things a coming together of people who have a common interest and wish to develop it. Once you drain an area of power over its own affairs you take a great deal out of life which cannot be given back either by the mere provision of jobs or by the proliferation of bureaucrats.'

There is an argument that lies still farther from that of administrative efficiency or economic advantage. How much weight is given to it will depend upon how much respect we pay to the personal possessions of islanders, their language and culture and way of life. These may appear paltry by other standards, but they happen to be their very own. As a matter of fact the intellectual vitality of Shetland, Orkney and the Hebrides are phenomenal if measured against population statistics or the economic level. But it would make no difference if they were not. Hebrideans do not write Gaelic poetry in order that it should be evaluated in English translation by outsiders.

It is noteworthy that the existence of a separate Faroese language was recognised by the Danish Government as a prominent reason for conceding self-government. There are still more than twice as many Gaelic speakers as Faroese speakers, and it is the language of the Hebrides. So it is essential to the integrity and future identity of the Western Isles to inaugurate a language policy based upon the present predicament of the language, and upon standards worthy of the mid-twentieth century.

The Gaelic Language,
Its Study and Development

Kenneth D. MacDonald

The Gaelic Language,
Its Study and Development [1]

Language is one of the most distinctive marks of any people's cultural identity, and to speak of 'Gaelic Scotland' is to apply to a part of Scotland a definition that is primarily linguistic. Strictly, the term can refer only to those parts of Scotland in which the Celtic language introduced from Ireland in the early centuries of the Christian era is still spoken. The developments political, economic, social and educational surveyed elsewhere in this volume, have played their part in determining the extent to which the language still survives and the kind of status which it enjoys. In this chapter, the attempt is made to examine that status, to review the attention Gaelic has received from scholars and preservationists, and to suggest possible directions for future developments.

One measure of the state of the language is that afforded by the returns for each decennial census, the most recent of which took place in 1961, when, as in previous inquiries, house-holders were asked to 'write "G" opposite the name of each person, 3 years of age and upwards, who speaks Gaelic only' and to 'write "G and E" opposite the name of each person who speaks both Gaelic and English'. The full report on the replies given to this question was published in 1966, showing that in 1961 the total number of persons in Scotland, aged 3 years and upwards, who spoke Gaelic only was 974, and the number of those who spoke Gaelic and English was 80,004, the total number of Gaelic speakers representing 1·66 per cent of the Scottish population. The figures produced for each locality give a clear picture of the geographical distribution of Gaelic speakers and their relative density in different areas. Leaving aside the settlements of Gaelic speakers in the towns and cities of the

177

south and east, of which the Glasgow total of 11,165 is by far the most substantial, the Gaelic area on the mainland is largely confined to the county of Argyll, the western parts of the counties of Inverness and Ross and Cromarty, and the western and northern parts of the county of Sutherland. The highest percentage of Gaelic speakers recorded for any of the landward areas of Perthshire was only 15·6, for east Inverness-shire 15·9 and for Easter Ross only 8·7. Over the mainland area as a whole, the percentage of Gaelic speakers exceeded 60 only in the western peninsular districts of Applecross and Ardnamurchan, while in the southern part of the county of Argyll it was less than 20. Of the islands, Bute and Arran showed returns of less than 2 per cent and 10 per cent respectively, but the proportion in the Inner Hebrides was substantially higher, only north Mull showing a percentage of less than 40, while the districts of Kilmuir and Bracadale in the north of Skye showed a Gaelic-speaking population of over 80 per cent. The Outer Hebrides emerged as the true heartland of the language, showing percentages of less than 80 only in the district of Lewis which contains the town of Stornoway, and in South Uist, where the dilution in the concentration of Gaelic speakers is due to the influx of armed services personnel.

The overall trend in the numbers of Gaelic speakers over the seventy years from 1891 to 1961 emerges clearly from the following table:

	(a) Speakers of Gaelic & English	(b) Speakers of Gaelic but not English	Percentage of population aged 3 years & over	
			(a)	(b)
1891	210,677	43,738	5·66	1·18
1901	202,700	28,106	4·89	0·68
1911	183,998	18,400	4·14	0·41
1921	148,950	9,829	3·26	0·21
1931	129,419	6,716	2·82	0·15
1951	93,269	2,178	1·93	0·05
1961	80,004	974	1·64	0·02

The Census Report table which sets out the number of Gaelic speakers counted in each census since 1891 as a percentage of the total population of each district shows that the reduction has been most drastic in those mainland areas most easily accessible to the English-speaking Lowlands. In the Outer Hebrides, on the other hand, the percentage has nowhere fallen steeply, showing over-all a slight downward trend, but in some areas, particularly in Lewis, remaining remarkably steady. The dramatic reduction in the number of monoglot Gaelic speakers is of particular significance, especially as a large proportion of the 974 counted in 1961 were in the 3–4 age group, and thus only transiently monolingual, while the proportion of monolingual persons in the over-65 group has fallen drastically over the years. This means that the monoglot Gaelic speaker is on the verge of extinction. The general picture that emerges, then, from the censal figures is of a steadily declining total of Gaelic speakers, diminishing much more rapidly in the mainland areas than in the remoter islands, and of a Gaelic-speaking population the great majority of whom are, and all of whom soon will be, bilingual.

Census returns, useful and significant though they are in assessing the position broadly, provide but a superficial analysis of the situation. Bilingualism is a highly complex condition, influenced by many variable factors, both linguistic and non-linguistic, and these the simple censal count cannot measure. The census gives no indication as to whether the bilingual individual uses Gaelic habitually or infrequently, whether in some situations and not in others, whether he can read and write the language, what the degree of his fluency in it, or how much mutual interference there is between each of his two languages. To answer such questions adequately would require numerous detailed surveys, after the manner of that on Gaelic-speaking children in Highland schools, published by the Scottish Council for Research in Education. Even in the absence of such research, however, there are some general observations that can be made about the bilingual situation in the Highlands and Islands of Scotland. It requires no detailed analysis to establish that English is the dominant language in this confrontation. The dominance of English in the educational system since 1872 has been crucial and decisive, and its effects are discussed in another chapter of this book. Arising out of the English orientation of the educational system and the resulting spread of English literacy, there has been the far-reaching influence of the English media of communication—newspapers, magazines, books, the cinema, radio and television are all vehicles by which the English language is transmitted in copious quantity to the bilingual Gael. The machinery of government and administration uses English, and English only, at practically all levels. Numerous scientific and technological advances percolate to the Highlands from the south, bringing with them their associated English terminology, and the expansion of the tourist industry has led to increasing contact between Gaelic speakers and those who are speakers of English only. The settlement of Gaelic speakers in places outwith the Highlands, and intermarriage between them and non-Gaelic speakers, cause a further feedback of English influence to the Gaelic area.

In the face of so many powerful forces ranged on the side of English, the Gaelic survival, precarious though it is by now, may fairly be regarded as remarkable, and to account for it note must be taken of a number of factors that have helped to slow down the Gaelic decline. Supreme among these has been the influence of the Church, as the principal institution which has maintained the use of Gaelic in public and corporate activity. The Church of Scotland since the late seventeenth century, and the Free and Free Presbyterian Churches since the mid and later nineteenth century, have exerted a tremendous influence on the social life of the greater part of the Gaelic-speaking area, and although in the earlier part of the eighteenth century evangelical Presbyterianism was not too kindly disposed towards the language, for the past two hundred years Protestant ecclesiastical policy in the Highlands has been consistently pro-Gaelic, even if not always very appreciative of certain aspects of Gaelic culture. The regular holding of church services, the catechising of parishioners, participation by laymen in public prayer-meetings and meetings at which spiritual and theological matters were discussed, and the reading of the Gaelic Scriptures at family worship in the home, have all done much to retain for Gaelic a dominant position in one important area of the people's life. The Presbyterian Churches still maintain their policy of appointing Gaelic-speaking ministers to parishes where the language survives, although the steep reduction in the number of speakers in some districts, and the shortage of ministers who are themselves fluent in the language, has led to a reduction in the number of Gaelic services held, and in some cases to the appointment of a non-Gaelic incumbent to a parish where formerly a Gaelic speaker would have been required. In general, altered social conditions in the Protestant areas have lessened the Church's influence on the life of the community, the minister is no longer accorded the honoured and influential place that he once enjoyed, is, on average, probably a less learned and cultured man than his counterpart of a century ago, and contributes less to the Gaelic cause in leadership and literary activity. While the Presbyterian Churches still play an important part in the perpetuation of Gaelic speech, and still make a contribution to Gaelic literature, they are not the bulwark of the language that once they were.

The Roman Catholic Church maintains its strongest influence in some western districts of Ross-shire, Inverness-shire and Argyll, in the islands of Eigg and Canna, and in the outer islands of Barra and South Uist. Although it has traditionally used Latin for the most important parts of its liturgy, in Gaelic-speaking areas a great deal of Gaelic has also been used, for example in the readings of Epistle and Gospel, in litanies, sermons, hymns and special services, and parish priests have been expected either to have or acquire sufficient knowledge of the language to enable them to carry out their pastoral duties. The ruling of the Second Vatican Council permitting the strictly liturgical parts of the Mass to be said in the vernacular will, it is hoped, lead to an increase in the amount of Gaelic heard at Catholic services, and should invest the language with an added dignity for the Catholic faithful. The Roman Church has always adopted a more permissive attitude towards social amusements than the Presbyterian Churches, with the result that a much greater wealth of traditional Gaelic song and story has been preserved in Roman Catholic than in Protestant areas.

Broadcasting has become one of the most influential media of communication in modern times, and almost since the institution of the Scottish Home Service of the B.B.C., over forty years ago, Gaelic has had some place in the programme output, and the total time devoted to Gaelic programmes has been gradually increasing over the years. In March 1950, for instance, the average weekly output of Gaelic was 1 hour 45 minutes, in March 1959 about 2 hours and in March 1967 about 3 hours. Independent television, not yet available over much of the Gaelic-speaking area, has screened several series of Gaelic entertainment programmes, mainly of a musical character. The regular content of B.B.C. Gaelic programmes at present comprises a weekly religious service with an additional service once a month, a monthly programme for children, a weekly talk, two evening programmes per week usually devoted to Gaelic songs but sometimes varied with the broadcast of a Gaelic play, readings from Gaelic literature, and a special programme for women. Five-minute news bulletins are broadcast at mid-day on five days per week, followed on four days per week by ten minutes of Gaelic records. There is also a weekly magazine programme which is broadcast on V.H.F. from transmitters in the north of Scotland, and there is one weekly programme devoted to bagpipe music. The B.B.C.'s Gaelic television programmes are mostly of a musical character, although a few religious programmes and one Gaelic play have been screened. The B.B.C. in Scotland thus devotes to Gaelic programmes a percentage of its total broadcasting time higher than the percentage of Gaelic speakers in the country's population. The influence on the linguistic situation is difficult to assess, but it will clearly be least in the case of programmes with a high musical and song content, and greatest with the news bulletins and other programmes in which contemporary affairs of all kinds are reported or discussed in Gaelic. It should be remembered, however, that when compared with the quantity of English programmes available to Highland listeners and viewers from the B.B.C. and the commercial stations, the total Gaelic output is very small indeed.

Community entertainments such as concerts and céilidhs, and community drama, where it exists, also help to preserve for Gaelic something of a public status. Other factors which have undoubtedly helped to slow down the Gaelic decline have been the recognition, in so far as this has been achieved, of Gaelic in the educational system, and the amount of Gaelic material published in books, magazines and newspapers. As these subjects are discussed in other chapters, they need only be mentioned here.

The uneven competition with English has had its effect not only on the number of Gaelic speakers but also on the quality of the Gaelic which they speak. The nature and extent of this effect will vary from speaker to speaker, depending on such factors as the situation in which the individual finds himself, the subject on which he speaks and the register of vocabulary which he uses, his fluency in the language, the kind of education he has had and the extent to which he is motivated by language loyalty, but in general it is inescapably clear that the dominance of English in the Gaelic–English bilingual situation has had its most obvious effect in the intrusion of English vocabulary into Gaelic speech. This intrusion involves not only those modern objects, processes and concepts for which Gaelic has no vocabulary of its own and which come to the notice of Gaelic speakers with their English designations already attached but also the substitution of English words for many of the commonest concepts for which Gaelic itself is lexically quite adequate. This shows that for many speakers repeated encounter with English words has rendered these more accessible to them than their Gaelic counterparts. The fact that practically all Gaelic speakers are practised in using the English sound system means that borrowed words, unlike the borrowings of earlier times, no longer undergo much phonological adaptation, and are made to conform to Gaelic usage only as regards word-order, initial mutation and the addition of some declensional and conjugational endings. Less obvious but no less real is the weakening effect which English has had on the idiom of Gaelic speech. Schoolteachers have observed that the pupils they now teach have a much poorer knowledge of Gaelic vocabulary and idiom than their counterparts in the same locality a decade or two ago; and even old people, who in their youth must have been possessed of flexible and idiomatic Gaelic, become increasingly influenced in their speech habits by the prevalence of English. It was this aspect of the Gaelic Decline—the degradation from within—that led Finlay J. MacDonald, in a perceptive analysis of the Gaelic situation contributed to the *Saltire Review* in 1958, to conclude that 'the cult of Anglicisation . . . may mean that the language we finally bury will not be the Gaelic we know, but a *patois* whose loss we need hardly mourn.'

Much of the scholarly attention given to Gaelic during the present century has been governed, in its priorities and emphases, by the realisation that the language and the culture which it represented were in danger of vanishing, that, indeed, much had already irrecoverably vanished, and so it was concerned with the recording and studying of what still remained. This applies to the actual sounds of the language itself, as represented in its various dialects. Different aspects of dialect study had been dealt with around the turn of the century in papers contributed to different periodicals by various people, notably C. M. Robertson with his articles published in the *Celtic Review* and the *Transactions of the Gaelic Society of Inverness*, but the first people to undertake systematic phonological and morphological descriptions of different dialects were the Scandinavian scholars, Nils Holmer and Carl Borgstrøm. Holmer published his *Studies on Argyllshire Gaelic* in 1939, and collected material for the more recently published volumes, *The Gaelic of Arran* and *The Gaelic of Kintyre*. Borgstrøm, having published his study of the dialect of Barra in the journal, *Norsk Tidsskrift For Sprogvidenskap*, in 1937, went on to provide two further volumes, *The Dialects of the Outer Hebrides* and *The Dialects of Skye and Ross-shire*, in a series published as a supplement to the same journal, under the general title of 'A Linguistic Survey of the Gaelic Dialects of Scotland'. In a preface to the first of these volumes, Carl Marstrander describes the object of the series as 'to give posterity a clear and reliable first-hand account of the phonetic and morphological system of these dialects, based not on written or printed sources but solely on the spoken, everyday language of the common people'. A third volume was added to the series in 1956, with the publication of Magne Oftedal's *The Gaelic of Leurbost, Isle of Lewis*.

By this time, a new and much more comprehensive survey was in progress, as part of the Linguistic Survey of Scotland, instituted at Edinburgh University in 1949–50, for the purpose of collecting and studying specimens of the dialects of Scots and Gaelic. The collection of Gaelic material was begun under Professor Myles Dillon, and has since 1950 been directed by Professor Kenneth Jackson, assisted by various researchers. The method employed was to tackle first those areas where Gaelic was most in danger of disappearing, using carefully picked informants whose parents as well as themselves had been born and brought up in the district whose dialect was being studied, avoiding, if at all possible, people who were married to speakers of other dialects, or who had themselves lived for a long time in another dialect area. These informants were taken through a questionnaire of some 1,200 items, designed to cover the phonology and most of the morphology of any dialect. Samples of the informants' speech were then recorded on tape and later transcribed into phonetic notation, to await analysis. These procedures were repeated in different dialect districts until the whole of the Gaelic-speaking area had been covered, and the whole corpus of material collected is now being analysed for publication. While this editorial processing of the primary collection goes on, more intensive dialect studies are being conducted in selected areas. The Survey came in time to study the language in many mainland districts where it was on the verge of extinction, and its published findings will constitute a most valuable record of Scottish Gaelic as it was in the mid-twentieth century.

Also concerned with recovery and preservation, this time in the realm of vocabulary and idiom, is the project directed towards the production of a comprehensive historical dictionary of Scottish Gaelic, an undertaking sponsored by Glasgow University with financial assistance from The Carnegie Trust for the Universities of Scotland, directed by Professor Derick Thomson, and begun in the Autumn of 1966. The aim of this venture is to present the Gaelic vocabulary in a way that will illustrate the range and development of its usage over the centuries, and the collection of material will consequently involve the exhaustive examination of the documentary sources of all periods, as well as the collection of dialect vocabulary both in Scotland and Nova Scotia. At the time of writing, over a hundred voluntary readers have been recruited to tackle the written sources, and it is proposed to have a number of the older texts requiring the fullest excerption prepared for scanning by electronic computer. An organising editor, provided with secretarial assistance, took up office in September 1966. For the collection of vocabulary in the field, it is proposed to appoint a full-time fieldworker who will collect material in different areas, using subject-questionnaires and a tape-recorder. It is hoped, too, that some helpers will be found to undertake part-time collecting in particular districts, and that interested persons in all areas will assist the project by transmitting unusual items of vocabularly and idiom to the dictionary headquarters. Secondary schools with Gaelic-speaking pupils are being supplied with questionnaires to be filled with the relevant material which pupils will collect by interrogating their parents, relatives and neighbours. The sense of urgency given to the Linguistic Survey by the decline of Gaelic in mainland areas is felt *a fortiori* in the collection of vocabulary for the dictionary, for in all areas the Gaelic vocabulary is becoming increasingly attenuated, and the collection of many words and idioms will depend on their being recorded in time from such speakers of the older generation as will be able to recall them. The chief problems envisaged in this large and many-sided undertaking are the adequate coverage of the remaining areas of living speech, and the recruitment of suitably qualified persons to assist in the excerption of the older written sources, particularly manuscripts, and to help with the vast amount of sifting and selection involved in the ultimate editorial process.

As long as Gaelic is spoken at all, something of its sounds, its syntax and its vocabulary will be available for study at first hand. The tradition of its oral literature, on the other hand, will cease once the kind of society which fostered and preserved it has vanished. Since the eclipse of the Gaelic learned class early in the eighteenth century, the custodians of traditional Gaelic song and story have been non-literate men and women, many of them descendants of the old learned families, who acquired their lore at the social gatherings where such material was publicly recited, and transmitted it to others in the same way. With the spread of English education and mass-literacy, the traditional *céilidh* gradually went into decline, and was almost obliterated by the socially disruptive influence of the First World War, with the result that the dwindling number of inheritors of Gaelic oral tradition in the second half of the twentieth century are the last of their line, and are most of them advanced in years.

The attempt to record and preserve Gaelic oral literature has had a continuous history for the past two and a half centuries. In the eighteenth century, the researches of Edward Lhuyd, the Ossianic controversy, and the prevailing vogue of antiquarian inquiry stimulated such collectors as Donald MacNicol, James Maclagan and Ranald MacDonald, and led to the publication of the first anthologies of Gaelic verse, as well as the assembling of a considerable quantity of material in manuscript. The early collectors' emphasis on verse was continued in the nineteenth century in the work of such compilers as John Mackenzie, Donald MacPherson and Archibald Sinclair. It was J. F. Campbell of Islay (1822–85) who first envisaged and executed an organised attempt at the collection of Gaelic folk-tales. Through the labours of the paid collaborators whom Campbell enlisted all over the Highlands and Islands, a great body of tales and traditions was written down, only a small part of which appears in the four volumes of *Popular Tales of the West Highlands*, published between 1860 and 1862. Campbell was conscious that he had only scratched the surface of the available wealth of oral tradition in the Highlands, remarking: 'There is no reason to believe that the stories now current in the Highlands are nearly exhausted by this collection; whole districts are yet untried, and whole classes of stories, such as popular history and robber stories have scarcely been touched; and yet new stories come in regularly.' It was an awareness of how much there was to be collected, and the knowledge that the opportunity would not last for ever, that motivated the collectors who, following Campbell, were active around the turn of the century. These were all individual enthusiasts, who sought to snatch what they could from the receding tide—men such as Lord Archibald Campbell, the Rev. J. Gregorson Campbell, the Rev. J. MacDougall, the Rev. Fr Allan MacDonald, Alexander Carmichael, the Rev. Kenneth MacLeod, and on the female side Amy Murray, Frances Tolmie and Mrs Kennedy Fraser.

It was Mrs Kennedy Fraser who first used a recording machine in the Highlands, and the continuing development of mechanical aids during the present century has greatly facilitated the work of more recent collectors, and has, in particular, meant a great advance on purely scribal methods in the recording of folk music. The leading figure in the recording of Gaelic tradition during the fourth, fifth and sixth decades of this century has been Dr J. L. Campbell of Canna, assisted by his wife, Margaret Fay Shaw. An American student of music, Miss Shaw came to the community of Glendale, on the south side of Lochboisdale, in 1929, and stayed there for six years, collecting and studying the local songs and traditions. The fruit of her researches was published in 1955, in the volume *Folksongs and Folklore of South Uist*, containing over a hundred songs with music, together with some prayers, ballads, short stories, proverbs, cures and recipes, and enhanced by some magnificent photographs illustrative of the local way of life. Dr Campbell's own interest in collecting traditional songs and stories was first aroused by the late John MacPherson of Northbay, Barra, himself a distinguished repository of Gaelic lore, and since 1937 he has concentrated his attention on the islands of Barra, South Uist, Eigg and Canna, with one collecting trip to Nova Scotia, using successive types of recording apparatus. The number of his recordings runs into many hundreds, comprising about 300 Ediphone records made in 1937, mostly of songs from South Uist and Barra, with about 85 songs from Nova Scotia, some 200 recordings on Presto discs made in Barra and Canna in the spring of 1938 and later, over 1,000 Webster wire recordings made in 1949 in Barra, Eriskay, South Uist, Benbecula, Canna, Glasgow, Paisley and Edinburgh, and some 500 tape-recordings made in South Uist and Barra since 1957. Some of the items first recorded were re-recorded later with improved machines, so that the number of individual songs and stories is considerably less than the total number of recordings made. Even so, Dr Campbell estimates that the separate items he has recorded or has had recorded for him, from over a hundred different reciters, amounts to some 1,200 songs, about 350 folk-tales and anecdotes, about 100 personal reminiscences and some 5 or 6 Ossianic ballads. Dr Campbell has published, both in Gaelic and in English translation, collections of some of the songs and stories recorded by him, and has contributed numerous articles to journals and newspapers on some of the outstanding personalities and reciters he has encountered.

In his collecting activities, Dr Campbell had the help of various local enthusiasts who were similarly interested in the collection and preservation of songs and stories, notably the late Miss Annie Johnston of Barra, who had a very extensive knowledge of local tradition. Other local collectors deserving of mention for their contribution to the over-all task of preservation are Mr Donald J. MacDonald of South Uist, who recorded much material from his father, Mr Duncan MacDonald, the late Miss Nandag MacLeod of Stornoway, whose collection of songs forms the basis for the volume *Eilean Fraoich*, published in 1938, and the late Mrs Katie Douglas of Skye, who submitted many local songs to successive National Mòds. Another important contribution was made by the late Mr K. C. Craig, who in the early forties wrote down over 150 waulking songs from the recitation of Màiri Nighean Alasdair in Snaoisbheal, South Uist, and 5 folk-tales from Duncan MacDonald of Peninerine, material which he subsequently published in the two volumes *Orain Luaidh Màiri Nighean Alasdair* and *Sgialachdan Dhunnchaidh*.

Until the mid-forties, the collecting of Gaelic traditions in Scotland had been undertaken solely by interested individuals, able to devote only part of their time and resources to the task, and receiving no support from the State or any central institution. In Ireland, by contrast, a Folklore Society had been in operation since 1927, a Government-sponsored Folklore Institute was established in 1930 and expanded in 1935 to become the Irish Folklore Commission, employing a number of full-time collectors trained in the methods used by Swedish folklorists, in addition to many part-time collectors and correspondents. The Commission organised the collection of material on a nation-wide basis, and maintained publication of the folklore journal *Béaloideas*, which was started in 1927. It was in 1945 that the late Mr Calum Maclean, one of the Irish Folklore Commission's trained collectors, was sent over to the Hebrides, to become the first professional collector employed full-time in the systematic recording of material in Gaelic Scotland. During his four years' work for the Commission in Scotland, Maclean assembled eighteen MS. volumes of material from Barra, South Uist and Benbecula, drawing on the repertoire of such outstanding reciters as Duncan MacDonald and Angus Macmillan, the latter of whom recited 165 tales, one of which took over nine hours to narrate.

The stimulus from Ireland, together with an acute awareness on the part of Scottish folklorists that far too little was being done to collect and study the oral traditions of Gaelic Scotland, led in 1947 to the founding of the Folklore Institute of Scotland, in order to undertake the collection, preservation and publication of Gaelic tradition, in collaboration with the Irish Folklore

Commission and other bodies. Dr J. L. Campbell was appointed president of this new body, which over the next five years organised the recording of hundreds of songs and a number of tales on wire, many of these recordings being made by Dr Campbell himself, with the help of a grant received in 1949 from the Leverhulme Foundation. Working in collaboration with the Folklore Institute was the Barra Folklore Committee, formed at Dr Campbell's suggestion in the winter of 1949–50, to organise the collection of material in Barra. The recording expenses incurred by the Committee were paid for out of the royalties from the *Book of Barra*, published in 1936, supplemented by a small grant from Inverness-shire County Education Committee. The Folklore Institute found itself continually hampered by lack of funds, and ceased to function as an organised body when it was felt that it had been superseded by the establishment, in 1951, of the School of Scottish Studies at Edinburgh University. The B.B.C. made its own contribution as a collecting agency. In the early fifties, Seamus Ennis from Ireland and the American folk-song collector, Alan Lomax, were at work in the Hebrides, collecting songs for the B.B.C. archives, and in 1957 Mr Fred MacAulay of the B.B.C. Gaelic Department made a further collection of songs in Lewis.

At its inception, Edinburgh University's Linguistic Survey, though primarily concerned with the study of dialect, applied itself to the recording of Gaelic tradition in general. A recording van was sent to the Highlands in the Autumn of 1948, and a number of Gaelic recordings were made by Professor Angus McIntosh and Professor Myles Dillon. Following the foundation of the Linguistic Survey, it was felt desirable to establish a research institute in which the interrelation of differing aspects of Scottish life and culture—language, placenames, folk traditions, folk music, material culture, social institutions—could be studied, and so there came into being at Edinburgh University in 1951 the School of Scottish Studies, the institute which henceforward was to take the principal role in the collection, preservation and study of the oral traditions of Gaelic Scotland. Calum Maclean was appointed the School's principal Gaelic collector, and from 1951 until his death in 1960 he travelled the length and breadth of the Gaelic area, exploiting not only such productive fields as South Uist but also those mainland areas where the tradition was much weaker and the need to record in time more urgent. Even in these areas, however, the latent deposit of tradition could turn out to be remarkably rich—as evidenced by the 524 Gaelic tales which Maclean recorded from a roadman in Lochaber. Another collector who worked for the School in the Gaelic area was Mr James Ross, and the work is now carried on by Mr Donald A. MacDonald and Mr John MacInnes, supported by an archivist, Dr Alan Bruford, and two transcribers, Miss Morag MacLeod and Mr Ian Patterson. The School has never been adequately staffed to undertake a thorough combing of all the Gaelic areas, particularly as the collectors are not on the job all the time, but have to intersperse their collecting trips with periods of research at the Edinburgh headquarters. They thus have to reconcile themselves to the fact that while they are engaged in collecting in one area valuable and untapped informants may be dying off in another. A further setback in the School's work arose from the deterioration of their earliest recordings, made when recording on tape was still a relatively new procedure. Much time and trouble had to be expended in the making of new copies. Despite the difficulties, however, the School has during its first fifteen years of existence built up an impressive archive of Gaelic traditions—international folk-tales, local history, personal reminiscences, songs, Ossianic ballads and proverbs—amounting to over 1,100 hours of tape, recorded from many reciters, among whom Duncan MacDonald, Angus Maclellan, Mrs Archie MacDonald and Mrs Neil Campbell, all from South Uist, Mrs Annie Arnott from Skye, and Donald Sinclair from Tiree may be named as outstanding examples. All these reciters have been found to be merely passive bearers of tradition, not themselves transmitting their inheritance to any cultural successors, but representing the tail-end of a long succession. This fact gives priority and urgency to the task of collecting what yet remains. The School is understandably preoccupied with the task of recording, and the concomitant labour of transcribing and indexing, but one may hope that before long it will be able to undertake the publication of part of its great store of material, in greater quantity, and including items of greater length, than can be accommodated in its half-yearly journal *Scottish Studies*, which has to represent all aspects of the School's work.

Kenneth D. MacDonald

Surveying the whole history of the collection of Gaelic folklore in Scotland, the most salient truth is the complete lack of interest shown in this work in official quarters. It was only when in 1965 the late Angus Maclellan, at the age of ninty-five, was awarded the M.B.E. for his contribution to the preservation of oral Gaelic literature that the State bestowed its belated and inadequate recognition on this aspect of the national heritage.

The Scottish Place-name Survey constitutes one distinct aspect of the work of the School of Scottish Studies. Directed since its inception by Dr W. F. H. Nicolaisen, now assisted by Mr Ian Fraser, the Survey has as its object the creation of a comprehensive archive of Scottish place-names, that these may be studied for the light they may shed on linguistic developments, on the past history of the country, the pattern of human settlement and social structures. The work of collection involves the culling of names from all the earliest documentary sources, as well as the recording from living speech of countless names which have never been written down. Direct sound-recording of names is undertaken, particularly in the Gaelic areas, and the collection of unrecorded names is further assisted by the work of many voluntary helpers who send in names from their own localities. Already the whole archive contains over 1,000,000 index slips, and about 100 tapes of Gaelic place-names have been recorded. The Gaelic place-name collector is confronted with the same disturbing possibility as the Gaelic folklorist, viz. that the best, or in some cases the only, informants may have gone before there has been time to record them.

Not all Gaelic scholarly activity is so dominated by a race with time as is dialectology, folklore collection and place-name study. Part of its concern is the elucidation of those texts whose survival we owe to the work of earlier collectors, the preparation of scholarly editions for use in the schools and universities. To help this work forward, the Scottish Gaelic Texts Society was founded in 1934, 'for the purpose of promoting the publication of Texts in the Scottish Gaelic Language, accompanied by such Introductions, English Translations, Glossaries and Notes as may be deemed desirable'. Since 1937 the Society has published nine volumes of material, both prose and verse, ranging in date from the sixteenth century to the twentieth, and a further two volumes are due to appear this year. In recent years, the publication programme has been reorganised in the hope of producing one volume per year, and the financial position has been eased by annual grants from the Universities of Aberdeen, Edinburgh and Glasgow, and by help from various trusts and societies. The chief difficulty in the way of a sustained programme of annual publication is the shortage of qualified editorial man-power.

Gaelic studies of a general kind have been promoted by the Gaelic Society of Inverness and the Gaelic Society of Glasgow. The former has since 1871 issued a distinguished series of published *Transactions*, extending now to over forty volumes, and containing much valuable material in the way of previously unpublished verse and folk-tales, papers on dialect study, historical subjects, and literary criticism. The Gaelic Society of Glasgow has rendered a similar service in a much smaller way, having to date published five volumes of *Transactions*. The journal *Scottish Gaelic Studies*, issued, since 1926, from the University of Aberdeen, has similarly concerned itself with a broad spectrum of studies philological, literary and historical. Recent numbers have witnessed a new departure in the papers by Mr Donald MacAulay, in which the analytic methods of the structural linguist have for the first time been applied to some aspects of Scottish Gaelic speech.

It is time now to turn to a consideration of some of the ways in which Scottish Gaelic studies might develop in the future. Now that the linguistic survey of Gaelic dialects has been well covered as far as phonology and morphology are concerned, there would seem to be room for a deeper investigation of the Gaelic–English bilingual situation by means of various surveys of a socio-linguistic and psycho-linguistic sort. Such surveys might set out to examine the level of Gaelic literacy in different age groups, different occupational groups, and groups of different educational background, to examine the varying degrees of interference from English vocabulary, idiom and syntax in different groups and different dialect areas, to measure relative word frequencies, to assess attitudes towards the two languages in different groups, so as to gain some impression of the way in which language loyalty operates.

Of basic academic tools, there is need for a good instructional grammar based on a descriptive examination of one major dialect, noting important deviations from other dialects, but shorn of the many doctrinaire anachronisms with which existing grammars are so much cluttered. There is need, too, for a new, historical grammar of Scottish Gaelic to replace Calder's outdated work, tracing the development of Scottish Gaelic phonology, morphology and syntax from the parent Middle Irish, and comparing developments with those in the Manx sisterlanguage. Another tool much needed by Gaelic scholars is a comprehensive catalogue of Gaelic manuscripts. The Rev. John Mackechnie, until recently Reader in Celtic at Aberdeen University, has for some years been engaged in the compilation of such a work, and it is hoped that it will be published before long. In passing, one may remark that it seems surprising that Scotland's National Library has not seen fit to appoint a suitably qualified specialist to take care of its extensive holding of Gaelic manuscripts. It is hoped that a revised edition of Maclean's *Typographia Scoto-Gadelica* will emerge as a by-product of the work being done for the Historical Dictionary, and that the research being undertaken by Mr Donald John MacLeod at Glasgow University will lead to the publication of a Gaelic bibliography for the twentieth century.

Gaelic literary criticism still suffers from the Victorian vogue for biographical notes on the author and emotive superlatives for the work. It was Sorley Maclean, in a series of papers read to the Gaelic Society of Inverness, who first jolted Gaelic literary criticism out of this sterile rut, and although his example has been followed in more recent times by Derick Thomson, Iain Crichton Smith, Donald MacAulay and Donald John MacLeod, in occasional published articles and in public lectures, there is still need for a critical survey of Gaelic literature in all its periods. This is a project on which those scholars who have most to contribute in this field could work in collaboration. Also lacking is a forum in which contemporary writers of Gaelic can have their work seriously discussed. There might be a case for devoting half of each issue of *Scottish Gaelic Studies* to contemporary literary review, if there were no possibility of producing a separate journal of criticism.

Scholars, qua scholars, are dedicated to the pursuit of truth, and with Gaelic culture as with other matters they are primarily concerned with the objective examination of what was and is.

Gaelic preservationists, on the other hand, among whom many scholars may number themselves, are concerned also with what will be, being anxious to ensure for the Gaelic language and Gaelic culture some kind of existence in the future. The spearhead of the movement for the preservation of Gaelic is An Comunn Gaidhealach, the association founded in 1891 with the object of encouraging and promoting the teaching and use of the Gaelic language, the study and cultivation of Gaelic literature, history, music and art, the native industries of the Highlands of Scotland, and the wearing of Highland dress. The constitution also lays down that 'in pursuance and furtherance of these objects, the Association shall hold an annual Mòd, at which competitions and exhibitions in conformity with these objects shall take place and prizes shall be awarded. The Association shall be non-political and non-sectarian.'

An Comunn has been much criticised for its approach to the Gaelic problem. It has been accused of not taking a sufficiently realistic view of the political, social and economic forces undermining Gaelic society, and of relying too much on over-optimistic and emotionally charged affirmations of the language's immortality. It has been held that the devotion of so much of its organisational energy and finance to the one major event of the National Mòd has led to a disproportionate emphasis on Gaelic song, at the expense of the spoken and written word, that the competitive nature of the Mòd encourages mere trophy-hunting and little real desire on the part of many competitors either to acquire or use the language, that the whisky-swilling image, annually projected in the popular Press, has tended to antagonise the Presbyterian Churches, and to preclude support from many people who would otherwise be sympathetic to An Comunn's basic aims. An Comunn's concentration of its branches and activities in the Lowland areas, largely among exile Gaels, has, it is claimed, alienated the movement from the real Gaelic heartland, encouraging merely a dilettante interest in things Gaelic, while the emphasis on Highland dress has served only to strengthen the impression of consciously contrived ritual. That these criticisms are in a measure justified cannot be denied. Nevertheless, An Comunn can boast of solid achievement in some of the less spectacular, but not for that reason less important, of its activities. It did much to obtain for Gaelic such recognition as it now enjoys in the educational system, and its most important contribution of all has been in the field of Gaelic publishing, particularly in the provision of the basic textbooks used for Gaelic instruction in the schools. There are signs that An Comunn is at present engaged in reappraisal of its aims and methods, and is making a fresh effort to promote Gaelic in ways relevant to the modern age. Evidence of this may be seen in the production of Gaelic lessons on long-playing records, in the fortnightly bilingual newspaper it has been issuing since April 1967, and in its recent success in persuading the Lewis District Council to hold its meetings in Gaelic.

If Gaelic is to have any future as a living language in the modern world, one large problem that must be systematically tackled is the modernising of its vocabulary. Every language has areas of particular strength and weakness in its vocabulary, depending on the total cultural context in which the language is used. We thus find that Gaelic, having been the language of close-knit, geographically isolated, rural communities, given to close observation of human personality and behaviour, is very rich in words descriptive of particular physical types or different kinds of character. Similarly, the strong influence of the Presbyterian Church from the eighteenth century onwards has brought it about that the Gaelic terminology of conservative evangelical theology has been very well assimilated in the Protestant areas. On the other hand, the many advances in science and technology and the increasing complexities of government and administration which now impinge on the life of the Gaelic speaker confront him with many objects and concepts for which his own language is lexically inadequate, and for which Gaelic equivalents must be found if the total erosion of the language is to be prevented.

A certain amount of experiment with new Gaelic words has already taken place in Gaelic writing and Gaelic broadcasting. In particular, the quarterly *Gairm*, since its birth in 1952, has contained articles on a great variety of what might be called 'non-Gaelic' topics, such as atomic energy, the processing of rubber, Japanese art, child psychology, fashions, household gadgets and cosmetics. On radio, the Gaelic news bulletins have a strategic role in the dissemination of new vocabulary, for news is of necessity contemporary, and may embrace the whole range of human experience and activity. Since the introduction, in December 1964, of daily bulletins, carrying a cross-section of local, national and international news, translators have had to find equivalents for many terms alien to the native Gaelic cultural context, such as *strike, merger, nuclear deterrent, satellite, submarine, radio-active isotope* and *the Association of Supervisory Staffs, Executives and Technicians.* On such occasions, new Gaelic words were tried out purely on an *ad hoc* basis. There has not yet been any organised attempt to bring the whole vocabulary up to date, though the necessity for it has long been acknowledged. For instance, G. C. Hay, writing in *An Gaidheal* in 1941, suggested the procedure to be followed in modernising the vocabulary, and Nils Holmer, in an article published in *Alba* in 1948, discussed the problem of absorbing alien words into Gaelic.

A systematic assault on the problem would require a thorough stocktaking of the existing linguistic resources, and this is already being undertaken in the collection of material for the *Historical Dictionary.* This will lead to the clearer definition of these areas in which Gaelic vocabulary is deficient or non-existent, and will also suggest Gaelic words which could be given a semantic extension and redeployed in a new context. One word which has already been treated in this way is *tearbadh,* used in a Gaelic context for the separating of lambs from sheep, and now commonly used by Gaelic newsreaders for a division at the end of a Parliamentary debate. There are doubtless many other Gaelic words which could be subjected to transference of this kind.

There will remain many instances, however, where new words will be required, and opinions vary widely as to the way in which these should be arrived at. Some advocate a policy of Gaelic elements only, breaking up the word to be translated into its basic parts, finding the nearest Gaelic equivalents for these, and combining them to form the new word. This, for instance, is the method employed by J. M. Paterson in his published list of new terms *The Gaels Have a Word for It!* The trouble with this approach is that the word to be translated has often acquired its modern sense only after a long process of semantic development which has taken it a long way from the basic meaning of

O

its constituent elements, and to use Gaelic elements in a corresponding way is, in many cases, to impose on them a semantic
strain which they cannot bear. A more fruitful approach is to
translate the idea of the alien word into Gaelic terms, if this can
be done without too much clumsiness, as in the case of *bàt'-
aigeil* used for submarine, and *carbad-eiridinn* for ambulance. It
seems clear, however, that in many sectors the Gaelic vocabulary will have to be augmented by direct borrowing from
English, but that, by contrast with the many English words
indiscriminately borrowed at present, these should be subjected
to the kind of phonological adaptation which they might have
undergone had they been borrowed into Gaelic at an earlier
stage. An example of this is the treatment of the word satellite.
By lopping off the ending and introducing some internal sound
changes, the form *saideal* was arrived at, giving a word with a
thoroughly Gaelic flavour and yet sufficiently close to its English
prototype to be easily recognisable in context.

To tackle the problem properly, a body would have to be set
up to undertake research into the ways in which a similar
situation was being dealt with by other minority languages, to
study the different ways in which neologisms could be formed,
to receive advice from experts in different fields as to those areas
of vocabulary for which it was desirable to find Gaelic equivalents, and to decide in individual cases which procedure was to
be followed, whether the semantic extension or transference of
an already existing Gaelic word, the translation of the term
into Gaelic, or the borrowing of the term from the other
language, with or without some simulated phonological
adaptation. It would be desirable that such a body should work
in close association with the compilers of the *Historical Dictionary
of Scottish Gaelic*, and should from time to time issue authorised
lists of Gaelic terms for particular subjects, with the ultimate
aim of producing an up-to-date English–Gaelic dictionary.

With regard to Gaelic conservation strategy on a broader
front, it is perhaps worth considering whether the time has
come to concentrate all the effort on the Outer Isles, where a
third of the total number of Scotland's Gaelic speakers live, and
to accept the fact that in other areas the battle is already lost. If
the Government could be persuaded to make the islands into a
single administrative unit, with their own local authority, the

area could be envisaged as an experimental Gaelic reserve, having its own all-Gaelic V.H.F. radio transmitter, and an educational and administrative policy favourable to the language. Such a scheme would, of course, require the prior consent of a majority of the inhabitants of the Outer Isles. Should it turn out that here, in Scotland's last Gaelic stronghold, the people had no strong desire to perpetuate their language, then it would have to be accepted, albeit regretfully, that the days of Gaelic in Scotland were numbered. In which case we should be all the more appreciative of the labours of those who have striven to gather and preserve.

NOTE

[1] I am indebted to Dr J. L. Campbell, the Rev. Mark Dilworth, Mr John MacInnes, Dr Alan Bruford, Mr Ian Fraser and Mr Fred MacAulay for information kindly given.

Selected Bibliography

BORGSTRØM, C. H. 'The Dialect of Barra in the Outer Hebrides', in *Norsk Tidsskrift For Sprogvidenskap*, Bind VIII, 1937.
—— *The Dialects of the Outer Hebrides*. Oslo, 1940.
—— *The Dialects of Skye and Ross-shire*. Oslo, 1941.
CAMPBELL, J. L. *Orain Ghaidhlig le Seonaidh Caimbeul*. Dunfermline, 1936; 2nd ed., 1937.
—— *Sia Sgialachdan: Six Gaelic Stories from South Uist and Barra*. Edinburgh, 1939.
—— *Gaelic Folksongs from the Isle of Barra*. Published by the Linguaphone Institute for the Folklore Institute of Scotland, 1950.
—— *Tales from Barra*, told by the Coddy. Edinburgh, 1959. 2nd edn., 1961.
—— *Angus MacLellan: Stories from South Uist*. London, 1961.
—— *Angus MacLellan: The Furrow Behind Me*. London, 1962.
Census 1961, Scotland: Volume Seven: Gaelic. H.M. Stationery Office, 1966.
Census 1961, Scotland: Gaelic: Supplementary Leaflet. H.M. Stationery Office, 1966.
COMUNN GAIDHEALACH LEÓDHAIS. *Eilean Fraoich: Lewis Gaelic Songs and Melodies*. Stornoway, 1938.
CRAIG, K. C. *Orain Luaidh Màiri Nighean Alasdair*, Glasgow, 1949.
—— *Sgialachdan Dhunnchaidh*. Glasgow, N.D.
HAY, G. C. 'Foreign Words in Gaelic', in *An Gaidheal*, May 1941.
HOLMER, N. M. *Studies on Argyllshire Gaelic*. Uppsala, 1938.
—— 'New Words in Gaelic', in *Alba*, No. 1, 1948.
—— *The Gaelic of Arran*. Dublin, 1957.
—— *The Gaelic of Kintyre*. Dublin, 1962.
JACKSON, K. H. 'The Situation of the Scottish Gaelic Language, and the Work of the Linguistic Survey of Scotland', in *Lochlann*, Vol. I, 1958.
MACDONALD, F. J. 'Last Days of Gaelic', in *The Saltire Review*, Vol. 5, No. 14, Spring 1958.
MACDONALD, K. D. 'A New Gaelic Dictionary', in *The Scottish Educational Journal*, Vol. 49, No. 47, 15 November 1966.
MACLEAN, C. I. 'Gaidheil Eireann agus am Beul-aithris', in *Alba*, No. 1, 1948.
—— 'Aonghus agus Donnchadh', in *Gairm*, No. 10, Winter 1954.

The Gaelic Language

—— Obituary notices of, in *Scottish Studies*, Vol. 4, Pt. 2, 1906.

OFTEDAL, M. *The Gaelic of Leurbost, Isle of Lewis*. Oslo, 1956.

ORR, J. 'The School of Scottish Studies', in *Scottish Studies*, No. 1, 1957.

PATERSON, J. M. *The Gaels Have a Word for It!* Glasgow, 1964.

ROSS, J. 'Bilingualism and Folk Life,' in *Scottish Studies*, Vol. 6, Pt. 1, 1962.

SANDERSON, S. F. 'The Work of the School of Scottish Studies', in *Scottish Studies*, No. 1, 1957.

SCOTTISH COUNCIL FOR RESEARCH IN EDUCATION. *Gaelic-speaking Children in Highland Schools*. London, 1961.

SHAW, M. F. *Folksongs and Folklore of South Uist*. London, 1955.

WEINREICH, URIEL. *Languages in Contact*. New York, 1953.

WOOLLEY, J. S. *Bibliography for Scottish Linguistic Studies*. Edinburgh, 1954.

Literature and the Arts

Derick S. Thomson

Literature and the Arts

The position of literature and the arts in Gaelic Scotland is affected by the structure of Gaelic society and by the society's economic strength. Public attitudes are coloured by the religious and dogmatic principles which inform the society, or part of it. The minority status of the Gaelic language and culture has repercussions on the range and the nature of the work that is done in the various artistic media. Historical events and attitudes still exercise a profound influence on all these matters, and on the texture of life in general in the Gaelic area of Scotland, or more widely, in Scotland's Gaelic community.

Aspects of these topics have been discussed in the Introduction and in the preceding chapters, so that the reader already has in his mind many facts and opinions that will help to fill out the background to this chapter. He will know something of the historical causes of the Gaelic community's minority status, the size and distribution of that community, the economic status of the Gaelic area, the educational pattern in the recent past and at the present time. It will already be clear that this Gaelic society is one which lacks the normal structure on which literary activity and artistic organisation are based in modern communities, although it still retains, in a fragmentary form, the archaic structure on which various kinds of artistic achievement were built in earlier times. Thus the oral literary tradition still retains some vitality, although the half-hearted way in which the educational system has come to terms with the native culture often has the effect of depriving the people of the best of both worlds.

Literature and the arts need some form of patronage, however flexibly we may define 'patronage'. At one extreme, that of truly popular generation, patronage is perhaps too well-defined a word to describe the generating impulse. Here it might be truer simply to say that literature and the arts need a public or an audience: the popular audience is the patron in this case. But in any highly organised society the artist tends to be supported directly or indirectly. He is supported directly by commissions, sales, office. But sometimes his support is largely a moral and intangible one: he is set aside from the community, and given a status or prestige which derives from his occupation. He goes about earning his living in other ways, as a civil servant or a bank clerk, and produces art in response, partly at least, to this intangible stimulus.

We can distinguish at least three separate if interconnected sets of conditions under which the artist has worked in Gaelic Scotland. In the earliest times art was generated through patronage of an artistic *order* by a ruling *caste*. The system is more clearly demonstrable from Irish sources, but there can be no doubt that it was firmly established in Gaelic Scotland, and on closely similar lines. The fullest illustration is provided by the court of the lords of the Isles, the premier MacDonald family, who maintained court poets for centuries, and whose officers at the end of the fifteenth century included both poets (who were also probably historians and genealogists) and musicians. The main bardic family, that of the MacMhuirichs, is known to have existed for over five hundred years, and examples of its work range in date from the thirteenth to the eighteenth century, if we include the work of the founder of the family. When we catch a glimpse of these elaborate arrangements for the patronage of art, in the sixteenth century, there seem to have been two separate families of musicians, designated as harpers in particular: the Ó Senógs and the Clann an Bhreatnaich, still represented in Kintyre by MacShannons and Galbraiths. At an earlier period there were doubtless artists of a different kind, silversmiths and perhaps goldsmiths, wood-carvers and stone-carvers, and certainly artists of this kind, and also illuminators of manuscripts, were at one time employed in Iona, and at other religious centres, maintained directly by the Church, but indirectly by the patronage of native nobles.

Secondly, there is art generated in the basic stratum of society. This art is known to us in the main in the form of folksongs and folk-tales and a certain amount of music. Part of this corpus, of course, only came to rest in the basic stratum of society when the patronage of the nobles and chiefs dried up. This seems to be particularly true of certain classes of tales: the historical and heroic tales. Other tales, for instance those of the international popular type, presumably took their local form in this basic stratum of society, by whatever avenue they first entered Gaelic culture. Again, we can probably conclude that religious compositions such as Alexander Carmichael collected and published in *Carmina Gadelica*, came to rest in the basic stratum rather than took their origin there. Also, we have to imagine a great deal of historical interaction between this basic stratum and higher strata in more modern times, explaining, for instance, how the work of Iain Lom (a seventeenth-century poet closely related to the ruling family of Keppoch) or Mac Mhaighstir Alasdair (a learned eighteenth-century poet and a political agitator) became a part of the folk repertoire.

Thirdly, we have art generated in a metropolitan centre or by a metropolitan nexus. I use the phrase 'metropolitan nexus' to avoid any hard-and-fast connection with a particular metropolis. Thus we find in the eighteenth century a good deal of literary activity, much of it of a collecting or antiquarian nature, connected with a group of men who were graduates of St Andrews University, or in the twentieth century much literary activity on the part of people who were graduates of Aberdeen University, although neither of these groups worked in any particular metropolis or centre. I would regard Alasdair Mac Mhaighstir Alasdair and Uilleam Ros in the eighteenth century, and Caraid nan Gaidheal and William Livingstone in the nineteenth, as being part of this metropolitan nexus. In the nineteenth century and the early twentieth, we can more confidently point to an actual metropolis: Edinburgh at one time would qualify, but more particularly Glasgow or the Greater Glasgow area, when the inflow of Gaelic-speaking population from the Highlands reached sizeable proportions. At this stage metropolitan centres of Gaelic publishing became established.

The main question to be considered in this chapter is how the third situation described above works in the specific context of Gaelic Scotland, and how it might be made to work better. What is being attempted, in current political terminology, is to

Derick S. Thomson

work out a National Plan. This entails some description of the existing situation, and an outline of strategy for the future, especially the near future.

Although it is convenient to deal separately with literature and music, we must not lose sight of the fact that these, together with the graphic and related arts, are expressions of a national or regional ethos, and combine to reflect that ethos, often inter-acting inevitably, since they draw on the same pool of experience.

It is in the nineteenth and twentieth centuries that a dichotomy between 'folk' and 'metropolitan' literature begins to show in a marked form. This was no new phenomenon in Gaelic literature, since it must have existed, though in a different form, at the earlier period when the professional litterateurs (the bards, etc.) formed the metropolitan sector. In modern times, however, the dichotomy stems from the rise of printing and the spread of popular literacy. These twin movements, in the Gaelic context, date from the second half of the eighteenth century. The first Gaelic printed book had in fact appeared in 1567, and the Gaelic Schools movement belongs mainly to the first half of the nineteenth century, but the second half of the eighteenth century remains the truly seminal period. The appetite of the new literate class of Gaels fed on the printed books, and these were mainly religious and ecclesiastical prose on the one hand, and poetry on the other. From 1830 onwards a stream of Gaelic periodicals widened the range of prose writings. The school curriculum, both in the pre-1872 era of Gaelic schools and afterwards, was slanted towards the metropolitan rather than the folk literature, and this no doubt increased the prestige of this metropolitan literature. Nevertheless, interesting crosses between the two types of literature continued to appear, and still do appear: in the late nineteenth century, the poetry of Mairi Mhór nan Oran, who adapted the technique of popular 'village' poetry to the needs of the Land League campaign, or in the twentieth century, those poems of Angus Campbell, of Dell in Lewis, written as a war prisoner in Poland during the Second World War.

In the nineteenth century and the early part of the twentieth publishing facilities in Gaelic seem to have been fairly adequate. There have never at any time been Gaelic publishing houses which could be described as flourishing, for the total publishing programme in Gaelic has always been modest, as is shown by the following examples of decennial totals in the middle and later years of the nineteenth century: 1830–40, 106 titles; 1840–50, 164; 1850–60, 115; 1860–70, 142; 1870–80, 169; 1880–90, 98; 1890–1900, 111. The total for the period 1900–14 is probably under 100. These figures, however, show a significant increase over the figures for the eighteenth century, and clearly the setting up of Gaelic colonies in the Lowland towns and cities provided a marked stimulus to Gaelic publishing. We are probably justified in interpreting the situation in the following way: the Highland emigrés, nurtured in a wholly Gaelic culture, wanted to assert their own individuality in their new environment, and they took advantage of the new opportunities which an urban environment offered, organising societies, schools, and classes for 'improvement', and making use of the printing presses. Gaelic publishers such as Norman MacLeod of Edinburgh, Archibald Sinclair of Glasgow and Aeneas Mackay of Stirling came into prominence, and were followed later by Alexander MacLaren of Glasgow. Meantime a few publishing societies were formed also, notably the Gaelic Society of Inverness and An Comunn Gaidhealach (publishing being a more important part of An Comunn's function in its earlier years). The entry of An Comunn Gaidhealach into this field probably indicates, as early as the turn of the century, that subsidised publication was beginning to be a necessary expedient. This has become more and more the recognised solution of the Gaelic publisher's problem as the twentieth century has moved on.

The present position reflects not only rising costs of printing and publishing, and a decrease in the number of Gaelic speakers: it reflects also a decline in racial pride and solidarity on the part of the Gaelic population. This pride and solidarity are already gravely undermined by the time the Gael has completed his school education, and he is already equipped to settle unobtrusively into an English-speaking environment. He may, indeed, be already conditioned to accept the values of that environment, and to reject the values of his native community, although he may be prepared to make certain exceptions, as in the case of enjoying Gaelic songs, or piping, or poaching. The total number of Gaels who are still prepared to assert their cultural identity would seem to have seriously declined.

Yet at the same time it is fair to emphasise that a hard core remains of people who still do assert this cultural identity, and it is clear that this assertion is usually a function of conscious thought and study. It is not surprising that the more vocal elements are largely recruited from the professional sectors of the population. One never fails to find culturally conscious Gaels among university students, whereas there is at least a temptation now to regard the non-professional Gael who shows a deep and wide-ranging interest in his Gaelic identity as a nineteenth-century survival.

Gaelic literature in the last thirty years, and more specifically and seriously in the last fifteen, has been passing through a period of radical reappraisal. The process of reappraisal has produced a very large cleavage of opinion. We need not regret this; it was inevitable. The literature, almost until the last War, was tied as it were to the apron-strings of the oral tradition. To put it in this way is to be highly offensive to certain susceptibilities, but in the interests of clarity, and in the interests of truth (as seen from one angle at least) it is necessary to put it this way. Gaelic society, which has been developing a bilingual ambience for the last hundred years, began in the last generation to produce, logically and inevitably, a literature which straddles two worlds, the Gaelic one and the 'outside' one. The responses from readers form a continuous spectrum. At one end we see the indifference and incomprehension of that part of the public which is rooted in a purely local literary tradition (that of oral song and story and 'village' verse). In the middle of the spectrum we have the selective approval and rejection by that other part of the public which is more familiar with the written tradition of Gaelic literature but which is naturally conservative in outlook. At the other end of the scale is the small section of the reading public which lives almost entirely in the present, and is impatient (as only an extremist can be) of 'tradition' as such. This latter section can be labelled a coterie. There have been a few vocal critics also, speaking from entrenched positions, such as the 'purist' one which regards all linguistic and conceptual innovation as suspect, as a corruption of the native tradition, as though literature and language existed to serve the purposes of antiquarians. One might also distinguish a small and not very significant body of opinion, especially among city Gaels, which is chiefly interested in preserving nostalgic links with the homeland, which is more interested in romance and superstitions than in fresh creation, and which bases its opposition to change on these flimsy foundations.

The spectrum, investigated here only at isolated points, is continuous. In a psychological sense it is not difficult to understand the mental attitudes which produce it, and the problem raised is in the main a psychological one rather than a literary one. On the other hand, there is a limited sense in which one can respect certain of these attitudes. If we were ever to reach a situation in which the Gaelic language became so attenuated, in vocabulary and syntax, and the conceptual basis of Gaelic writing became so divorced from the Gaelic tradition, as to constitute a complete break with the past, one would then have to pose the question, 'Is this Gaelic, and Gaelic literature, at all?' To suggest that we are anywhere near this stage is to be irresponsibly alarmist. Yet I would not dismiss the attitude out of hand, but rather emphasise, to the writers in particular, that they need constantly to look to their roots, in native life and in the literary tradition, as well as outwards, and that they need also to avoid any tendency to attach themselves too exclusively to any one external literary tradition, notably that of English. Our argument is not the negative one that Gaelic literature and thought should not become equated with English literature and thought, but the positive one that it should retain its own identity, thus making its individual contribution to the total pool of experience. Yet it cannot be too strongly emphasised that this contribution should not be a trickle of stagnant water.

If we use the word 'literate' in a wide sense, to imply not only a familiarity with written works but also, or alternatively, a familiarity with the content of an oral literary tradition, we find that 'literacy' of this kind is widely diffused in the Gaelic area, and that its connotations vary according to the spectrum referred to earlier. The literate public can be seen to form two main sectors, while there is an intermediate sector, less clearly defined but not properly identifiable with either of the other two. The first of these may be called the 'local' sector. Within it we find a public well rooted in local traditions, familiar with a corpus of folk-song, folk-tale and folk anecdote, and still falling heir to a body of folk wisdom and communal knowledge.

Thus, a large number of people within this sector will know hundreds of Gaelic songs, ranging in date from the sixteenth to the twentieth century; a much smaller number will be familiar with folk-tales, many of them much older in origin than the songs; a large number will have some traditional knowledge of a handful of stories, some ancient and some modern; most people will have some familiarity with proverbial lore, lore about natural life and local genealogy. The size of this corpus of knowledge varies, of course, from one individual to another. Few will rival the repertoire of Nan Mackinnon of Vatersay, who recorded some five hundred songs and much proverbial and other lore in the 1950s; the species of traditional story-teller represented by the late Duncan MacDonald of Peighinn-nan-Aoirean in South Uist, or the late Angus Macmillan of Benbecula, both of whom told stories lasting for many hours, is now very rare. But repertoires which, while more modest than these are still very considerable, are common enough. The size and the content of the folk repertoire also vary regionally, with a strong tendency for the more isolated localities, and the Catholic communities, to produce larger and more varied repertoires, and to retain more ancient material, while in certain regions the literary repertoire may be restricted in some ways by the climate of dogmatic religion.

Again, in the local sector one finds a corpus of local literary tradition, as, for example, a good knowledge of the poetry of the eighteenth-century bard John MacCodrum in North Uist, or of the more recent bards Neil MacLeod and Mairi Mhór nan Oran in Skye. This interest merges with that in the work of contemporary local bards, such as Domhnall Ruadh Chorùna in North Uist, or 'Am Puilean' or 'Red' in Lewis. The tradition of what has been dubbed 'village poetry' remains strong throughout the Gaelic area. Some of the 'village bards' confine themselves to composing on purely local topics, often in a humorous or satirical style: making broad fun out of the topic of cattle-breeding by Artificial Insemination, or greeting the advent of margarine into the diet with ribald disrespect. Others of these bards are less confined or localised as to subject-matter. We should remember that a large part of the work of such eighteenth-century poets as John MacCodrum and Rob Donn belongs to this genre, and that its local origins do not debar it from universality. Such a poet may live and compose in the Islands, or in Wester Ross, or in Glasgow or Paisley or Greenock. His subject-matter and his style are not so much a function of geography as of social environment and education.

We may include in this sector also the writers of sketches, dialogues and monologues for dramatic presentation at public entertainments.

It is noteworthy that in the field of contemporary creation in this sector, prose does not appear at all.

The other main sector is that of the Modern Coterie, which usually communicates with its public via paper rather than by word of mouth. Before going on to summarise the activities of this group, we may look briefly at the intermediate sector, which shows some of the characteristics of the other two. The writers we are concerned with here draw directly on the traditional resources of language and literature, and their work is fairly directly related to the communities in which they live, whether these be in the Gaelic area or Gaelic colonies in the Lowlands, or indeed in London. But if we except the occasional use of radio, their communication with the public is by the printed page, not by oral channels. These writers can be recognised as the lineal heirs of the nineteenth and early twentieth-century poets and essayists, most of whom lived and published in one or other of the urban Gaelic colonies, but kept their lines of communication with the Gaelic homeland in good repair. In the period since the First World War such writers have been able, as it were, to address the reading public without first moving their domicile to the cities. I have in mind writers such as James Thomson (poet and essayist), John N. MacLeod (dramatist and essayist), Donald Lamont (essayist), Norman MacLeod (poet and prose-writer), the latter better known by his pseudonym Am Bàrd Bochd. Norman MacLeod, for example, draws on the rich vein of comic and racy expression which has for long leavened both verse and conversation in Gaelic. He has his serious moments too, but his main inspiration comes from a zestful and sardonic appraisal of the life around him. He is not, however, confined to this environment, as appears most notably in his hilarious verse and prose account of an imaginary Summit meeting between Harold Macmillan, President Kennedy, de Gaulle and Khruschev. Another recent example of work which belongs securely to the Gaelic tradition but ranges freely in subject-matter is the poetry of the late Donald Macintyre of Paisley. His collected poetry, close on 10,000 lines of it, is to be published this year.

Many of these writers use prose as well as verse, mainly for discursive writings on general topics. An interesting tradition of humorous prose writing may be said to have been established by a group of writers associated with Portree High School. Their high-priest, if he will forgive this appellation, is John Steele, and the genre was established, strangely enough, in an all-Gaelic school magazine, *An Cabairneach*. Writers in this genre later contributed to *Gairm*, the most prolific of these being Finlay J. MacDonald. Their style is extremely racy, and the overall effect, which is often hilarious, is produced by a combination of wit and humorous description of incongruous situations. These writers may be said to have close links with the native Gaelic tradition which produced, and produces, the humorous and witty verse of the village poets, but their medium is prose. Their work is also an interesting vindication of creative teaching in Gaelic, for almost without exception these writers took Gaelic as a Secondary School subject, and indeed the majority of them are university graduates.

In the third sector, that of the Modern Coterie, the great majority of the writers live in academic and professional circles, and the degree of formal education achieved clearly influences recruitment to this sector. To some extent these 'entry qualifications' have set the writers aside from their contemporaries, and the odd complaint has sometimes been lodged that these writers are too intellectual in their outlook. The dichotomy, however, is a real one, and there is often a failure to communicate between the writer and the public. Usually the writer is blamed, but in fairness one should inquire about the public to whom the writer addresses himself. Not every writer addresses himself to Everyman, nor does there seem to be any good reason why he should. The fault, however, is not all on one side, even in the matter of complaining, for the intellectual sometimes objects that the work of the pop-song writer makes no appeal to him.

The work of the Modern Coterie flowered first of all in poetry, predictably, since verse rather than prose has had a long ascendancy in the Gaelic literary tradition. The first faint beginnings can be seen in the work of First World War poets such as Murdo Murray and especially John Munro, both Lewismen and both graduates of Aberdeen University. The earliest major figure, however, was Somhairle MacGhill-Eathain (Sam Maclean), a Skyeman and graduate of Edinburgh. His main work belongs to the thirties and the earliest years of the forties. His first publication, a joint one with Robert Garioch, has symbolic significance. Here new work in both Gaelic and Lowland Scots appeared within the one collection, as if to symbolise Hugh MacDiarmid's thesis that Gaelic and Scots were but two facets of Scottishness, and the title chosen, *17 Poems for Sixpence*, may have been intended to suggest that this was literary fare within the reach (financially) of the proletariat. There is no evidence that the poetry was as well designed, for these ends, as the price, but in a literary context the poetry was significant. The Gaelic part included four numbered poems from the sequence *Dàin do Eimhir*, to be published in 1943, and an extract from Maclean's long poem 'An Cuilthionn', most of which is still unpublished. Maclean's first full-scale collection, and his only one to date, appeared in 1943. This was entitled *Dàin do Eimhir agus Dàin Eile*; it was published by William Maclellan in that publisher's most significant decade, and it was illustrated strikingly by William Crosbie. It was clear that the renaissance, or revolution, in Gaelic poetry had come. Already by this time non-traditional poetry by other writers was appearing in the periodical *An Gaidheal*. The next ten years saw the consolidation of the new poetry, with published collections by George Campbell Hay and others, and with the founding of the Gaelic quarterly *Gairm*, which was sympathetic to new work, and was indeed founded largely to make the publication of such work possible. From 1952 to the present time there has been a constant stream of new verse published in *Gairm*, and a steady recruitment of young poets. The publication of collections has lagged behind this development, but it seems likely that this delay is temporary.

What is the nature of the new poetry? It is clear that it has veered away from the tradition of the preceding period. In some ways it has veered away from the whole tradition of Gaelic poetry, in that it is more personal, more introspective, less inhibited in terms of personal emotion. Personal and introspective elements occur, of course, in earlier Gaelic poetry, as in the work of William Ross, Dugald Buchanan and the folk poets of the seventeenth and eighteenth centuries, but perhaps in less sophisticated forms. The main difference may be traced to the poet's relationship with society. The new poet is no longer a member of a close-knit Gaelic social group, but seems to stand apart, sometimes indeed on the fringes of Gaelic society, sometimes in overt rebellion, as against the Calvinistic assumptions of part of the society, certainly living in a bilingual world, and in constant touch with the non-Gaelic world. From the point of view of the innovator or the experimenter this may be a good vantage point, and if poetry is steadily becoming a cosmopolitan art, as seems probable, it may be a realistic stance. In the purely Gaelic context it makes for difficulties of communication.

If we agree, however, that poetry must be relevant to the age in which it is written, it is difficult to see how the values of a bilingual society, or the trends of thought of an international world in which communications have been enormously accelerated, can fail to influence Gaelic poetry in our time. The writer who opts out of such a social contract must at least make sure that he does so for adequate reasons. He is at liberty to cultivate his own garden, but not to prescribe his blooms for the general market. I do not wish to give the impression that only the New Poets show an involvement with the outside world, but it is true to say that their involvement is both on a wider front and more consistent. This has resulted in much innovation, both in technique and in subject-matter.

To look first at technique, there would seem to be two quite distinct reactions to the problem of escaping from the tyranny of a poetic tradition. The first of these is iconoclastic, and may result in a rejection of the good in the tradition along with the bad. The other is more cautious and considered, and perhaps more difficult. Yet anyone who wants to say something new, and to elicit a fresh response, must be careful about how he uses familiar techniques. Metrical patterns and poetic rhythms can have a mesmeric effect both on poet and on reader. They are capable of pulling the poet's thought off its original course. This is true to an extraordinary degree of Gaelic verse, in which vowel music has played a large part, particularly since the seventeenth century. The poet, if he is to express his own thoughts, must be constantly on his guard against succumbing to former patterns, lest these should lead him to use other people's words, and hence other people's thoughts. Gaelic poetry, like any other, is full of instances where writers have succumbed to this temptation, whether on a small scale as in clichés, or on a larger as in the long successions of closely similar poems on the Highland clans, or on the homeland, or on the effects of whisky on behaviour. So, when John Munro wrote about the First World War, the necessity of using his own words seems to have led him to use also untraditional forms of metre and rhythm, as in 'Ar Gaisgich a thuit sna Blàir'. Munro in 1917 did not want to write about Blàr na h-Eiphit, or Culloden or Inverkeithing, and it must have seemed to him that the war he was describing demanded new metrical forms as surely as it used new weapons and called forth new psychological reactions. Similarly, in the Second World War George Campbell Hay, writing of the burning town of Bizerta, did not use that metre in which a seventeenth-century poet celebrates the 'firing' of 'little Glasgow'. When we read Hay's 'Bisearta' we are brought face to face with a twentieth-century catastrophe, with minds uncluttered by irrelevancies, for the poet is allowing himself to ponder over and recreate that particular experience, which the reader in his turn recreates, without blurring its outlines with half-remembered thoughts of other battles, other poems.

Similarly, when Donald MacAulay writes of Bernera, Lewis and his reactions to the people, the life, the traditions of this place, when he wants to say that they are in a sense improvident about the future of their identity, he does not use the metre or style of 'Am faigh a' Ghàidhlig bàs?' ('Will Gaelic die?'), with its confident brash assumption that rhetoric is sufficient to save the Gaelic language. Instead he uses a tentative, hesitant rhythm, broken by doubts, a rhythm which is dictated by his thought rather than one to which his thought must bend:

> Tha thu a' fasgnadh an aghaidh na gaoithe
> sìol brìgh á calg is nasg,
> bhon thuig thu nach b'aithne dhaibhsan
> o'n d'fhuair thu fuath

do͡ghràdh;
tha thu a' deasachadh siol-cura
a chionn gun dh'aithnich thu an eu-comas,
gun chuir iad a sìol uile gu muileinn.
(You are winnowing, in the face of the wind,
seed that will germinate, separating it from the husks,
since you have understood that they did not recognise—
those who showed hatred to you—
your love;
you are preparing seed for sowing
because you saw that they could not,
having sent all their seed to the mill.)

The poet, plying his ancient craft, is preparing something new to add to the poetic storehouse, instead of living on his capital—sending all the seed to the mill for grinding. The imagery of the poem comes out of the traditional background, but its literary application is new, and so is the metrical form which carries it.

It is clear that this is not the only way in which poetry which is modern in thought and in idiom can be written. The metre of 'Bisearta' is not George Campbell Hay's most characteristic metre. His poem 'Atman', for instance, in which he contrasts the situations and the characters of an Algerian petty thief and the judge who tries him, is written in a traditional metre. Here metre and rhythm are used to assimilate new subject-matter to the Gaelic poetic tradition. This tends to be the method of Iain Crichton Smith also, in his Gaelic verse.

It is often the method used by Somhairle MacGhillEathain in *Dàin do Eimhir*. Maclean's metres are for the most part traditional, but much of his subject-matter is not. His political attitudes are new to Gaelic poetry, and the social conscience which colours so much of his published work had not appeared before allied to such considerable poetic power. When to these elements we add Maclean's wide literary interests and sympathies, and his appreciation of the unity of artistic endeavour, we can see that there was bound to be a formidable novelty in his verse. He was able, in the main, to bend the vocabulary and the metrical norms of the Gaelic poetic tradition to these new purposes. He knew this tradition intimately, and he brought to it also fresh resources of colloquial expression. In his work the traditional metrical patterns are transcended, and this is achieved by the novelty of much of his subject-matter, by the freshness of his thought, including his power of poetic imagery, and by his abandonment of the traditional Gaelic sequence of thought within a poem, that is, the artistic development of the poem. In all these respects he was no doubt influenced by the poetry of other literatures, particularly that of English.

Similar influences can be seen in the work of all the non-traditional poets now writing in Gaelic, and this has helped to produce an interesting variety of styles and techniques. *Vers libre*, sometimes with very subtle rhythms, is common enough, and in the work of Donald MacAulay in particular there is often a highly ingenious pattern formed by imposing many layers of meaning. Yet in all this verse links with the Gaelic poetic tradition are strongly preserved, and can be clearly seen by anyone familiar with the tradition—unless indeed the observer's eyes are blinded by some stylistic or ideological prejudice.

Yet it is also true to say that this new poetry demands, for its adequate appreciation, some awareness of the modern English poetic tradition. This is a natural enough parallel to the bilingual situation which exists on the linguistic plane in Gaelic Scotland. I do not regret this infusion of fresh blood, but rather welcome it, and foresee the time, in the near future, when the new influence will be thoroughly assimilated in the Gaelic poetic tradition, as Latin and Norman–French influences were at earlier periods.

Although the poets were clearly the leaders in the revival of Gaelic writing which has taken place in the last thirty years, the work of the Modern Coterie is not confined to poetry, and this is a sign of literary health. The Gaelic situation in this respect is considerably more healthy than that of Scots. The Scots renaissance of writing was led by the poets and largely confined to poetry; it has long passed its zenith, and seems in danger now of fading completely. In Gaelic, on the other hand, a small but steady stream of prose continues to appear, and this prose is marked by innovation and experiment as the new poetry is. The short story in particular has developed in range and depth. Two of the most original and prolific short-story writers are Colin Mackenzie and Iain Crichton Smith. Smith is perhaps the more prolific of the two, but Mackenzie in his stories of mystery and his space-fiction shows that he has a lively imagination and a well-controlled skill in plot construction. Smith has published two collections of short stories: *Bùrn is Aran* (also including some poetry) in 1960 and *An Dubh is an Gorm* in 1963, and he has published regularly in *Gairm* and occasionally in *An Gaidheal*. Smith's themes are psychological ones, and much of his writing is basically introspective. The work of Kierkegaard has a marked influence on him. There is a good deal of symbolism in the stories, and frequently one can see close connections between his prose and his poetry: poetic themes are sometimes worked out in prose. His work has considerable imaginative subtlety. It is occasionally flawed by mannerisms and a forced use of imagery, and up to 1960 in particular his work was, and no doubt had to be, experimental. We can see him, for example, experimenting with the balance of narrative and dialogue in his stories, sometimes tipping the balance too far one way or the other.

Some critics object that Smith is too exclusively concerned with the close examination of psychological states, and they would welcome a more extroverted element in his work. This would be a more valid criticism of a *corpus* of short stories than of an individual writer, and no doubt we need a greater variety of writers, and more publication in depth of writers' work. There has been some publication of translations of short stories, for example, from Italian, Irish and Welsh, but it would be salutary to have a greater volume of translation, not so much from English as from Russian, French and other foreign literatures. Smith has demonstrated something that might have seemed obvious but was not: that the background of a Gaelic story need not be Highland, and that a Gaelic writer can comment freely on such burning contemporary issues as nuclear disarmament and the emergent African races. For a Gaelic writer to do this is unexpected, but no worse than that; there are, however, strong literary taboos which are still in force. Sexual topics are subject to these taboos, and so are religious and clerical topics. I recall, for instance, that Finlay J. MacDonald's short story *Air Beulaibh an t-Sluaigh* drew sharp protests from the self-righteous in 1958. But there seems no acute danger of Gaelic ever having a pornography problem (apart from that raised by the writings of earlier poets such as Mac Mhaighstir Alasdair), and more risks could safely be taken.

Gaelic literature throughout its history has been sadly lacking in dramatic work. In the context of a legalistic and self-righteous Calvinism, which was one of Gaeldom's least happy imports, this would not be surprising, but the Gaels are not all Calvinists, and there was a pre-Calvinist era. More serious, perhaps, was the lack of towns and connurbations in Gaelic Scotland. Such Gaelic drama as there is had its beginnings, significantly, in Glasgow, and the annual Gaelic Drama Festival is held there, although it now attracts entries from teams in the Highlands, notably from Islay, Oban, Skye and Lewis. Iain Smith has in recent years written plays for this Festival, but the most significant entries have been those written and produced by Finlay MacLeod, and presented by a team of Island students from Aberdeen University. MacLeod has a fine sense of dramatic timing, a thorough understanding of his medium, and a lively wit. Some of his plays combine an infectious surface gaiety with an underlying seriousness or with mordant satire. He is much more than a gad-fly, but it should be said in passing that his function as a gad-fly is an important one, especially in a society which tends towards ingrowing and self-righteousness. It is to be hoped that he will stay outside the Establishment as long as possible.

All of MacLeod's plays have been broadcast; sometimes the radio versions have come first, sometimes the stage versions. The Gaelic Department of the B.B.C., and Mr Fred MacAulay in particular, is to be congratulated on a most enlightened piece of patronage.

Gaelic prose is used for a wide variety of other purposes. As in the case of the short story, the main impetus for this range of use comes from the B.B.C. and the periodical *Gairm.* Both these media have encouraged writers to deal with a wide range of topics: literary criticism, agricultural matters, crofting law, foreign travel, industrial processes, current affairs generally, women's fashions, careers and hobbies, and so on. At times this range has imposed some strain on writers, who may have to excogitate or manufacture suitable terminology for subjects which are novel in Gaelic. This activity is clearly a salutary one, forcing writers to use language creatively, and to exploit their resources more fully. In the end this must result in a tensing and pointing of these linguistic resources, and an increased flexibility, and this in turn will give the imaginative writer a more flexible and complex linguistic instrument for his own uses. The role of journalism, then, is an important one, in the present situation of Gaelic, and a wider variety of journalistic media would be warmly welcomed. A great impetus would be given to general writing in Gaelic if one or more of the Scottish newspapers introduced regular Gaelic features, provided by competent journalists.

The number of persons able to speak Gaelic in Scotland is in the region of 80,000. Accepting various degrees of literacy, we might say that there is a potential reading public of over 60,000 for Gaelic books. This is small, not so small as in the Faroes, which support much publishing, but still small. Yet there are two ways of looking at the problem of the production and consumption of Gaelic literature in this situation. One view would be that the figures should obey the crude economic logic of supply and demand. This would lead one to say that this small community cannot afford to support the publication of specialised reviews, or of novels or of collections of poetry, that penalties must be paid for smallness. One could argue, perhaps oversubtly, that since the pressure of the majority culture 'squeezes' the minority one, making it less viable than even its numerical basis suggests, the majority culture owes the minority one a bonus, a subsidy, in much the same way as the State pays compensation to a farmer for appropriating some of his land for road or housing or military development. But these latter conventional economic sums are easier to work out—the community accepts this straightforward way of thinking. In cultural matters it prefers a laissez-faire policy, and will wax philosophical over the 'natural' fate of minorities, and the inevitability of 'progress', although 'progress' is a word that has become a cliché, a shibboleth, a dirty word almost to those whose values are not those of the mass-society, or of the majority culture.

What of the kind of progress which enables a people to work out the more complicated sort of sums, to introduce intellectual and spiritual items into the balance-sheet, and even to give them equal weight with financial and economic items?

The societies, Utopian and actual, which are founded to some extent on ideals, attempted to do this, and of course we can find many instances in the society of this country. This should be another instance. How is it to be done?

A Literary Programme for the next Ten Years

A desirable literary programme for the next ten years will have to be couched in rather general terms, indicating the media for publication and the types of publication which are desirable, at least in the writer's view, and which seem possible, making a realistic but not a pessimistic assessment of the writing potential available and of the reading public which exists or may exist. The assumption is made that the age group 15–25 will be rather more literate in Gaelic than has been the case in recent generations, as a result of the educational policies pursued in Inverness-shire and Ross-shire over the last decade. It is clear that unless this extended teaching in Gaelic leads into the provision of suitable post-school reading material, the increase in Gaelic literacy will evaporate.

There is a certain oddity about setting out to design a ten-year programme for Gaelic literature, and the designer must be prepared to be proved wrong in his forecasts. Nevertheless, the exercise can be a very useful one if it sets a target and provokes discussion of detailed recommendations.

The programme can conveniently be broken into sections: School textbooks, Reading for Adolescents, Periodicals (including children's periodicals), Adult Fiction, Poetry, General Literature.

SCHOOL TEXT-BOOKS. Gaelic textbooks for schools have been provided, in the main, not by commercial publishers, who find the market too small, but by societies or publishing bodies, the main one in this century being An Comunn Gaidhealach. For a long time the main range of Gaelic textbooks (*Leabhraichean Leughaidh, Bàrdachd Ghàidhlig, Rosg Gàidhlig*, etc.) was published by An Comunn. In recent years they have added a series of illustrated readers for very young children, but have made few other contributions in this field. Several books have been provided by Gairm Publications and by the Departments of Celtic at Aberdeen and Glasgow Universities (*Crìochan Ura, Làithean*

Geala, Bùrn is Aran, Rosg nan Eilean, etc.); these are mainly intended for use in the Secondary School. There is a clear need for a wider range of textbooks, but the existing agencies mentioned should be able to provide these if they accept the challenge implicit in the present situation. The Local Authorities have been ready to co-operate in buying and using all textbooks produced, and publishing of this kind can be undertaken without financial loss. Some subsidy for this type of publication is desirable, however, if fees or royalties are to be paid to authors, and if a good range of books is to be produced.

In increasing the range of these textbooks we should move away from the idea that Gaelic textbooks are needed only for the teaching of Gaelic language and literature. We should also provide textbooks for History and Geography, Introduction to English, Nature Study, Gaelic Songs, Modern Studies for example. There is a great need to rethink the methods of presenting Gaelic as a specific subject in schools, and this calls for the design of a complete new range of books: graded readers, work-books, books of a 'First Aid in Gaelic' type, spelling books, anthologies of prose and poetry, abridged texts of Gaelic authors and so on. Some of these need advance research, which might well be the concern of University Departments of Education or more especially of the appropriate Departments in the Colleges of Education. It would be useful if the Scottish Education Department were to make arrangements for the secondment of suitably qualified and experienced teachers either to the Colleges of Education or to the Universities, to carry out the research necessary for the development of such textbooks. Such a concrete expression of interest would be far more valuable than the somewhat meaningless expressions of goodwill which appear from time to time in the Department's official publications.

READING FOR ADOLESCENTS. There is at present practically no provision in this sector. *Gairm* for some years has featured a short section intended for teenagers: this includes careers and hobbies articles and articles on fashions and cosmetics. The *Stornoway Gazette* has published abridged translations of adventure classics such as *Treasure Island* and *Kidnapped*. There is a large field here for development. Some further translations of adventure stories could be undertaken, and it would be valuable to have a native Gaelic series of such stories, directed at the age range 10–20, the books at the lower end of the range being more generously illustrated. In addition, books on hobbies, introductions to careers, publications like the English *Finding Out* or *Knowledge*, and song books might be published. There is no existing publishing body which has a clear claim in this field, and an opportunity exists for creating an entirely new body. It seems likely that publications of this sort would attract some subsidy from the Secretary of State for Scotland, who has recently declared his support of the principle of some public subsidy for general Gaelic literature.

PERIODICALS. The provision of an adequate range of periodicals is basic to the encouragement of new writing. At present there is only one all-Gaelic periodical: the quarterly *Gairm*, founded in 1952. Various Church magazines include short Gaelic supplements. *An Gaidheal*, until March 1967 the official publication of An Comunn Gaidhealach, was a bilingual monthly. It had the wrong format and formula for a literary periodical, was inadequate in size and scope, and tended to fall between two stools: publishing in Gaelic and English, aiming at native speakers and at learners of Gaelic, and trying to be both a general publication and a 'house' magazine. An obvious development would have been to erect *An Gaidheal* into a full-scale literary and general periodical, doubling its size and increasing its circulation and advertising revenue, and if necessary appointing a full-time Editor to run it: this would have been a more constructive way to use the subsidy of some £600 which An Comunn applied annually to *An Gaidheal*. Meantime, An Comunn is attempting a different type of solution, by publishing a fortnightly bilingual newspaper, *Sruth*. Fortnightly publication should make it possible to develop a strong current affairs section, designed not on a local or parochial scale, but offering comment on national and international affairs, in Gaelic. Full-time staff is now more necessary than before. I am far from being convinced that a bilingual newspaper can for long remain both solvent and of vital benefit to the Gaelic community, but it is as yet too early to judge.

Gairm is in the process of developing a stronger current affairs interest, but its emphasis remains literary, and as it is a quarterly there are advantages in retaining that bias. *Gairm* from time to time has had to be subsidised by extra-mural enterprises, but has managed to remain solvent, mainly by keeping circulation and advertising revenue buoyant. Its circulation is a world-wide one, with university and public libraries strongly represented, but with a steady sale in the Gaelic area.

Another periodical, perhaps a quarterly, might well be run by the Highlands and Islands Development Board and the Crofters Commission. The emphasis here might be on practical topics: industry, crafts, land use, tourism. This should be designed as a bilingual publication, on a strict 50–50 basis, and it could command a reasonable amount of advertising (tourism, crafts, agricultural, small industry, government). The Crofters Commission has made fairly regular use of Gaelic in recent years, and the absence of any Gaelic affiliations in the Board to date must surely be put down to administrative blundering rather than to conscious policy.

Recently, the suggestion was mooted within the B.B.C. of producing an occasional *Listener*-type publication entirely in Gaelic, in which selected talks and features could be published. This might well be a quarterly publication. The B.B.C. in Scotland has shown much goodwill towards Gaelic, and we can perhaps hope that this idea will come to fruition when the present financial stringency eases.

There should be a further attempt to found a children's periodical, to succeed the short-lived *Sradag*, published several years ago by An Comunn Gaidhealach. This should be at least a monthly, if not a weekly, well illustrated and professionally produced, with no doctrinaire nonsense about including Gaelic lessons for learners. An Comunn seems the obvious body to undertake this, perhaps in close liaison with a revitalized Comunn na h-Oigridh (Gaelic Youth Movement). Possibly the one person could have editorial oversight of both this and *Sruth*, although such a dual function could only be justified in terms of financial expediency. It is surely not too much to hope that An Comunn, now showing a new vigour in its top echelon, will put its house in order in the matter of publications.

ADULT FICTION. The current production of fiction in Gaelic is too small to build up an appreciative and discriminating reading public. There can be little doubt that more encouragement from publishers, and the provision of attractive prizes and royalties, would bring more books on to the market. But subsidy would be required here more than in other categories. The subsidy must not be used, however, as a pair of crutches. It is necessary also to organise a regular reading and buying public, and this can best be done by establishing a Book Club which can offer a guaranteed sale for any book accepted. The Book Club could be a co-operative of publishers, possibly with an independent Reading Panel. It could also commission works independently, especially translations of foreign works of fiction, and work of this kind might attract some subsidy from UNESCO. As to native Gaelic work, collections of short stories would be more readily available than novels, but strenuous efforts should be made to interest Gaelic writers in submitting novels for publication. The Book Club would not be confined to works of fiction, since it would be wasteful and unrealistic to attempt to establish several specialised types of Book Club.

POETRY. The possibilities for verse publication are considerable, due to the bias towards verse in the tradition. In addition to the anthologies and abridged editions which should be made available for schools, there is ample room for anthologies of songs, collections of local and regional verse, as, for example, Lewis or Uist or Islay verse, and collections of the work of well-known contemporary bards such as Angus Campbell, Ness or Dòmhnall Ruadh Chamustianabhaig, Skye. There could also be a series of collections of verse by the writers of the 'metropolitan' school who have been publishing in the periodicals. The Scottish Arts Council is already giving a grant to *Gairm* for this latter purpose. The publishers who are already in this field, such as *Gairm*, Alexander MacLaren and the *Stornoway Gazette*, might be expected to continue this work, but there is room for several more to make a contribution.

GENERAL LITERATURE. The field of general literature is the largest of all, and the one in which there is the greatest potential for development. From the point of view of encouraging the public to read more Gaelic, this may well be the crucial sector. There might be a ready market for war stories, sailors' accounts, autobiographies, biographies, works of piety or religious doctrine, discussions on crofting and fishing, travel books. There is, for instance, wide scope for biographical writing, some possible subjects being the lives of famous religious leaders in the

Highlands, historical characters and persons who have played some interesting part in Highland life in modern times, as, for example, Lord Leverhulme or Tom Johnston or Compton Mackenzie. Biographies in Gaelic might well be written of people whose reputation is international, such as Nehru, Churchill, Stalin, De Valera or Billy Graham. It is worth emphasising—again because Gaelic writing tends to look inwards—that the writer's topics are not confined by any geographical border, and there should be more written in Gaelic about international politics, German music, the Faroese fishing industry, Italian art or Tibetan folk customs, to name only a few topics. To return home again, there could well be anthologies of Gaelic folk-tales, translations of Irish folk-tales and sagas, collections of historical and other anecdotes, collections of proverbs and so on. In this sector the only limits that could be imposed are those of finance and man-power. They are both severe enough limits, but neither is so close as we often imagine.

A programme as ambitious as this calls for much organisation and for the development of incentives. The greatest incentive is probably guaranteed publication of a work which reaches an agreed standard, but there should also be some financial reward from fees or royalties, and in some instances it would be useful to offer prizes for literary work. The provision of prizes is perhaps the least troublesome of these requirements. Publishers should make some effort to make reasonable prizes available for selected classes of work, e.g. fiction or biography. We might reasonably expect An Comunn Gaidhealach to offer more substantial prizes for a more interesting range of literary work. The National Mòd Literary Competitions have a low status, and have had this low status for a good many years, largely because they are so static and unadventurous, and the prizes offered are so paltry. A glance at the Irish situation underlines the truth of this assertion. There prizes of £2,000, £1,000 and £500 have been offered in literary competitions. Arrangements have been discussed recently for granting prizes or bursaries to one or two Gaelic writers, through the good offices of the Scottish Arts Council. But An Comunn and the other Gaelic publishers should not rest content with this, but rather widen the field by making their own separate arrangements also.

The question of guaranteed publication and the provision of fees and royalties depends largely on setting up a strong and efficient organisation for both publishing and distributing Gaelic books. In view of the rather limited public, there is a strong case for some public subsidy, and indeed this case has already been conceded by the present Secretary of State for Scotland. The Welsh parallel is instructive. In recent years approximately £30,000 of public funds has been spent annually on providing and buying books in Welsh. A large part of this sum is channelled through the Local Education Authorities, and a smaller part takes the form of direct subsidy to the University of Wales Press Board. In addition, the Public Library service gives a guaranteed market for Welsh books. The net result of these arrangements has been a marked upsurge in the number of Welsh books published and sold, the figures for books published being at least ten times the Gaelic ones in the last decade, while the figures for books sold show a still larger multiple. It might plausibly be argued that the case for public subsidy of Gaelic publication is an even stronger one, since the potential book-buying public is a smaller and less viable one.

It was suggested to the Secretary of State for Scotland that an annual sum of £10,000 should be set aside, for an experimental period of five years. This money should be used to provide grants in aid of publication, to set up a modest distributing agency, to provide secretarial assistance where required and to pay honoraria to authors. The appointment of full-time Editors in the more active publishing concerns would have the effect of stimulating the production of books markedly.

The administrative arrangements for such a scheme present some problems. It is first of all crucial to its success that the active co-operation of the maximum number of Gaelic publishers should be ensured. It therefore seems desirable that policy should be formed by a small body representative of Gaelic literary interests, with one or more assessors appointed by the Secretary of State. This body, which should have its own premises and secretariat, should draw up a list of desirable literary projects, bringing these to the attention of potential authors and publishers; make grants to specific publications; help to subsidise the appointment of persons of editorial status, who could expand the production of a publishing body; keep a register of books in print, and act as a clearing-house for information; handle publicity and advertising for publishers; set up a system of distribution of books.

Whatever this body does should not have the effect of stifling enterprise. With a reasonable degree of goodwill among existing publishers such a body could work for the general good of all, and these arrangements might well have the wholly desirable effect of encouraging new publishing bodies to enter the Gaelic field. This field is in desperate need of new man-power, fresh ideas and business drive. If these can be conjured up by the expenditure of a very modest amount of public funds and the co-operation of a few men of goodwill, results quite out of proportion to that outlay can be anticipated.

Some loose similarities can be seen between the literary and the musical situation in Gaelic Scotland. In music also there are both 'folk' and 'metropolitan' traditions, the latter represented, let us say, in different ways by the work of Marjory Kennedy Fraser and the music associated with the National Mòd. There are many examples of an uneasy crossing between two traditions: the tradition of the sub-literate folk composer and that of the composer who publishes his music. This usually results in an unsophisticated end-product, neither good folk music nor good sophisticated music. A different class is formed by the choral settings for folk-songs which are produced for Mòd competitions. These settings have often been made by musicians preoccupied with other musical traditions, and frequently they cannot be said to have added much of artistic value to the Gaelic musical tradition. There are, however, choral settings, notably some of the puirt-a-beul ones, which have added a new dimension to Gaelic music. Just as the renaissance of Gaelic writing in this century was founded on a deep and developed literacy, so any worthwhile revival of Gaelic musical composition must be founded on a deep and developed musical literacy, and this presupposes a great deal more scholarly work on the Gaelic musical tradition than has been done as yet. There certainly exist the beginnings of that scholarly work, notably in the publications of Frances Tolmie (*Journal of the Folk-Song Society*, No. 11 [1911]) and Margaret Fay Shaw (*Folksongs and Folklore of South Uist* [1955]) and more recently Francis Collinson (*The Traditional and National Music of Scotland* [1966]), but this work has not yet leavened the general musical consciousness.

A marked revival of interest in Gaelic, especially Hebridean, music was brought about as a result of Marjory Kennedy Fraser's publications and concert tours in the earlier part of this century. Marjory Kennedy Fraser understood well what she was about, and her Introductions are positive contributions to an understanding of the music she became so absorbed in. She was not content with this sober analysis, and went on to alter the rhythm and tempo and shape of many of the songs, and to provide ornate settings, in the romantic style of her period, or of the preceding one. Similarities can be seen between her musical style and the general style of the Celtic Twilight school, whether in literature or in painting. It was perhaps the last blow of 'Ossian' Macpherson's trumpet, though 'trumpet' is too robust a word. Yet she achieves a dramatic intensity in some of her settings, and they are worth savouring for their own sake. The mistake lay in assuming that this was an inevitable treatment of the folk-songs, and some acquaintance with the work of Greig or Bartók, Ravel or Kodály, and other composers who have used folk material, might quickly have dispelled this false notion.

A counter-campaign was needed to get Gaelic music back into perspective. The indigenous tradition of Gaelic folk-song needed to be investigated rigorously, its style defined and savoured, and the many points at which Mrs Kennedy Fraser's treatment was at variance with this pin-pointed. This counter-campaign has been in progress since the 1930s, and wide acceptance has been won for its views. Francis Collinson's balanced statement in his recent *The Traditional and National Music of Scotland* may sum up the modern critical attitude to Mrs Kennedy Fraser's work: 'With all praise due to Mrs Kennedy Fraser for her great work in collecting and popularizing the songs of the Hebrides the world over, this [referring to the turning of a lament into a bridal song] is only too typical of the legacy of confusion which she and her collaborator Kenneth MacLeod left to traditional Hebridean song, a confusion which will probably never be properly cleared up.' In some ways, however, the counter-campaign has gone too far. For we are concerned not only with scholarly investigation of the nature of Gaelic folk-song but also with the question of a growing, developing tradition of singing and songs. The questions are different. Mrs Kennedy Fraser neglected one (but not entirely), her detractors neglect the other. We should not shut our eyes to the possibility of Gaelic song developing in a tradition *other than* a 'folk' one. We should welcome a new professionalism, provided that it is prepared to think its way into new standards of performance of Gaelic song, and not rest content with an imposed set of values which belong to another tradition. To say this is not to take the arrogant and ignorant view that the singer of Gaelic songs has nothing to learn from other singing traditions but rather that he should be well-founded in his own tradition and assimilate to it what is of value and what can bear assimilation. Such professionalism would of course involve some stylisation, and if it is an interesting stylisation there is no reason why it should not be accepted gratefully.

There is a strong tendency to blur the outlines of different traditions within the corpus of native Gaelic song music. The newspaper critic, for instance, who reviews a Gaelic concert at the Edinburgh International Festival will tend to think of all he hears as 'folk-song', being insufficiently aware of the existence of an old type of art-song within the native Gaelic tradition. These art-songs are bundled into the same class as work-songs, dance-music, nineteenth-century songs with derivative metres and melodies, modern ditties whose melodies are dredged from half-remembered phrases of Irish and Lowland song, and translations of the pop-songs of the thirties and forties. But many of the *òrain mhóra* (elegies and praise-songs of the seventeenth and eighteenth centuries) were probably set to melodies which were originally conceived as art-songs, when music was still being composed for the clàrsach. These songs can stand instrumental arrangement and concert performance, and this may imply a 'high gloss' being put on them, a fairly rigid stylisation of performance. There is no reason to suppose that such songs require an 'intimate' or 'rustic' setting for their performance, or a piece of jolly introduction by a compère. Indeed, it is an impertinence to treat them in this way, as it would be an impertinence to introduce *lieder* with a joke about Schubert. The direction of the singer's stylisation is not of course necessarily that of German *lieder* or operatic *aria*, but neither is it reasonable to assume that the concert style should be equated with the folk style, which develops in a different set of circumstances.

It is beyond doubt that there are a number of Gaelic songs which deserve international recognition as art-songs, and should form part of the repertoire of singers in the international music world. It should also be recognised that the two classes of folk-song and art-song are not mutually exclusive in the context of public performance, although the techniques of folk-song are, of course, to be studied academically only in their native setting.

There are other classes of songs which could make an effective transition from the folk tradition to that of the public stage. The effectiveness of waulking-songs sung under concert conditions is a hit-or-miss affair. These songs are virtually dead *as labour-songs*, that is to say in the milieu in which they developed, but enjoy an extended lease of life as entertainment, on a private or public scale. I see no reason why the waulking-song sequence, with stylised setting and props and dramatisation, should not be accepted as a piece of concert spectacle. The rhythms are mesmeric and some of the melodies are lovely. This type of sequence is already being presented at concerts and in television programmes, but it needs further shaping and development, in addition to judicious selection of the sequence and rigorous production. Again, stylisation should be accepted here, so long as it is understood that such a concert or programme item is presented for its intrinsic interest of music, rhythm and spectacle, and not as a museum piece whose details must be carefully checked for authenticity. If the latter, then let us have the cloth steeped in urine, and let the audience hold their noses.

To study the authentic folk tradition in music, in the study, and to present the art-songs of the past in stylised form, is still not enough. There is no natural law which lays down that there shall be no fresh creation in Gaelic music. I should like to see many modern settings for Gaelic songs, and the composition of melodies and settings for Gaelic poetry which is not composed, as was usual in the past, with a particular air in mind. We can hardly assume, for instance, that Gaelic melody *requires* to be set to words arranged in particular metrical sequences, or to put the matter differently, that Gaelic melodies cannot be

made for Gaelic verse which does not rhyme, or which is
irregular in its line length, or which is composed in metres not
previously used in Gaelic. To assert this is to deny the composer
musical inventiveness or imagination. It should still be possible
to compose music which can be seen to belong to the Gaelic
tradition but is not stultified by it. And there is a considerable
field also for the composer who will use themes from Gaelic
music to build into some larger composition with a flavour as
national and international as the music of Carl Nielsen or
Bartók. On a less ambitious scale, perhaps, there is room for
experiment and creation in the genre of folk opera. The pool
of sophisticated musical ability in Gaelic Scotland is small. This
is underlined by the notorious difficulty of finding native Gaelic
musicians who might adjudicate at the National Mòd. A frank
assessment of this type of musical poverty, and a more wide-
ranging discussion of the place of music in Gaelic Scotland, may
make it easier for fresh musical talent to break to the surface,
for there is now a tendency for the professional to keep his
distance, leaving the amateur to pontificate. The Scottish Arts
Council might consider it a part of its obligation to search out
and to encourage musical talent of the type we have been
considering.

Another important facet of this subject is programme design
and production. In general this tends to be desperately old-
fashioned, and the need here again is for artistic professionalism. We have to move away from the old formulae which have
produced the hotch-potch concert programme, with an assortment of singers and instrumentalists, selecting an assortment of
songs and pieces, which are then juggled with until they form
some arbitrary pattern. The recital needs to be developed as
one alternative, and the 'show', with a greater use of costume,
sets, spectacle, with an over-all design, as another. One should
anticipate new developments of this kind taking place only on a
small scale at first, and not appealing to the mass audience,
although there is some evidence that the mass audience itself
is tired of the old formulae. Again, the Scottish Arts Council
might be able to show a lead here.

Some steps have already been taken in this direction with
television programmes of Gaelic music. Since there is at present
only one regular, or rather periodic, T.V. programme of this

kind, the scope for experimentation is reduced. The programme is inevitably beamed towards a large and somewhat 'pop' audience. A second programme, for an audience which can survive without constant rhythmic 'kicks', is needed.

Glasgow in particular has provided a considerable circuit for Gaelic singers, with its seven-month season of Annual Gatherings (of clan and territorial associations), concerts and céilidhs. A great deal of organisation and resource goes into keeping this circuit going, and the whole machinery compares more than favourably with that devised for Scots musical activities. The organisers of these events, however, tend to cater for their 'mass' audience, so that an insufficient range of musical events is provided. It may be partly as a result of this that the general Scottish musical public regards Gaelic music with a fastidious condescension, while there is some evidence that professional musicians actively resent any tendency to take it seriously. On the other hand, it should be clearly recognised that Gaelic music has a large following in the non-Gaelic areas of Scotland. I would suspect that it is a somewhat more sophisticated following than the organisers of public entertainments are prepared to concede.

The Mòds (National and Provincial) affect the tradition of Gaelic singing in other ways. The National Mòd has indeed produced a marked stylisation of Gaelic singing, but unfortunately not one which is exciting in a creative sense. It is rather a stylisation designed for competitive purposes. This imposed solution has done much harm to Gaelic singing, robbing it of its flexibility, in which a great part of its interest lay, and sometimes substituting crude competition, of a personal or regional kind, for artistic exploration. Too often, at least in terms of audience reaction, personalities dominate the Mòd musical competitions, instead of musical experience. This is, of course, a danger inherent in competition, but there could with profit be a greater degree of depersonalisation in the proceedings, and more emphasis on creativity. The redesigning of classes, and the introduction of new classes might help towards these ends, and a larger part of the Mòd's programme might consist of concerts and recitals by invited artists, thus reducing the competitive bias of the festival. One fears, however, that this suggestion will not commend itself to the Mòd organisers, since it carries with it the risk of reduced audiences, at least in the early stages of the experiment.

The influence of the National Mòd reaches out all over the Highlands, and so does that of the Glasgow 'circuit'. Though we should freely admit that the Mòd, like Mrs Kennedy Fraser, has done good in spreading an interest in Gaelic song, we should look critically at it, and try to improve it. The schools are often drawn into the Mòd network. They have too seldom used the local material to form a foundation of Gaelic musical appreciation, although there are of course exceptions to this charge. It would be unrealistic to expect the schools to set more rigorous standards, or to alert people to the dangers of the current situation, when there is so little appreciation of our musical malaise, in the field of public performance or in that of fresh creation, anywhere in the society.

In this connection it is of the greatest importance to raise the standard of musical criticism, establishing regular and rigorous criticism of concert, radio and television programmes, and of records. At present such criticism is almost totally lacking, and what passes for criticism is usually either crude propaganda (for example, pro-coterie or anti-Mòd propaganda) or a recital of names of singers and songs, accompanied by some jejune personal comment. The native Gaelic publications should try to give a lead here, but it would be valuable if newspapers such as *The Scotsman* and *The Glasgow Herald* could persuade some serious music critics to look into this aspect of Scottish musical life. Serious pipe music deserves the same service.

The topic of pipe music is one which I can refer to only in the most general terms. This music has experienced a remarkable spread of popularity, not only in Lowland Scotland but also in many other parts of the world. The reasons for this popularity are not all musical ones, but it is important to appreciate that this branch of Highland music has crossed so many racial and linguistic borders, yet has made little impression on orthodox musical citadels in Scotland. The scale and tonality of pipe music remain obstinately foreign to those within closest earshot of it. Perhaps, after all, the explanation is a simple if unflattering one, connected with earlier, emotional reactions to the sound of the Highland war-pipe. Yet it seems true to say that *ceòl mór*, the classical music of the pipes, constitutes Scotland's major individual contribution to musical experience. Fortunately it has a fair-sized band of dedicated enthusiasts and exponents within Scotland. There is no lack of organised competitions, and *ceòl mór* has its regular radio programme. Occasionally one hears a short pibroch played at a Gaelic concert. Glasgow has an active College of Piping, and holds summer schools in different parts of Scotland, as well as providing teachers abroad. Two recent Scottish composers, Ian Whyte and Erik Chisholm, were influenced by *ceòl mór*, and Francis Collinson, a convert to this musical cult, composed a pibroch *c.* 1960. A competition in new pibroch composition, promoted by the Broadcasting Council for Scotland in 1964, attracted sixty-six entries, forty-three of these from Scotland. In 1966 the B.B.C. published eleven of these for private distribution. But again, orthodox musical circles in Scotland remain aloof and incurious.

Such attitudes remind us of the strange exclusion of Gaelic and pipe and clàrsach music from the researches of Music Departments in the Scottish universities. Edinburgh has made some amends with its School of Scottish Studies, and the first fruits of its musical studies appear in Francis Collinson's book referred to above, two-thirds of which is concerned with Gaelic music. It is time that the Music Departments in the universities took such studies seriously, both at undergraduate and at post-graduate level.

There are still many people in Scotland, and elsewhere throughout the world, who are not resigned to the thought that the Gaelic tradition now surviving is only 'the end of an auld sang'. The developments of the last twenty years have shown that there is still a great deal of life in this tradition. This life should be guarded, and nurtured, and fostered, for the common weal.

Selected Bibliography

An Cabairneach. Gaelic School Magazine produced occasionally by Portree High School

An Gaidheal. Gaelic and English monthly; the official Magazine of An Comunn Gaidhealach (65, West Regent Street, Glasgow, C.2). Ceased publication in March 1967.

CAMPBELL, ANGUS, For poems written in Poland, see *Gairm*, Vol. XI. Gairm Publications: Glasgow, 1963.

CAMPBELL, JOHN LORNE. *Gaelic in Scottish Education and Life*, 2nd edn. revised and extended. W. and A. K. Johnston Ltd.: Edinburgh, 1950.

Caraid nan Gaidheal. A Choice Selection of Gaelic Writings by Norman MacLeod, D.D. John Grant: Edinburgh, 1910.

CARMICHAEL, ALEXANDER. *Carmina Gadelica*, Vols. 1–5. Oliver and Boyd: Edinburgh, 1928–54.

COLLINSON, FRANCIS. *The Traditional and National Music of Scotland.* Routledge: London, 1966.

Gairm. Gaelic Quarterly. Gairm Publications, 227, Bath Street, Glasgow, C.2.

HAY, GEORGE CAMPBELL. *Fuaran Sléibh.* William Maclellan: Glasgow, 1947.
—— *O na Ceithir Airdean.* Oliver and Boyd: Edinburgh, 1952.

IAIN LOM. See Annie M. Mackenzie, *Orain Iain Luim, Songs of John MacDonald, Bard of Keppoch.* Scottish Gaelic Texts Society: Edinburgh, 1964.

KENNEDY FRASER, MARJORY, and MACLEOD, K., *Songs of the Hebrides.* London, 1909–21.

LAMONT, DONALD. See Thomas M. Murchison, *Prose Writings of Donald Lamont* (1874–1958). Scottish Gaelic Texts Society: Edinburgh, 1960.

LIVINGSTONE, WILLIAM. *Duain agus Orain*, Glasgow, 1882.

MACASKILL, ALEX. *Rosg nan Eilean.* University of Glasgow: Glasgow, 1966.

MACAULAY, DONALD. *Seòbhrach ás a' Chlaich.* Gairm Publications: Glasgow, 1967.
—— 'On Some Aspects of the Appreciation of Modern Gaelic Poetry', in *Scottish Gaelic Studies*, Vol. XI, Pt. 1. University of Aberdeen: Aberdeen, 1966.

MACCODRUM, JOHN. See William Matheson, *The Songs of John Mac-Codrum.* Scottish Gaelic Texts Society: Edinburgh, 1938.

MACDONALD, DUNCAN, of Peighinn-nan-Aoirean. See *Fear na h-Eabaid,* a Folk Tale by Duncan MacDonald. Private Publication. University of Glasgow, 1953.

MACDONALD, FINLAY J. 'Air Beulaibh an t-Sluaigh', in *Gairm*, Vol. 6, 1958.

MACDONALD, JOHN A. *Crìochan Ura.* Gairm Publications: Glasgow, 1958.

MACINNES, JOHN. 'Gaelic Songs of Mary MacLeod', in *Scottish Gaelic Studies*, Vol. XI, Pt. 1. University of Aberdeen: Aberdeen, 1966.

MACLEAN, SAM. *17 Poems for Sixpence*, 2nd edn. Edinburgh, 1940.
—— *Dàin do Eimhir agus Dàin Eile.* William Maclellan: Glasgow, 1943.

MACLEOD, FINLAY. For an account of a tour by his group of players, see *Gairm*, Vol. 15, 1966.

MACLEOD, JOHN N. *Litrichean Alasdair Mhóir. Stornoway Gazette*: Stornoway, 1932.

MACLEOD, MURDO. *Làithean Geala.* University of Aberdeen: Aberdeen, 1962.

MACLEOD, NEIL. *Clàrsach an Doire*, 3rd edn. Edinburgh, 1902.

MACLEOD, NORMAN (AM BÀRD BOCHD). See *Gairm*, Vol. 10, 1961, for prose and verse account of Summit meeting.

MAC MHAIGHSTIR ALASDAIR. See A. and A. Macdonald, *Poems of Alexander MacDonald.* Inverness, 1924.

MAIRI MHÓR NAN ÒRAN, i.e. MARY MACPHERSON. *Dàin agus Orain Ghàidhlig.* Inverness, 1891.

MORRISON, RODERICK. *Daibhidh Balfour*, translated and abridged from R. L. Stevenson, *Kidnapped*. *Stornoway Gazette*: Stornoway, n.d.

MUNRO, JOHN. See J. Thomson, *An Dìleab*, and an article on Munro by Murdo Murray in *Gairm*, Vol. 5, 1957.

New Pibrochs. B.B.C.: Edinburgh, 1966.

Report on the Welsh Language To-day. H.M.S.O., 1963.

ROB DONN. See Hew Morrison, *Orain le Rob Donn*. Edinburgh, 1899.

SHAW, MARGARET FAY. *Folksongs and Folklore of South Uist*. Routledge: London, 1955.

SMITH, IAIN C. *A' Chùirt*. An Comunn Gaidhealach: Glasgow, 1966.
—— *An Coileach*. An Comunn Gaidhealach: Glasgow, 1966.
—— *An Dubh is an Gorm*. University of Aberdeen: Aberdeen, 1963.
—— Article on Kierkegaard, in *Gairm*, Vol. 11, 1962.
—— *Bùrn is Aran*. Gairm Publications: Glasgow, 1960.
—— *Bìobuill is Sanasan-reice*. Gairm Publications: Glasgow, 1965.

Sradag. Children's comic; eight issues published by An Comunn Gaidhealach. Glasgow, 1960–62.

Sruth. Fortnightly bilingual newspaper, published by An Comunn Gaidhealach. Inverness, 1967– .

THOMSON, DERICK S. *An Dealbh Briste*. Serif Books: Edinburgh, 1951.
—— *Eadar Samhradh is Foghar*. Gairm Publications: Glasgow, 1967.
—— 'Gaelic Poets of the Eighteenth Century', in *An Gaidheal*, 1958–61.
—— 'The MacMhuirich Bardic Family', in *Trans. Gaelic Society of Inverness*, Vol. 43. Inverness, 1966.

THOMSON, JAMES. *An Dìleab*. Stirling, 1932.
—— *Fasgnadh*. Stirling, 1953.

TOLMIE, FRANCES. *Journal of the Folk-Song Society*, No. 11, 1911.

UILLEAM ROS. See Calder, George, *Gaelic Songs by William Ross*. Oliver and Boyd: Edinburgh, 1937.

WATSON, W. J. *Bàrdachd Ghàidhlig*, 3rd edn., An Comunn Gaidhealach: Stirling, 1959.
—— *Rosg Gàidhlig*, 2nd edn., An Comunn Gaidhealach: Glasgow, 1929.

WHYTE, IAN. For a series of modern settings by Ian Whyte of Gaelic songs, see *Gairm*, Vols. 1–7.

Highland Administration

Magnus Magnusson

Highland Administration

'Fundamentally, the Highland problem is to encourage people to live in the Highlands by making it possible to secure there, in return for reasonable efforts, proper standards of life and the means of paying for them.'

(*A Programme of Highland Development*, 1950)

'The Government's Highland policy is in general terms to promote economic growth in the Highlands, and to provide suitable amenities and social services so that viable communities with modern standards of living and opportunities for useful employment may be established and retained there. This policy involves the improvement of basic services and amenities such as roads, houses, electricity and water supplies. It requires, too, the progressive development of the principal Highland industries of agriculture, forestry and fisheries, of manufacturing industries that may be found suitable for Highland conditions, and of other economic resources such as the tourist industry . . .'

(*Review of Highland Policy*, 1959)

'The Highlands and Islands are very different from any other region of the U.K. Much earlier work on them takes this difference as a reason for treating the region as something *sui generis*, justifying its own set of standards and insulation from criteria applied elsewhere in Britain. This tendency has been fed both by Highland feeling itself and hardly less by outside sentiment which would preserve a distinctive Highland way of life. Undeniable benefits have been won as a result of special treatment. But it is arguable that in the long run the Highlands have lost more than they have gained.'

(*The Scottish Economy, 1965–70, A Plan for Expansion*)

Thus, in three succinct postwar declarations, Government policy for the Highlands was outlined, reviewed and finally judged. That it has failed is all too obvious. In the decade after

243

the 1950 White Paper, new investment totalled more than £220,000,000 (which, with other government expenditure, generated more than half the income of the region); yet despite this massive injection of capital, the population of the Highland area fell more than twice as fast as it had done in the previous twenty years—by 10,300, a drop of 3·6 per cent compared with a significant increase of 1·1 per cent for Scotland as a whole—and is still falling sharply (there has been a further fall of nearly 4,000 since 1961).

The population decrease is even more serious than these figures suggest, for the figures were shored up by increases in Caithness (4,700) and Inverness (1,700); without these, the population decrease between 1951 and 1961 would have been 7·2 per cent. In addition, the average unemployment rate in the Highlands and Islands runs at a rate of 7 to 8 per cent, double that of Scotland as a whole, and four times the rate for the United Kingdom as a whole. In the light of all this, it is considerably more than merely 'arguable that in the long run the Highlands have lost more than they have gained'.

Yet the failure could hardly be said to have been due to government neglect, or to Treasury meanness: indeed, the Highland area, with only some 5 per cent of the population of Scotland, has consistently received about 10 per cent of the provision for Scotland as a whole. Fundamental to the whole problem of the Highlands is the administrative machinery available to implement policies of development. It has been obvious for many years that what the Highlands needed above all, much more than isolated gestures of indulgent charity, was coherent and co-ordinated administrative machinery that could put into effect a systematic programme of development. As the Highlands and Islands Advisory Panel pointed out in its celebrated resignation ultimatum in December 1963: 'No policy of development in the Highlands, local or general, could have a prospect of success without the *grouping* of financial incentives or advantages for existing or prospective industries.'

It is, let it be said at once, an extraordinarily difficult and diverse area to administer; even its boundaries and internal divisions defy the logic of geography and geology. The seven so-called 'Crofting Counties' that make up the Highland area (Argyll, Caithness, Inverness-shire, Orkney, Ross and Cromarty, Sutherland and Zetland) have only one thing in common—that they lie to the north and west; and it doesn't include adjacent upland areas which are patently 'Highland', like the Grampians, and Bute.

As it is constituted at present, the Highland Area comprises 9,020,474 acres, roughly 47 per cent of the area of Scotland and more than a fifth of the total area of Great Britain. It includes more than a hundred inhabited islands, and stretches for more than 400 miles from the north of Shetland to the Mull of Kintyre. Its declining population of 276,043 is more or less confined to the coasts, the islands and the eastern straths; the average density of population is 20 people per square mile, compared with a density of 554 for the United Kingdom as a whole, and 863 for England. Less than two-fifths of the population (104,961) live in burghs, only one of which, Inverness, is classed as a 'large burgh'; another one-fifth live on crofts, and the remaining two-fifths are widely scattered throughout the countryside. Most of the region is mountainous, barren and uninhabitable; distances are vast; villages and townships are in the main isolated; and communications are still (as the Taylor Report commented bluntly in 1954) 'poor and terribly costly'.

Within this disparate area, the counties themselves show huge differences. The largest in every sense is Inverness-shire, with a population of 81,689, a land area of 2,695,094 acres, and a rateable valuation of £1,483,496. Against this, Sutherland has a population of only 13,240, Orkney has a land area of only 268,527 acres (including 18,962 acres of foreshore and 9,089 acres of water), and Zetland has a rateable valuation of only £123,870 (see Figures 1, 2, 3). All the counties have a larger landward than urban population except Caithness, where the coming of the Atomic Energy Authority establishment at Dounreay has swollen the population of Thurso from 3,200 to 9,000; the greatest disparity between landward and urban populations is in Sutherland, where the only burgh, Dornoch, contributes a mere 959 to the county population of 13,240.

Considering the vast areas involved, the imbalanced scatter of the population, and the diversity of local problems and needs, the difficulty of creating an efficient and fair administrative machine is obvious. However, no one would seriously claim that the administrative machine for the Highlands has actually been *created* at all—it would be more realistic to say that it has merely *happened* over the years in a proliferation of sometimes despairing expedients designed to deal with immediate or marginal aspects of a huge problem that has defied effective solution for more than two centuries. Responsibility for administering the Highlands is now vested in a bewildering array of local, regional and national agencies. Farquhar Macintosh, a Skye headmaster, recently counted forty-seven different bodies among whom responsibility was dispersed (*Glasgow Herald*, 2 March, 1965), and the Highland Panel referred to 'more than thirty'. The 1950 and 1959 White Papers, and the Labour Party's *Programme for the Highlands and Islands* in 1953, listed many of the agencies then involved: the Scottish Office with its four main departments, the Treasury, the Board of Trade, the Ministry of Labour, the National Assistance Board, the Ministry of Transport and Civil Aviation, the Ministry of Supply, the Ministry of Fuel and Power, the North of Scotland Hydro-Electric Board, the Herring Industry Board, the White Fish Authority, the Forestry Commission, the Crofters Commission, the Scottish Tourist Board, the Scottish Council (Development and Industry), the Scottish Agricultural Organisation Society, the Scottish Country Industries Development Trust, the Highland Fund, the Scottish Council of Social Service, the Scottish Board for Industry, the Highlands and Islands Advisory Panel, the Scottish Land Court—the list was apparently endless; and at the tail of the list—'finally, the Highland local authorities are responsible for most of the local services and amenities and can also exercise an important influence on economic development' (1959 White Paper).

There have been certain changes and developments since these lists were compiled and published. Other agencies have come (or gone), like the Red Deer Commission or the short-lived Highland Transport Board, whose responsibilities were taken over in January 1967 by the Highlands and Islands Development Board after a three-year existence. The setting up of the Board itself in 1965, replacing and dramatically extending the scope and responsibilities of the old Highland Panel, is the most important single development in Highland administration this century; and in the foreseeable future the Royal Commission on Local Government in Scotland, which is taking evidence at present, could well change the whole structure of local authority administration in the Highland area.

But there is still a great plethora of agencies responsible for various aspects of Highland administration, usually with relatively specialised functions, often working in a vacuum without proper relationships with other agencies, or without the authority to implement courses of action effectively.

Apart from the United Kingdom ministries, some of which maintain branch offices in the Highlands, these agencies come under the authority of the Secretary of State for Scotland, who is responsible for a wide range of functions which in England are divided among a number of departmental ministries. One might expect from this a greater unity of purpose and execution where the Highlands are concerned; but in reality the administrative structure in St Andrews House merely reflects the anomalous and dispersive nature of Highland administration as a whole.

All the four main departments of the Scottish Office have functions that impinge on the Highlands. The *Scottish Education Department*, naturally, deals with education policy there. The *Scottish Home and Health Department* deals generally with law and order, and with the health and welfare services. The *Scottish Development Department* is concerned with physical development, including things like town and country planning, new towns, housing, roads, water and sewerage, coast protection, flood prevention, river and air pollution and electricity policy. It is also responsible for general policy in regard to local government, including its financial aspects (such as valuation and rating); and it also deals with the allocation of government grants to local authorities, which make up about half the revenue of Highland local authorities. So, clearly, the Scottish Development Department has large and vitally important responsibilities towards the Highlands; but although it is responsible for electricity policy (i.e. the North of Scotland Hydro-Electric Board), it is *not* responsible for the atomic energy policy represented at Dounreay—that comes under the United Kingdom Atomic Energy Authority. And though the S.D.D. is responsible for physical development in the Highlands, as in the rest of Scotland, Highland development as such (in the shape of the new Highland Development Board) *doesn't* come under its aegis. Nor does the most vital ingredient in economic development—industry; that is the general responsibility of the Board of Trade, which has an Office for Scotland in Glasgow.

General supervision and co-ordination of Highland affairs used to be the responsibility of the former Scottish Home Department; but when the St Andrews House departmental set-up was extensively reorganised in 1961, the Highlands came under the wing of the *Department of Agriculture and Fisheries for Scotland*, whose secretary is Sir Matthew Campbell (he was, incidentally, the first secretary of the Highland Panel when it was established in 1947).

'Ag and Fish', as it is familiarly called, naturally has general responsibility for agriculture and fishing in the Highlands and Islands, and also has functions relating to harbours, and to steamer services to the Islands. But surprisingly, it *doesn't* have control over the other main natural resource in the Highlands—forestry; the Forestry Commission is a separate United Kingdom department, responsible directly to the Minister of Agriculture in England and Wales, and in Scotland to the Secretary of State for Scotland. So in this crucial area of land-use policy, administrative responsibility and policy-making is divided, not unified.

The divisions are further reflected in the political structure of the Scottish Office. The Secretary of State for Scotland, William Ross (M.P. for Kilmarnock) is assisted at Ministerial level by a Minister of State and three Joint Under-Secretaries of State. Each has particular areas of responsibility—and a curious hotch-potch they are in some cases, with Highland affairs shared between them all.

The Minister of State, Dr Dickson Mabon (M.P. for Greenock), deals with general aspects of regional development, including Highland affairs and forestry.

One Under-Secretary, Lord Hughes from Dundee, deals with electricity policy and tourism.

Another, Bruce Millan (M.P. for Glasgow Craigton), looks after education, but has no other direct Highland responsibilities except health and welfare.

And the third, Orcadian-born Norman Buchan (M.P. for West Renfrewshire), deals with agriculture, fisheries and crofting.

Thus, the three most important aspects of land use in the Highlands—forestry, agriculture and recreation—are divided among three Ministers, instead of being unified in one central department.

Within the Department of Agriculture and Fisheries itself, Highland affairs are handled, generally speaking, by three divisions, each headed by an Assistant Secretary, under the direct supervision of an Under-Secretary—Ralph Law; Law succeeded Sir Matthew Campbell as secretary to the Highland Panel, and is now the top civil servant, under Sir Matthew, dealing with Highland affairs. The three divisions in the department cover the work of the Highland Development Board (William Russell), agriculture and crofting (Tom Lister) and Highland transport (Angus Mitchell).

Such, in bald outline, is the way that responsibility for Highland affairs is divided at governmental level. There are provisions, of course, for more or less formal interrelationships between departments to prevent excessive compartmentalisation —the rather shadowy 'Highland Committee'. But despite the calibre and ability of the civil servants at the Scottish Office (which should not be under-rated), the structure is such that no really coherent planning or co-ordinated development has ever been possible; administration of the Highlands has perforce been piecemeal and haphazard, dependent on far too many unrelated agencies to be able to achieve effective results. Thus, a new £40,000 harbourage for the island of Stroma was not built until *after* the protesting population had sunk below the minimum level of viability. Different departments and agencies compete for land for different uses. One agency subsidises the building of fishing boats, another subsidises the catching of fish —but no one is currently responsible for where to land it, or how to market it effectively. Another agency will spend thousands of pounds encouraging industrial development, but communications and transport charges, which would militate against industrial enterprise, are the responsibility of someone else. Tourism is frequently cited as a cure for many Highland ills—but there is no attempt to co-ordinate efforts to build it up.

More and more, these things will have to become central responsibilities, if the planning is to be on a broad enough front. But what effect will this have on the existing local authorities?

Already the power of the central government has increased greatly, usually at the expense of the local authorities. The remit of the Royal Commission under Lord Wheatley is 'to consider the structure of local government in Scotland in relation to its existing functions, and to make recommendations for authorities and boundaries, and for functions and their division, having regard to the size and character of areas in which these can be most effectively exercised, and the need to sustain a viable system of local democracy'.

It seems certain that there will be far-reaching changes, eventually. But to what extent is there 'a viable system of local democracy' at present? How good are the local authorities in the Highlands? And how do *they* see the problems of administering the Highlands?

Local government structure in the Highlands, as in the rest of Scotland, was established by the Local Government (Scotland) Act of 1929, which had two principal aims: to simplify local government by reducing the number of different kinds of authority, and to replace authorities exercising single functions by multi-purpose authorities covering a defined area and elected by the people of that area. It consists of county councils, town councils and district councils.

There is only one 'large burgh' in the Highland area, namely Inverness with its population of 30,716; in large burghs, the town council is responsible for most functions except education, valuation for rating and, in some cases, police, which are administered by the county council. In the 'small burghs' (broadly speaking, burghs with a population of under 20,000), the town council has fewer powers, mainly connected with housing, water, sewerage, lighting and cleansing, whereas the more significant functions are exercised by the county councils on the principle that the county council should undertake those functions which require greater resources or are more efficiently discharged over a wide area.

In the 'landward areas' (the parts of the counties that are left when burghs are excluded), the county council is responsible for all the main work of local government; and the county council can delegate certain limited functions to District Councils, which also carry out some minor statutory duties in their own right. County councils are directly elected as regards the landward area, but the burghs within the county nominate members of their town councils to serve on the county council. All the Highland county councils are non-political; but some of the burghs, like Campbeltown, for instance, are elected on party lines, so one does sometimes find 'politicians' sitting on county councils. The Highland local authorities are not usually regarded as nurseries for politicians, as the Lowland councils are apt to be; only two instances come to mind of Highland M.P.s who were previously local authority councillors—Alasdair Mackenzie (Liberal M.P. for Ross and Cromarty), and Major Sir Basil Niven Spence (who was M.P. for Orkney and Shetland from 1935 to 1950).

Town councils are the rating authorities in the burghs; county councils are rating authorities only in the landward areas, and requisition on the town councils to meet the cost of services which they discharge in the burghs. District councils requisition on the county councils for their expenditure, but their budgets are ludicrously small; for example, the 1966/67 budget for the 7-member Northern District Council of Caithness, comprising the districts of Canisbay (population 846) and Dunnet (population 681) was a mere £320!

There are 65 *District Councils* in the Highland area: Ross and Cromarty and Zetland have 12 each, Argyll, Inverness-shire and Orkney have 10 each, Sutherland has 6 and Caithness has 5. It is difficult to generalise about their powers and functions, for these are apt to depend on the discretion of individual County Councils and the initiative of individual District Councils. But in the main, District Councils are primarily concerned with administering churchyards and cemeteries, local scavenging and lighting and sewerage, and footpaths; they usually have some functions relating to open spaces and amenities like village halls, and are asked to administer local welfare schemes such as domestic help arrangements, or recommending tenants for county council houses, or drawing up priority lists for minor and township roads in the area. But these functions are not executive, they are purely advisory.

District Councils vary greatly in size. Skye, for instance (population 7,772), has nine electoral divisions, each of which elects one District Councillor and one County Councillor who is *ex officio* a member of the District Council, making 18 in all. Harris District Council, on the other hand (population 3,285) has only 3 electoral divisions and a District Council of 6 members; whereas Lewis District Council (population 16,700) has 19 members, half of them County Councillors.

In many of the smaller and more scattered District Councils, however, this 1:1 ratio between district and county councillors does not apply. There are 5 District Councillors on Jura, for instance, of whom only one is a County Councillor; Assynt District Council in Sutherland has 2 County Councillors among its 7 members; in the Mainland District Council of Orkney, and in Tain District Council, the ratio is 2 District Councillors for each County Councillor. Elections are held every three years, early in May; voting for District and County Councillors is simultaneous, but on different ballot papers. District Councils usually meet quarterly, although some meet as often as monthly; and meetings are often held in different parts of the parish to ease Councillors' travel difficulties—Tongue and Farr District Council in Caithness, for instance, meets at Tongue, Borgie, Melvich and Bettyhill.

District Clerks are usually part-time, and some serve two or more Districts; they are appointed by the District Council, which pays a very small part of their salary (about £150). The rest of their salary is paid by or through the County Council, although the bulk of it, about two-thirds or so, is actually provided by the Ministry of Social Security, for whom District Clerks act as local social welfare agents.

But what are they really like, these District Councils? The general public seldom hears much about their activities except when local controversies make the headlines of the national newspapers—Skye District Council, for instance, made its voice heard forcefully during the controversy over Sunday ferries to the island. In general, the island District Councils are apt to be more active than their mainland counterparts—no doubt because the remoteness of control from the mainland encourages the local community to look more to its local council.

An outstanding example of this is the 11-member District Council of the island of Yell, in Shetland, which has been in the forefront of attempts to revive the island's sinking economy.

District Councils can also reflect local feelings and aspirations strikingly; for instance, although Harris District Council conducts all its deliberations in English, the other District Councils of the Outer Hebrides use Gaelic to a large extent—North Uist always, South Uist and Barra as the fancy takes them. And in November 1966 Lewis District Council passed a formal resolution 'that to take account of the present development in the sphere of Gaelic education, and to give the language status to encourage its development in the conduct of local government business, Gaelic would have equal validity with English in council meetings. To achieve this in the initial stages in a bilingual council, reason, patience and goodwill would have to prevail. Members would therefore be at liberty to make their contributions in the language of their choice.' Naturally, a policy of this kind creates difficulties for any non-Gaelic speakers on the Council (there are two at present), and for the Clerk who has to record the minutes in both languages; but it illustrates how a District Council can have an influence in matters outside its direct statutory scope.

There is no doubt that a vigorous District Council and Clerk can be an essential part of a community, as a clearing-house for inquiries and appeals on innumerable aspects of county and central government, and as an effective voice on local problems. But all too many District Councils are apt to regard themselves as merely sub-committees of the County Council, and County Councils are apt to encourage this view and look askance at District Councils that take their responsibilities as *separate* local authorities too seriously and try to spend too much money.

And since County Councils can delegate functions at their own discretion, and, moreover, act as paymasters to the District Clerks, they can bring considerable pressure to bear; in the notorious case of Assynt District Council, Sutherland County Council stripped the District Council of all its delegated functions because it disapproved of the District Clerk's appointment as a part-time member of the Crofters Commission (*The Scotsman*, 6 February, 1967).

To get a clearer picture of the composition and aspirations of the District Councils in the Highlands, I wrote to the sixty-five District Clerks for information about their Councillors, and their views on the effectiveness of local authority work at district level. A very large number of them took the trouble to reply, often at considerable length. All of them stressed the importance of local representation to deal with local problems, and while admitting that the present system was by no means perfect, they expressed considerable concern at the prospect of any further centralisation:

'We fear that centralisation would destroy the close and intimate links with the local communities, and restrict future elections to the few unrepresentative persons who have the time and facilities to serve on a centralised authority.'

'When the units get bigger, there will be less interest in local affairs, and District Councils such as ours will lose their identity and administration will suffer.'

'This Council feels that local matters are dealt with better and more cheaply at local level because many of the problems are insular and they are understood better by local people. But considerable frustration is felt at delays in important projects, which happen at both County and Government level.'

'Greater centralisation would lead to full-time, paid Councillors, which would be a retrograde step, and would require an army of officials in a central authority to provide the same services. Administration costs would inevitably soar, as is usual, and the whole administration would become uneconomic.'

'Remoteness and sparseness of population in the Highlands would destroy the present roots of local democratic government as we know it today if they were to be replaced by very much larger units—local government ceases to be local if the little power that some of them have is to be handed over to regions or larger authorities.'

'No system of administration could operate successfully without a small unit body such as the District Council. The District Council is the only body with the time, interest, and local knowledge necessary to deal with the multitude of small local matters, often affecting only a small number of people but none the less important.'

'My Council have taken the attitude that amalgamations, centralisation and less representation of this wide area of scattered small communities would be to our disadvantage, with loss of local representation, loss of the links from ratepayers upwards, and loss of excellent voluntary elected representatives with their local knowledge.'

'The de-localisation of functions which are as immediately local as burial grounds, scavenging, secondary roads, caravan sites, etc., is a major contributory factor to the existing disinterest and apathy in local government and, indeed, such a proposal would appear to me to be a negation, not only of local government, but of democracy itself.'

'I think that grouping of local authorities might well be good for highly populated areas of the country, but in the Highlands some unit about the status of District Councils would be necessary, to maintain contact with the population.'

Some of this might be dismissed as special pleading, although it would be foolish to ignore the very real need for some sort of grassroots representation in widely scattered areas. But under the present statutory limitations, there is very little that District Councils can do apart from keeping alert to essentially local problems and needs that might not get much attention in larger council chambers a hundred miles away. This lack of real authority was the main theme in most of the letters I received:

'When the Parish Councils were abolished by the Local Government (Scotland) Act of 1929, practically all power went to the County Council. As a result, local government, so far as the inhabitants having any say in guiding their own affairs, is practically nil. All the District Council can do is to recommend to the County Council a very small number of things they would like to see done. Only about two meetings a year would be quite sufficient to do the little business we are empowered to do.'

'District Councils, as such, have very little autonomy, and in sparsely populated areas like ours, very little money to spend. The advent of the Exchequer Equalisation Grant in recent years has been a good thing, but does not go far enough.'

'District Councils have very limited powers, and more often than not act only as an advisory body for the County Council and the local population. The fact that the District Councils are so intimately concerned with local affairs within their areas renders their *potential* capacity for dealing with matters very great, but they themselves have neither the finance nor the technical staff to bring about any essential local improvements.'

'My Council have always been frustrated by a lack of statutory powers and financial provisions from playing the part which they would like (and are capable) of playing in the development of their district. When you realise that a service as fundamentally local as the provision and maintenance of burial grounds has actually been a

County Council responsibility since 1929, you realise that District Councils have had a very frustrated part to play in local government.'

'Mostly district councils have powers of recommendation only, and in cases such as proposed new township roads we have to wait until our own top priority case comes up first on the County list before it is even submitted by the County to the Scottish Development Department in Edinburgh for final approval.'

(The classic case of local interests being flagrantly ignored was in Harris three years ago, when the District Council there made a list of roads that needed building in order of priority, headed by the township of Manish; but higher officials struck Manish off the list altogether because it commanded no means of livelihood and 'is an example of a community rapidly becoming extinct'—and little wonder, without a road!)

'The question which has been exercising my Council is by what means they could most effectively play a greater part in the economic and social development of their district at this time. They feel that sweeping reorganisation of functions and financial arrangements is essential. In remote, scattered, depopulating communities, the District Council is invariably the body which concerns itself with these problems. It is right that they should so concern themselves. But it is manifestly wrong that they are quite unable, because of legislation, to take positive action to try to effect these remedies that are so essential. In any two-tier reconstruction of local government, all local functions should be the responsibility of the second tier, and each tier should be autonomous and independent, and should have complete fiscal resources to ensure its ability to fulfil its obligations. The statutory powers of the second tier, in particular, should not be restrictive. In this way, the rapid and continuous changes in society could be foreseen and allowed for by local authority without the necessity of always having to wait for statutory legislation to catch up.'

But if local government at District level is to play a dynamic part in economic development, it does not merely require legislation—it requires dynamic people as well. What about the people who serve on the District Councils at present? With the help of the returns sent by the District Clerks, I have built up some profiles of District Council representation in the Highland area.

Many of the Councils reflect their communities with re-markable fidelity. The *Mainland District Council* of Orkney, for instance, has 19 members—and no fewer than 16 of them are farmers, as befits this intensely agricultural island. On the other hand, the 5 members of *Mull District Council* are a farmer, a doctor, an author, a retired army officer and a retired surgeon, with an average age of 63—which fits pretty accurately the popular conception of Mull as a haven for retired gentry.

The difference between Lewis and Harris is equally marked. *Lewis District Council*, which has the largest mainland population to serve in the Highland area (16,700), has 19 councillors—8 crofters, 2 shopkeepers, 2 retired headmasters, a fisherman, housewife, tweed-weaver, tweed-manufacturer, sub-postmaster, farmer/auctioneer and a haulage contractor—with an average age of 57. The 6 members of *Harris District Council*, however, have an average age of 66—the highest I came across: 3 shop-keepers, a crofter, a fisherman and a mason.

Crofters predominate on the 11-member *Yell District Council* in Shetland, whose average age is 52—there are four of them in all; but the Council profile shows a good cross-section of island life—a retired education department officer, a ferryman, weaver, driver, shopkeeper, bus-operator and a postman. *Lerwick Landward District Council*, however, is distinctly urban in character (a sheriff's clerk, retired builder's labourer, building contractor, school teacher, market gardener and a farmer), with an average age of 61.

In fact, the average age of the District Councils is disturbingly high: Mid Argyll, 59; Assynt (Sutherland), 58; Tongue & Farr (Sutherland), 62. Few District Councils have an average under 50—South Uist and Stronsay (Orkney) are two exceptions, at 48. And there is a very high incidence of Councillors who are retired people—3 out of 6 in Tain District Council, 2 out of 6 in Harris, 2 out of 7 in Assynt, 4 out of 10 in Mid Argyll.

This partly reflects the general age structure in the High-lands, where there is a relative surplus of people over the age of 65 and of the older working age groups, and a relative deficiency in the younger working age groups and of children under 15. Partly it reflects the difficulty of recruiting younger candidates who may be deterred by the time and trouble involved in travelling long distances to meetings in sparsely populated areas.

But it reflects too the apathy that is widely felt towards local government in general, aggravated in the case of District Councils by their impotence to achieve effective results on matters of vital importance to a community. Young people of energy and vision will certainly not be tempted to serve on them, and they tend to become the preserve of the well-meaning old with time to spare on their hands for tinkering with affairs.

The younger and more realistic County Councillors who are *ex officio* District Councillors tend to be briskly intolerant:

'District Councils are unnecessary and could well be abolished.'

'Electoral districts were formed in the days of the horse-and-gig; now we have Jaguars and Minis. A great many electoral districts could well be combined, thereby affecting a saving in expense and time.'

'I find being a District Councillor more or less a waste of time. We have no real power to do anything in a big way.'

'District Councils are nothing but a dreadful bore, dealing mainly with the erection of headstones in local burial places and their up-keep. In my opinion this could be dealt with by the officials, with any difficulty that may arise being handled by the County Council.'

'I am convinced that District Councils could be done away with, they merely tend to prolong matters which could be dealt with directly at County Council level.'

Other Councillors took a directly opposite view:

'I would like to stress the value of the District Councils. I would be very sorry to see them swept away, but they should be given more authority, and the time-lag caused by having to refer decisions to the County Council at times creates unnecessary and undesirable delay.'

'One is often left with the impression that the powers that be are not sufficiently in touch with the day-to-day problems of the more remote parts of their domain. While not advocating the creation of a local government unit for each parish, I feel there is still a place for the smaller unit of local government.'

It is interesting, and significant, that there has been a development recently to bypass the frustrating statutory limitations placed on District Councils—the growth of non-statutory local bodies like the Councils of Social Service, particularly in the islands (and even, in the case of Yell, a community Development Council). They usually have some sort of official standing *vis-à-vis* the local authorities, and can act as pressure groups elected from the community. It has become very sophisticated in Mull, for instance, where after years of consistent and successful pressure for things like a small hospital, an airstrip, improved communications and comprehensive development (the local body even persuaded the School of Town and Country Planning in Edinburgh to bring out an ambitious *Study in Rural Planning* for Mull recently), area branches are being strengthened to form 'mini-Parliaments' all over the island.

Organisations of this kind have been extremely effective in many places—in Islay and Shetland, for instance—and it is significant that the Highland Development Board takes them pretty seriously as sources of local initiative and ideas. In any reorganisation of local authority structure in the Highlands and Islands, these organisations could well have an important part to play as nodes of public energy and enterprise in the smaller communities, taking over from frustrated, moribund District Councils whose outstanding characteristics seem to be longevity and impotence. The District Councils have clearly been made ineffective by the statutory limitations placed on their activities; the aim of any reorganisation must surely be to give truly local units greater, rather than less, opportunities for initiative.

Much the same could be said about the seven *County Councils*, which are also finding their powers and authority being steadily eroded by the growing weight of bureaucratic machinery in the Highlands that is ultimately controlled by St Andrews House and Whitehall. Here, too, the picture is one of relatively elderly councillors who have served on their councils for a very long time.

To get an accurate profile of the County Councils as at January 1967 (that is to say, *before* the triennial elections in May 1967), I sent a brief questionnaire to all the 317 County Councillors in the Highlands, asking for details of age, occupation, length of service, special interests, etc., and inviting comments on Highland administration in general. The response was most gratifying—196 returns out of 317 at the time of writing, over 60 per cent—and many Councillors took the trouble to write long and thoughtful assessments of their views. The seven County Clerks obligingly filled in any gaps, to enable me to complete the picture. (See Figures 4, 5.)

On the basis of this 60 per cent sample, the average ages of the Councils turned out to be rather high: 61·8 in Ross and Cromarty, 59·5 in Orkney, 57·7 in Argyll, 57 in Sutherland, 56·4 in Zetland, 55·7 in Caithness and 55·6 in Inverness-shire. Caithness can boast the oldest Councillor in the Highlands— 92-year-old John Abrach Mackay, with 40 years of Council service behind him; and Inverness-shire the youngest—23-year-old John Matheson, a farmer's son.

The average length of service is also high: 15·4 years in Caithness, 12·5 in Ross and Cromarty, 11·4 in Sutherland, 11·3 in Inverness-shire, 10·6 in Argyll, 10·5 in Zetland and 8·8 in Orkney. (See Figure 4.)

The largest of the Councils, in terms of population, acreage and rateable value, is *Inverness-shire County Council*, which has 84 Councillors (59 landward members and 25 burgh members, of whom 21 come from Inverness itself), and which sits like a miniature Parliament for a week at a time, handling an annual budget of about £7,000,000. Its profile is more or less what you would expect; it has the highest number of landowners of any of the councils (9), and a remarkable number of shopkeepers (19). Three of the five peers sitting in Highland councils sit for Inverness-shire—Lord Lovat, Lord Burton of Dochfour and Lord Macdonald of Sleat, all landowners (Ross and Cromarty has the other two); and the County Convener, Sir Francis W. Walker of Leys Castle, is one of the three other Highland Councillors with a title. Inverness-shire also includes a high proportion of clergymen, 7 in all. There has been a recent increase in crofter representation (now 8), while the burgh representatives follow the usual pattern of garage-owner, shopkeeper, publican and so on. As befits the major Council in the area, it contains more nationally significant figures than the other councils—men like Col. Donald Cameron of Lochiel, and Iain Hilleary of Skye; and there are the widows of other notable men, like Mrs Evelyn Hobbs and Mrs Mary Fraser.

And what do the Councillors themselves think of their Council?

'From my short experience I find that our C.C. is very conservative in its approach. There is not enough forward planning; subjects are dealt with the same way as it was done twenty years ago.'

'It is non-political, but in fact it divides into the Ascendancy and the Peasants and the Placemen . . . Senility sometimes becomes valued, being mistaken for "long experience" and seniority.'

'For a variety of reasons, county representation in the Highlands is in the hands of those with time to spare, and it may be that we have a surfeit of gentry and clergy.'

'The membership of Highland Councils does not reflect the population accurately, being overweighted with lairds, clergymen, shopkeepers and the retired, and largely lacking in representation from those in regular employment and of the professional classes.'

'The average age is too high—beyond the stage of creative thought. The whole system seems to be very ponderous, probably due to the difficulty of getting a quick decision by the committee system, which is nevertheless highly democratic.'

'The present set-up in this County is suitable and efficient for the County.'

'The present Highland administration is the product of common sense, of experience of the hard facts of life, and the mature judgment resulting therefrom. I have little confidence in the originators and promoters of the changes now envisaged.'

'I consider the Inverness-shire County Council an extremely efficient administrative unit, of the maximum size workable.'

'It is democratic and fortunately does not suffer much from the political beliefs of the members.'

'If Council business was made more attractive to the younger section of the community instead of the retired or semi-retired, we might get more forward-looking Councillors.'

The consensus of opinion seemed to be that Inverness-shire County Council was as large as was feasible, and they viewed the prospect of amalgamations with dismay. And many Councillors wrote feelingly of the amount of 'dictation' from St Andrews House—a sore point that occurred again and again in letters from all over the Highlands.

The next largest Council in all respects is *Argyll County Council*, which has 53 Councillors. Here, 10 farmers and 4 landowners, 4 Lt.-Cols (retd.) and a Brigadier, seems the right image for the Michael Noble country. The County Convener, J. G. Mathieson of Oban, is the doyen of Highland Conveners at 76, with 46 years of service behind him, and a notable record of public service on several other Highland bodies (his brother, incidentally, is a former Provost of Auchtermuchty). But on the other hand, Argyll also has the highest number of manual

workers (7) to balance the farming/landowning representation
—the 5 members of the Labour-controlled burgh of Campbeltown consist of 2 colliery workers from Machrihanish, 2 technical
workers from the Post Office and the Hydro Board, and a
retired civil servant. Dunoon's representatives are mainly small
shopkeepers (3 of the 5 are a chemist, a baker and a fruit
merchant). Tobermory sends a hotelier, Provost A. R. Mac-
Leod, better known as Bobby MacLeod the bandleader.
Inverary's representative is the wife of a coal merchant, and
Oban's 5 representatives are a good cross-section. There are
only 3 clergymen (2 Church of Scotland, 1 Free Church), but
Miss Maclean of Ardgour was the Church of Scotland's first
woman elder.

And the Councillors' comments?

'Practically every decision of a local authority has to be approved
by the Secretary of State for Scotland, which makes him a virtual
dictator over Scottish affairs.'

'There tends to be far too much parochialism and narrow-
mindedness in Highland administration. Too many Councillors can
only think of how matters affect their own area and do not consider
the county as a whole. The sooner there are changes in the present
system the better—increasing the area of an authority and cutting
down the number of Councillors.'

'I cannot visualise an alteration that would be an improvement
of the present system as far as our remote area is concerned.'

'The present system works reasonably well, and it is difficult to
see how larger units of local government councils can help where the
areas of land are large and the population very sparse.'

'Local government reform may speed up the local government
machine, but at the expense of councillors losing their close and
intimate touch with their constituents.'

'Many of the elected representatives are completely isolated from
the problems of working-class people in a rural community. Senior
members are nominated for representation on various other bodies
purely for prestige, and take no active interest. . . . The landward
area representatives have far too much power in proportion to the
number of electors they represent in comparison to the burghs.'

'Argyll has a very fair representation from all walks of life. We
have from the humble labourer to the wealthy landowner a very fair
balance of opinions and assorted abilities.'

'My main comment is the horrible delay in getting business
attended to by the Scottish Office.'

Again, several letters voiced the fear that enlargement through amalgamations, with the corresponding increase in the amount of work and travel involved, would tend to discourage able and busy people from local authority work, and leave it more and more to landowners, businessmen and retired people. The alternative—paid councillors—found little favour.

In *Caithness County Council*, the impact of Dounreay is very marked—no fewer than 10 members are technical staff, compared with only one in Inverness-shire and none in the other counties. But this block is balanced by 13 farmers from the landward areas. Most of the Dounreay employees represent burghs; 7 of the 10 Thurso representatives are Dounreay men, and 4 of Wick's 10 work at Dounreay. But there is a certain ill-feeling over the fact that although the burgh population of Caithness is larger than the landward population, the landward area has 22 members on the 42-man Council and can thus out-vote the more populous burghs.

The County Council submitted written evidence to the Royal Commission on Local Government in October 1966, which was claimed to be unanimously approved by the Council; it recommended an amalgamation of Caithness, Sutherland, Orkney and Zetland under the two-tier system. But the replies from individual Councillors suggested anything but unanimity about this matter:

'I am not convinced of the arguments for larger counties, since I believe the advantages gained on administration will be more than offset by the inability of the average person earning a living to spare the time in attending meetings on a large geographical basis.'

'I most certainly hope we don't get broken up into larger areas where only retired people or full-time Trade Union officials can become Councillors. I have no desire to see party politics enter local government here, and no wish to be paid for the honour of acting as a Councillor.'

'I maintain that regionalisation is a decade overdue.'

'There are too many salaried officials with big staffs (Caithness has 700 full-time and 50 part-time employees). The combination of two or three counties would reduce the number of officials and the cost of administration, and give top men more competitive salaries.'

'Retention of a county council in every county—abolition of District Councils—payment of County Councillors!'

'The grouping of counties is not the answer, as the difficulty of administering scattered areas will outweigh the advantages.'

In *Ross and Cromarty County Council*, landowners (7), farmers (7), and businessmen/company directors (9) form the largest categories among the 50 councillors. The Convener is a Free Church minister, but Ross and Cromarty, like Inverness-shire immediately to the south, has a liberal sprinkling of grouse-moor lairds and other bigwigs—like the Earl of Cromartie and the Marquess de Torrehermosa (it's an old Spanish title), Sir Kenneth Murray (former chairman of the Royal Bank of Scotland), and Sir John Stirling, a former County Convener and Forestry Commissioner. There are 4 clergymen in all—2 Free Church, 1 Church of Scotland and 1 Episcopalian (it is noteworthy that 2 of the 15 Highland County Councillors who are clergymen are Episcopalians, which is relatively a high proportion of representation). Mrs Marjorie Linklater, wife of novelist Eric Linklater, is also a member.

Perhaps because Ross and Cromarty is clearly threatened with amalgamation in one form or another, and is rather conscious of its illogical yoking of Lewis, the letters I received from this county were exceptionally candid and thoughtful, and deserve extended quotation:

'My own view is that there are far too many County Councillors and that we are all too old. I am not at all certain that one elected but properly paid Councillor would not offer a better service to his electors, than the fourteen, including burgh representatives, who now represent the area between Dingwall and Ardgay. If the job was full-time and paid, it might attract some competition; at the moment only the Grim Reaper seems to remove a councillor.'

'Most of us Councillors are far too old. Yet younger men don't have the time to do the job properly. At present, only retired people like myself can do a Councillor's job with any thoroughness—one whole week per month plus many odd days for sub-committees, visits, etc., etc.'

'The threat to enlarge areas is likely to dissipate local interest in public affairs.'

'In the Highlands one should not think of tiers of local authority on a population basis, but on an area basis. It has not been proved to me that the present system fails or could be bettered, except that small burghs should be absorbed into one all-purpose local authority. Our proposed amalgamation with Sutherland is intended to show the Secretary of State we are prepared to do something, in the hope that we may not be forced into a greater amalgamation.'

'I consider that local government administration as at present suits the Crofter Counties best, and would oppose any major change involving more centralisation.'

'The average age of our Councillors is too high. Electors in the Highlands are too courteous ever to reject long-serving Councillors, however inefficient or ill or absent.'

'The present local government set-up could only be improved by the setting up of District Councils with greater responsibility and keeping the Town Councils as we know them, and that Police, Education, Fire service and all Highways, Water and Sewerage be regionalised.'

'I think it is a very good set-up of excellent people, who put in good hard work in a conscientious manner and devote a lot of time to the benefit of the country and the county. I would be sorry to see it changed.'

'The present system of administration is working quite well, but the number of people willing and able to attend meetings in Dingwall—a whole week at a time—is very limited. Any enlarging of the area of administration will make this a very serious problem. Paid professional councillors are not wanted.'

'In the projected administrative changes, I would wish to see Lewis as a separate county.'

'Even as a young man, with far less local government work going on than now, I found it hard to keep in touch with activities in this county. Any enlargement of our 2,000,000 acres would make it impossible today. Population does not come into it; geography is what counts.'

'What is appropriate for the industrial built-up areas would not work efficiently in this area. The formation of larger units than at present exist would in my view be detrimental to good local government work in the Highlands.'

'There is far too much reading-matter and reports to get through. And too few people to do all the necessary unpaid work on committees, etc.'

'I am convinced that a wider grouping is necessary up here, preferably a North Highland area—Inverness, Ross and Cromarty, Sutherland, Caithness and perhaps Nairn, with the disappearance of "independent" burghs and the hiving-off of Lewis and Harris.'

'The system of allocating committees gives rise to much dissatisfaction. Some members have been on the same committee for as much as twenty years. The claim is made that such members have gained so much experience that it would be unwise to replace them with less experienced ones—but when they retire from the Council their committeeships are allotted to their successors as if they were family heirlooms, regardless of the experience or interests of the new member!'

'The present system of integrating the Islands into mainland counties is wrong. Island problems are in many respects entirely different from mainland ones, and tend to be misunderstood in a mainland setting.'

'I see nothing very far wrong with the present system, but would like to see more local autonomy. I am opposed to regionalism except possibly for strategic policy. There could well be too much power in the hands of the executive; on the whole the democratic system is preferable, though it has its limitations.'

'I think the present system is quite good.'

By far the smallest of the councils is *Sutherland County Council*, with only 20 councillors representing 13,240 people; it seems certain that its days as a separate authority are numbered, and that it will be amalgamated either to the north or south. It is the most imbalanced of all the councils, with only one burgh representative (for Dornoch), as compared with 8 farmers and 4 hoteliers who dominate this essentially rural county. Because of its concentration of population on the east coast and the remoteness and difficult terrain of the west coast, it is a difficult and expensive county to administer; the Council staff, including teachers, is about 700, and the current education budget of £774,000 for 2,300 children works out at over £330 per child. There seems no reasonable alternative to amalgamation in one form or another—but not all the councillors see it that way:

'The present system is functioning satisfactorily, and any attempt to amalgamate the Crofting Counties into one administrative group would be unworkable. In a county like Sutherland, if amalgamation took place, the rural areas would lose their identity.'

'The present system is perfect for Sutherland.'

'May we not just be imagining that the present system is inadequate? By creating larger units for administrative purposes, we would only accelerate depopulation in many of the already depleted glens. The human and personal touch would tend to get lost, and the areas most needful of help tend to get least. Who will there be to speak for them?'

'I cannot for the life of me see but that councils in the Highlands are made up of as shrewd men as you can get anywhere; whether amalgamation will cure any ills, I am doubtful, but one thing is certain—it will not cure the financial difficulties but only make them worse.'

'Too much time is taken up discussing trivialities.'

'Education and Class 1 Roads are much too heavy a burden on the rates for sparsely populated areas.'

'In my opinion there is too much advice and inquiry about the "troubles" of the Highlands. Had the Government simply made available grants and loans at low rates of interest, and also substantial tax concessions to the local population and substantial incentives to industry in general to come to the Highlands, we would have cured our own ills.'

Zetland County Council, with 36 members, is the larger of the two councils for the Northern Isles, although its population is slightly smaller than that of Orkney. With 8 crofters, 7 shopkeepers, 6 white-collar workers and 5 businessmen, Zetland gives a more balanced democratic profile of representation than most of the Highland councils. The Convener is a retired farmer, and also on the council is the Lord Lieutenant of the County, Robert H. W. Bruce of Sandwick, who has a distinguished record of public service on many important Highland bodies. And yet, despite the apparent good balance of the council profile, there is a hidden imbalance; for although only 12 of the 36 members are representatives from the burgh of Lerwick, the majority of the island constituencies are represented by people who live in Lerwick, because of the difficulties of travel involved; the member for the remote island of Foula, for instance, is a Lerwick bank manager. It is extremely difficult to enable the outer islands to get local representation—which should be a warning to those who think that Shetland's affairs could be managed better from some regional centre on the mainland of Scotland. In a Joint Submission to the Royal Commission in December 1966, Zetland County Council and Lerwick Town Council argued flatly against any conceivable form of amalgamation with a mainland county—and here the councillors really were unanimous:

'Shetland, as its geographical situation would indicate, has problems peculiar to itself. I share the opinion of all other local councillors that there should be no thought of amalgamation with mainland areas. The present system, within human limits, is quite satisfactory.'

'I have no opinion on *Highland* administration. I am an Island councillor, and I hope that our administration will remain in Shetland.'

'My worry is not Highland development but Island development, which is inclined to be overlooked.'

'Completely opposed to any form of amalgamation with any authority on the mainland of Scotland.'

Apart from this closing of ranks on the question of separateness from the mainland (with which I, personally, wholeheartedly agree), not all councillors were satisfied with the present situation:

'There is far too much duplication of work and effort—separate county and town councils, for instance, when the two could well be amalgamated with benefit to both and more especially to the ratepayers.'

'One weakness arises from the fact that councillors are not paid, with the result that the majority of representatives are successful businessmen with staffs able to run the business in their absence. It is also presumed that since they can run a business successfully, they can do likewise with local administration bodies when, in fact, they are the least suitable; their thinking is conditioned by profitability, not by community service.'

'I think there should be some statutory ruling to prevent councillors *en masse* concerning themselves with minutiae; at present, broad principles are poorly debated. Also, greater inducements should be considered to raise the standard of councillors; at the moment no authority is getting anywhere near the best available.'

'I feel quite strongly that there should be a more equitable division of committee chairmanships. Far too often we come across *one* person being chairman of a number of different committees, and in this way monopoly *does* reign.'

'There is too much mere rubber-stamping. And in St Andrews House there is total ignorance of our geographical position, and callous indifference to the problems arising therefrom. "Consultation" is a farce; whatever *we* want is ignored, and we are simply ordered to do something else—this is useless, time-wasting and utterly frustrating.'

'Local authorities are largely influenced and, in many ways, controlled by the policy of the central government and by the interpretation of the policy by St Andrews House. There is insufficient scope for local initiative.'

Finally, in *Orkney County Council*, considering the intensity of the island's agricultural industry, it is not surprising that 14 farmers dominate all other groups on the 32-man council. All 14 sit for the landward areas, which have 21 members compared with 7 for Kirkwall and 4 for Stromness. No teachers, no clergymen, no supervisor/white-collar workers, no shopkeepers, no crofters, no manual workers—Orkney has the fewest number of categories represented; but there are 5 businessmen/company directors, and no fewer than 5 housewives, the largest number in any of the seven Counties—2 from Stromness, 2 from Kirkwall and one from the landward area. In addition there is another lady on the Council, Mrs Firth, who is a doctor. Six out of 32 members gives the ladies an unusually large, but welcome, voice in the affairs of the county. The County Convener, Col. Henry Scarth of Breckness, is also Lord Lieutenant for Orkney, a 67-year-old landowner and farmer with immense experience in local authority work and public service that goes back for several generations of his family.

Orkney's councillors were no less vehement about the folly of amalgamation with mainland counties than Shetlanders were:

'Nothing in our geographical position, language or culture has the slightest affinity with the Highlands. That is why the proposed mergers of police and water systems with the mainland of Scotland seem so utterly ridiculous.'

'The affairs of Island counties can only be successfully administered within the Islands.'

'We must remain an independent council on our own.'

In common with other councils, remoteness seems to add to the delays in getting things done:

'Our only common ground with the Highlands is the abiding difficulty and delay in persuading St Andrews House to approve our proposals: one small housing scheme in Stromness has taken ten years, an essential harbour improvement scheme is still hanging fire, and Kirkwall seems unable to get approval for the removal of a line of old scullery/wash-houses in Palace Road affronting (yes!) the Cathedral.'

'Owing to the remoteness of these islands, and the centralisation of administration in London and Edinburgh, far too little is known of the real needs and difficulties of the county. Travel is expensive and time-consuming, so that there is too little personal liaison between the authorities and their subjects. One has the feeling that the islands are considered to be expendable. It is extremely disheartening to those living here, especially the young, who wonder if there is any future for them here at all. Policies are formulated which may suit industrial and city areas and even other rural areas, but which may be ruinous to an island community.'

'The outstanding problem is fiscal weakness, caused by the very heavy burden on the rates imposed by education. Since the central government wills the ends anyway, it ought to pay the means of achieving them.'

It was the threat from outside that dominated most councillors' thoughts; the present system satisfied them with only a few minor exceptions:

'No chips on our shoulders here. We're happy to maintain the status quo.'

'I cannot see any better system of local government for a place like Orkney than the present set-up.'

'We want to be a single, self-contained, all-purpose authority. Our semi-isolation gives us a community of spirit that easy communication has stolen from other areas, and we have the people behind us. In short, we feel that the administration of this archipelago is being butchered to make a holiday for the planners in St. Andrews House, and we don't take kindly to the process.'

Over all the county councils there hung the prospect (or threat) of reorganisation in the foreseeable future, and this has probably distorted attitudes to a certain extent. How much of the complacency revealed by some answers was a defensive gesture of defiance, born out of a fear of change? There is in northern councils today, I think, a very real sense of frustration, an inability to get things done with any speed, a growing awareness of impotence, a sense of being stifled by a proliferating bureaucracy. The crux of the problem was succinctly summed up by one county councillor: 'One has to try to reconcile the paro-

chial with the practical, and the immediate with the imaginative.' And it isn't easy. Is parochial democracy really com-
patible with the kind of large-scale, all-embracing development
planning now being undertaken? Is the problem of administering the Highland area growing too complex and burdensome
for volunteer 'amateurs' undertaking public service, unpaid,
from a sense of duty? Should geography, or populousness, be
the basis for administering local budgets?

Some sort of reorganisation is bound to come, for whatever
the merits or demerits of individual councils and councillors,
the present system has signally failed to cope with the chronic
problems of the area, or the acute challenge of new developments. The most striking example of this is at Fort William,
where a virtual New Town is being created by the huge pulp
mill there. Yet the town and county councils have been at
loggerheads for years over urban development; and each year,
Fort William is being slowly strangled by traffic and clogged
facilities. The division of responsibilities there is clearly harm-
ful, and would be avoided by the kind of reorganisation that
seems to be most in favour at present. It was adumbrated by
two White Papers published by the Conservative Government
(*The Modernisation of Local Government in Scotland*, 1963, and the
First Working Party Report that followed it next year), which laid
down general guidelines: there would be amalgamations (unspecified) into larger units (unspecified), in order to create a
two-tier structure consisting of enlarged county organisations,
and new landward councils centred on burghs.

Within this broad framework, a host of ideas have been aired
and submitted to the Royal Commission. Some want six
regional councils, with a second tier of up to 90 burgh/landward
councils; this would give the Highland area one top-tier
regional council, and a series of second-tier authorities for
Orkney, Shetland, the Outer Isles, Caithness, Sutherland,
Ross and Cromarty, Skye and the smaller islands, Lochaber,
North Argyll with Mull, South Argyll with the Inner Isles,
Bute, Inverness and Badenoch, and Highland/Western/Central
Perthshire. The administrative pyramid envisaged by the
S.T.U.C., however, puts the (non-elected) Scottish Economic
Planning Council at the top, with 7 elected regional councils to
deal with rating, housing, planning, roads, employment and

development, and 30–40 land-states or city-states to deal with housing, amenities, social welfare, etc.

Any redrawing of boundaries in the Highland area will arouse fierce passions; even something as theoretically sensible as the union of Lewis and Harris will draw vigorous protest from Harris ('I'd rather be ruled by a Turk than a Lewisman'), and there are few signs that Orkney and Shetland want to renew an ancient association that grew up in the days of the Norse Earls. Sutherland has little relish for a union with Caithness and/or Ross and Cromarty.

But to my mind, the problem of finance is going to prove far more stubborn. The Highlands alone cannot raise the revenue required. Dwindling populations and soaring administrative costs have forced the county councils to rely more and more on government grants; sparsely populated counties cannot afford to build new roads to attract more tourists (who would contribute little to the rates in return), or initiate development projects, or attract new industries. Finance of the required scale has to come from the central government; but I would like to see local authorities being given greater scope to dispose of it as they think best, and for that reason I see no better alternative to the idea of an elected Regional Council for the Highland area, consisting of about 20 or 25 paid councillors. This would enable the present county council boundaries to be redrawn where necessary into more viable and logical units—in many cases *smaller* units—based on burghs as the foci of landward areas. These new second-tier authorities would have to be given greater powers than they have at present, however, if they are to attract people of calibre to serve on them—and not so much power of administration, but power of initiation. These councils should also have the power of co-option, so that the local representative of national concerns like BEA and British Rail could serve on them. Below them, I would like to see the District Councils being abolished as limited statutory authorities in favour of voluntary Community Development Councils, which would have the right of representation on the second-tier authority. Their function would be to act as ginger groups, harnessing local energy and ideas at parish level.

By this means, I would hope to see the Highlands utilising to the best advantage their best natural resource—people. The ultimate future of the Highlands lies in the self-help and co-operation of the people themselves, and the aim of any re-organisation must be to give local initiative a chance to thrive. This seems to me to be the central importance and value of the Highlands and Islands Development Board, which will be discussed later in this chapter; regeneration cannot be imposed from outside, but only assisted and encouraged. But the mere presence of the Board before the reorganisation of local authority administration takes place poses its own problem: how is it to fit in? The H.D.B. has its own (non-elected) consultative council; in the future, I would like to see it as the executive arm of an elected Regional Council, a small Board of skilled specialists in different fields.

No democratic system will ever be ideal; and since there will never be enough finance to do everything desirable, any system of defining priorities will disappoint someone, somewhere. But the crasser blunders the Highlands are all too used to can be avoided in the future if national policies can be planned, co-ordinated and executed at regional and local level, and if local people can be given a greater opportunity of participating in decision-making and execution. This will undoubtedly mean paying some Councillors for their work; but it should also mean a reduction of some of the more time-wasting procedures that at present discourage people of ability from any participation at all.

Any future reorganisation must also take into account the astonishing plethora of government or semi-government agencies that are at present engaged in Highland work, for their future functions (and existence) will have to be rethought in terms of any new administrational structure.

Not only are there far too many of these agencies, but not one of them has been endowed with sufficient authority to cope effectively with the problem it was created to solve. Let us glance first at some of the agencies concerned with land use in the Highland area.

The *Red Deer Commission*, based in Inverness, was set up in October 1959 as a result of the Deer (Scotland) Act of 1959. Like so many other specialised agencies, its whole existence is anomalous: it was established to deal with an irksome problem that was just as much social and political as it was physical, but not endowed with sufficient statutory power to deal with it with any conviction. It was charged with the apparently incompatible dual function of 'furthering the conservation *and* control of red deer'. It consists of 13 members: a chairman, two representatives of the Nature Conservancy, and 5 representatives each from two of the most incompatible of all Highland interests—land-owning and sporting on the one hand, farming and crofting on the other.

At present there are an estimated 180,00 red deer which are to be found over some 7,000,000 acres of land in the Highland area, although deer forests as such cover only 2,500,000 acres. This deer population is demonstrably too high to prevent them encroaching on agricultural land—but the Commission doesn't have the power to order or enforce an overall reduction; its powers are limited to killing marauding deer that are proved to have caused damage to agricultural or forestry property. In its first six years of existence, the Commission's field staff of seven killed 2,400 marauding deer on receipt of complaints from farmers; yet it has no power to act in anticipation, even if it knows that severe damage is likely to occur because of a rise in the local deer population. In the same way, landowners who have the right to exploit exclusively the commercial or sporting value of the deer on their land, cannot be forced to bear responsibility for controlling them.

It is known that stags start marauding when the number of hinds rises out of proportion; but the Commission has no power to compel ignorant or idle or selfish landowners to cull their hind stocks to reasonable proportions. The use of so much land for deer is economically unjustifiable at present—yet the Commission has no power to ensure that the existing deer forests are economically exploited to the full (it is argued that with proper care and control by landowners, the present annual export figure of 1,200 tons of venison could be very considerably expanded).

Most of the Commission's work until now has been concerned with the control of marauding animals. On the question of conservation its powers are even more meagre, and little more than advisory; in 1965, only three requests for advice were submitted by private owners. And even though the Commission believes that deer stocks could be improved in quality by providing adequate grazing and shelter areas for wintering, it has no power to ensure that this is provided; so in the perennial conflict between sporting interests and forestry and agriculture, the Commission can only say rather wistfully from the sidelines, 'The Commission would welcome requests for advice on this problem.'

So in this, as in so many other areas of conflicting interests in the Highlands, it seems that a Commission was set up more as a buffer than an instrument with sufficient authority or funds to deal with the problem thoroughly and objectively. Indeed, the Commission admits this by implication in the last paragraph of its Report for 1965: 'The Commission do not claim to have solved the "deer problem" during the last six years, but they have taken some of the heat out of it.' And that, probably, is no more and no less than the politicians intended—the sort of faint-hearted political expedient that has all too often been substituted for policy in the Highlands.

The *Crofters Commission*, set up in 1955 after the Taylor Report of 1954, is another example of a Highland agency having the will but being denied the authority to deal with a deep-rooted problem inherent in the Highland situation, another example of pious hopes and exhortations having to substitute for effective action.

To most outsiders, 'crofting' and 'the Highland problem' are practically synonymous. It has acquired the most enormous psychological significance which politicians find excessively intimidating. And yet in reality it is a marginal problem, confined to just over a fifth of the population of the Highlands and Islands, and physically to the periphery of the area—the extreme north and north-west of the mainland, the Outer Isles, Skye and the Hebrides. About 60,000 people (some 16,000 crofter households) are gathered in some 700 crofting townships, contributing about a quarter of the gross estimated agricultural output of the Highlands (which is valued at about £20,000,000 a year).

The numbers are declining—but declining too slowly for the sterner economists; by 1980, according to the so-called Scottish Economic Plan of 1966, the number of crofting households will have fallen by '*only* about 2,000. . . . If action were taken by stronger powers to accelerate this trend towards more viable units, it is doubtful if the reduction in units and holders would be greater than another 1,000.'

The crofting problem is complex, but can be stated fairly simply: crofting, for the most part, is uneconomic; uneconomic to the crofter (less than 20 per cent of crofting households are supported by full-time agricultural work), and uneconomic for the nation, in that the agricultural potential of the land is not exploited to the full, and an enormous amount of public money is spent on subsidising it (the *Economist*, in a special supplement on the Highlands on 17 September, 1966, rather snappishly totted up all the subsidies available to crofters and concluded: 'The crofters would probably be worse off if all their special subsidies were dropped in exchange for a hand-out of £20 a week per household for ever. But the cost of trying to keep the crofters on the crofts can never be officially calculated, for fear that English—or Lowland—M.P.s might get to hear'). To solve the problem, to put crofting on an economically viable basis, massive reorganisation would be required; but the Crofters Commission that was set up to 'reorganise, develop and regulate' crofting was not given the authority to do so, and has signally failed to do so as a result.

The present work of the Crofters Commission is fully discussed in the chapter on 'Economic Life' by Farquhar Gillanders, and it is unnecessary to go into detail here. It seems to me to be doing a useful if limited task, tidying up loose ends and encouraging self-help and amalgamation where possible. But those who lament the failure of the Commission to transform crofting into a viable system *agriculturally* seem to my mind to miss the point, just as the point was missed by the legislators who failed to endow the Commission with suitable authority: crofting is *not*, for the most part, an agricultural occupation. It is a way of life—and a way of life that can be valuable to the nation not just because of its independence and freedom 'which is worth preserving for its own value' (Taylor Report), but because the best crofting townships could be growth-points of people 'whose services are useful to the community in other ways—services which could not be easily or cheaply replaced if the crofting population were to disappear' (Scottish Economic Plan). Now, the Taylor Commission believed that the crofting communities were capable of restoration and survival (not necessarily as agricultural communities), 'if the proper measures were taken *in time*'; and the proper measures, surely, were not merely amalgamations and reorganisations of township lands. The Crofters (Scotland) Act of 1955 empowered the Crofters Commission 'to keep under review wider social and economic problems'—but in fact it is powerless to do anything effective about these problems.

Here is the nub of it. Crofting communities do not wither and die because the land is not being properly used; it is because the young men cannot earn a living there, or find the living too uncomfortable—and amalgamating crofts is only one answer to this. The 'wider social and economic problems' are just as important—the provision of facilities and amenities that are taken for granted in other parts of the nation, like electricity or water or a road; social amenities like access to a cinema or a pub; economic amenities like the availability of jobs. Yet here, where it ought to have powers, the Commission is powerless.

There was the celebrated and ludicrous case of the 'Tail-End Charlies', where higher officialdom decreed that all the houses in a crofting township *except the last one* should be supplied with basic services like mains water. Why on earth not the last one? Yet neither the Crofters Commission nor the local council could do anything to unravel this preposterous bureaucratic tangle.

There was the equally celebrated case of the scattered and dwindling crofting community on the coast of north Applecross, in Ross and Cromarty—fifty-five people in all, living in eight townships. It had no road at all, only a bicycle track unfit for the elderly and useless for any sick who required to be taken to hospital; it was a community that had grown and prospered when the sea was their highway, and they had been left out of every road-building programme. In January 1964 the County Planning Officer recommended that it would be a better economic proposition to evacuate the survivors of this beleaguered part of the mainland than to build a road for them! This suggestion at least had the virtue of shocking the county council into action, and now a road is being built; but this may well be insufficient without the provision of other basic social services. I had the privilege of attending a meeting in Dingwall in which all the various agencies involved in the area came together in a sort of unofficial development council; the Forestry Commission would do a survey to evaluate potential, the Crofters Commission would advise on fencing grants and improvement schemes—everyone tried to pitch in with ideas and offers of help. But I remember the gradual feeling of helplessness that spread over the meeting; for they discovered that no one had the money, no one had the power, no one had the authority to get things done urgently—and everything depended, anyway, on the whim of an absentee landowner as to whether he would grant permission for a road to be built at all! Keeping under review the wider social and economic problems? That is a sour joke in north Applecross—and a bitter one for the Crofters Commission. The administrative machinery bequeathed by the legislators was simply not up to the complexities and difficulties of the task involved throughout the crofting counties.

'Crofting law', as one might call it, comes under the jurisdiction of the *Scottish Land Court*, a judicial tribunal that was established in 1912 as a result of the Small Landholders (Scotland) Act of 1911. Although its function is to arbitrate on agricultural land problems throughout Scotland, its primary concern (and favourite subject) is crofting problems in the Highland area; its task is to fix fair rents and deal with questions of alleged bad husbandry, evictions, resumptions, enlargements, assignations and even sheep-stock valuation.

As a tribunal it is unique, the only court of its kind in the world (and so, too, are the problems it deals with—where else does the tenant own everything on the land he farms except the land itself, for which he pays a miniscule rent, and on which he has an almost unassailable security of tenure for himself and his descendants?). Essentially, the problems it deals with relate to issues between landlord and tenant, and so its membership includes practical and expert laymen; at present only the chairman, Lord Birsay, is a lawyer—the other four members are agriculturalists and one of these, by Act of Parliament, must be a Gaelic speaker.

Its proceedings have a flexibility and informality suited to the circumstances, for its sittings are held *in situ*, sometimes in crofting kitchens or even in the open air, with the bonnet of a car acting as the clerk's table, and the court is more likely to wear gumboots and oilskins than wigs and gowns. Evidence can be given in Gaelic, with an interpreter; and considerable latitude over the rules of evidence is allowed (even 'second sight' evidence has been taken on occasion). Indeed, within the statutory requirements of the law, its proceedings are astonishingly inexpensive (it costs only five shillings for an application, and the crofter can present his own case) and summary; decisions by the full Court are final on questions of fact, and only appealable to the Inner House of the Court of Session on questions of law.

The Court deals with an average of 1,000 to 1,500 cases a year, and now claims to have travelled to every part of Scotland there is to go; the record was completed by a memorable visit to the island of Foula, in Shetland (CLOSE-UP in *The Scotsman*, 23 July, 1966).

The other main government agency dealing with land use in the Highland area is the *Forestry Commission*, established in 1919. Although its headquarters are in England, the major part of its activities take place in Scotland, where the Commission owns (September 1965) 1,530,256 acres of land at 240 separate forests. Over half of this acreage is in the Highlands, where the Forestry Commission is far and away the largest landowner, with 858,000 acres of land, 316,000 of which have already been planted in 95 separate forest areas (the rest is mostly unplantable land on mountaintops, or farmland reserved for agricultural purposes). The tempo of the Commission's activities in the Highlands is now increasing quite briskly; by 1969 the Commission will be planting 20,000 acres a year in Highland forests, compared with 14,000 acres at present.

The Commission has a 'social clause' built into its constitution, and takes its responsibilities towards the Highlands seriously—to the dismay of economists who are concerned at the Commission's vast annual subsidy of well over £13,000,000 to cover the yawning gap between its capital expenditure and its receipts from timber sales (these amounted to £4,615,620 in 1965); they find the Commission's dispersal of effort over a large number of small forest areas wasteful, even though it provides pockets of employment that have stabilised or even increased many dwindling communities. The Commission now provides employment for 2,000 people directly on its plantations, and has built some 600 houses (mostly grouped in new forestry villages) and some 1,500 miles of forest roads, as well as helping to improve and maintain public roads where necessary. It has also developed a system of modern-style crofting—pastoral Forest Workers' Holdings on Commission land, whereby the tenant is guaranteed at least 150 days' work a year in the forest if he so wishes.

Forestry is by nature a slow-maturing business; timber production, now running at 20,000 tons a year, will be over 90,000 tons by 1985, and only now is the major harvest of the 50 years of planting beginning to be reaped in terms of large-scale industrial employment. The massive new £20,000,000 pulp and paper mill at Fort William now provides direct employment for about 1,000 workers, and, overall, for some 3,200; by the 1980s, capacity should be doubled.

Yet there are some who think that the level of planting is still much too low. William Scholes of the T.G.W.U., now a part-time member of the Highland Development Board, has demanded (through the S.T.U.C.) a 30-year planting programme to cover no fewer than 3,000,000 acres—which would cost some £750,000,000. But this huge investment would be worth it, in his eyes, for it would provide 130,000 new jobs in the Highlands.

But here we run up against one of the Commission's major problems, and the old problem of split administration that bedevils the Highland area—the acquisition of land. For large areas of the Highlands, forestry is the most practicable activity in terms of employment—the number of people employed per 1,000 acres planted is six, compared with only one, on average, per 1,000 acres employed on land devoted to raising sheep, deer or grouse. But social remit or not, in many parts of the Highlands (particularly, recently, in Mull) there is considerable resistance from farming and sporting interests over the Commission's land acquisitions; some claim that good agricultural land is being taken and wasted. And although the Commission can fairly claim that it takes great care to cater for tourists, and tries to be tactful in its relations with others, it is arguable that some areas of land would be better used as a combination of forestry, farming, sport, and tourism, rather than being devoted exclusively to forestry.

But there is no machinery available at present to effect such a co-ordination of interests. Of these four basic uses for land in the Highlands, only one—forestry—is directly within the scope of a public authority. The Commission is a separate department of the Secretary of State for Scotland (in England it comes under the Minister of Agriculture), and naturally maintains close relations with the Department of Agriculture and Fisheries in St Andrews House; but little control is possible over sporting interests, which guard their preserves with jealous vigilance.

As for tourism—the *Scottish Tourist Board* was given the princely sum of £15,000 a year for five years (ending in 1965) for the promotion of tourism in the Highlands; most of this went on administration costs, and in grants to local tourist associations. The following year, as if admitting that it had never had the faintest idea what tourism was about, the Government gave the Tourist Board £25,000 for three years *for research only*.

Both tourism and forestry have been extolled (in the Scottish Economic Plan, *inter alia*) as important growth industries for the Highlands ('Both forestry and tourism can utilise a dispersed local population for their labour and resident services which would otherwise be increasingly difficult to obtain'). But neither industry has been exploited, and tourism has been frankly left to struggle along on its own; no funds have been available to finance hotel-building, and in one of the most incomprehensible decisions ever made by a government department, the Board of Trade turned down an urgent request for a £50,000 loan to help the Cairngorms Development Board exploit the growing ski-ing boom on Speyside. A spanking new 'tourist' road between Sheildaig and Torridon was built in Wester Ross for £360,000—but nothing at Aviemore, where massive private investment in hotels and holiday centres has attracted hordes of skiers who can scarcely make their way to the ski-ing grounds. Salmon and trout fishing, which could be developed for the benefit of all instead of as a preserve of the rich and the upper classes, according to the Hunter Report in 1965, is still the preserve of the rich and the upper classes.

It was against this background that the Highland Panel produced a revolutionary report on 'Land Use in the Highlands and Islands' in December 1964—practically on the eve of the

Highland Development (Scotland) Bill in February 1965. It called for the establishment of a Land Department, or at least a combining of the activities of the Forestry Commission and the Department of Agriculture and Fisheries, as a first step towards rationalising the situation. It was tantamount to a call for land nationalisation (reflecting with startling promptness the change of government in October 1964), in view of the 'under-use, and in some cases gross mis-use' of a good deal of land in the Highlands which, the Report said, was the basic natural resource of the Highlands. This new Department should have powers of compulsory acquisition of land for forestry and for creating family farm units, and the acquisition of rivers and lochs to enable fishery boards to administer them for recreational purposes; land acquired for forestry was to be administered as estate units, to be managed comprehensively for agriculture, forestry, sport and tourism.

So far, nothing of this scope has come about. The Highland Development Board has a rather ill-defined roving brief; it is not responsible for deciding forestry programmes, but where clashes of interests occur, as in Mull, it seems to be trying to act as a kind of arbitrative tribunal—although its preliminary efforts there were hardly distinguished for their tactfulness or judiciousness. In the field of tourism, it has infuriated the Scottish Tourist Board by simply setting up its own tourist organisation for the Highlands, and announced that it will build five hotels in the Islands at a cost of £1,000,000 for letting to private hoteliers. Another project, a scheme to build an ultra-modern camping and caravan centre has infuriated not only Macdonalds but Campbells as well; and another of the Board's well-meaning gestures towards tourism—a £1,000 grant to assist an organisation hunting for the Loch Ness Monster—was received without amusement or enthusiasm.

Nevertheless, in my opinion the Board is undoubtedly right to take these steps. It has powers of compulsory acquisition of land, which it has not had occasion to use at the time of writing; but the use of land in the Highlands has for so long been the subject of squabbling and bickering between different interests, the development of tourism has been so grossly neglected, that it is more than time that some agency tried to impose an over-all planned pattern on it.

The other major natural resource in the Highlands—the fishing grounds—show a similar division of administration. Despite the recommendation of the Fleck Report that there should be a single Sea-Fishing Authority, responsibility for the Highland fishing industry is divided between the *Herring Industry Board* and the *White Fish Authority*, with occasional sorties into the field by the Scottish Development Department and, recently, the Highland Development Board. To compound the division, the financial vote for the Herring Industries Board is handled by St Andrews House, whereas the White Fish Authority vote is dealt with by Whitehall. The dividing line between the two seems to be that if a fisherman decides that he will be fishing predominantly for herring, he comes under the wing of the H.I.B., whereas if he intends to concentrate on white fish or prawning, he goes to the W.F.A. But there is some difference of attitude between the two.

The fishing industry is of considerable importance to the Highlands, and to Scotland. Total fish landings at Highland ports in 1965 were a quarter of the value of all landings in Scotland, worth well over £4,600,000, and more than a third of the total United Kingdom herring catch is landed at Highland ports. The Highlands' share of the fish landings in the United Kingdom has been growing steadily since 1961, and the growth of the shellfishing industry in the last decade has been most spectacular.

As a source of employment, the number of full-time fishermen in the industry has increased slightly over the last decade, to the 1965 total of 1,530, but the number of crofter–fishermen has dropped sharply from 4,000 in 1938 to 870 in 1965. In all, however, there are 3,250 fishermen, full-time and part-time, employed in the industry, and another 1,920 in ancillary industries—representing a total of roughly 4 per cent of the working population of the Highlands, compared with about 1 per cent for Scotland as a whole. And yet the figures could be considerably better; about two-thirds of the fish landings at Highland ports are made by boats from outside the Highland area; and Highland fishermen, by landing their own catches at non-Highland ports, have inhibited the expansion of ancillary industries—the ratio of ancillary workers to fishermen in the Highlands is 1:1, compared with 2:1 in Scotland as a whole.

Both the two main agencies administer grant-and-loan schemes for the purchase of fishing boats (government subsidies for the fishing itself are provided through the Department of Agriculture and Fisheries). The White Fish Authority was set up in 1953, replacing the White Fish Commission and the Scottish Fisheries Advisory Council; it has a Committee for Scotland and Northern Ireland, run by a chairman and five other members. The Herring Industry Board, on the other hand, is based in Edinburgh, and was set up as a statutory body in 1935; it consists of a chairman (at present George Middleton), and three members appointed by the Government, backed by a Herring Industry Advisory Council, also appointed by the Government.

From 1953 to 1966, the W.F.A. provided grant and/or loan assistance for the purchase of ninety-four inshore boats in the Highlands and Islands, involving a sum of over £800,000, equivalent to 12 per cent of the total of grant-and-loan aid given to all Scottish inshore boats. In the same period, the Herring Industry Board provided grants and loans totalling some £200,000 for about twenty new boats. But whereas the H.I.B. has moved into the marketing field, by operating two quick-freezing factories at Stornoway and Mallaig, where the trade is too vulnerable to tempt investment by commercial concerns, the W.F.A. prefers to stand aloof (after burning its fingers somewhat over an early venture in Shetland). And where the H.I.B., under George Middleton, is fiercely enthusiastic about the need to expand the Highland herring industry, the W.F.A. is austerely objective, and rather disapproved of the special (and successful) Outer Isles Fisheries Training Scheme that provided twelve new boats for the Highlands and Islands under specially favourable grant-and-loan schemes sponsored by the Scottish Development Department. The W.F.A. has no 'social clause' in its remit, and the interests of the industry as a whole outweigh any sense of special responsibility it might harbour for the Highlands.

The W.F.A.'s coolness towards the Highlands seems to be approved by the Government. The Scottish Economic Plan stated that 'it would be quite wrong to imagine that fishing can be looked to as a significantly expanding sector of the Highland economy'; although it qualified this by saying that 'agriculture and an improved fishing industry will continue to be essential to the Highland economy and, even if they afford less employment, stability based on increased efficiency could, if carefully directed, help to strengthen selected communities'.

But once again, the Highland Development Board has jumped in with a new scheme to provide more fishing boats for the Highlands and Islands—a scheme for no fewer than twenty-five boats for the Outer Isles, to the pained disapproval of the W.F.A., which will be required to supply the loans for two-thirds of the boats. It is difficult not to believe that if the Scottish Committee of the W.F.A. were a separate authority (as it would like to be), its attitude to the Highlands would be a little warmer, as two of its present members (Ewen Robertson from Mallaig, and Roderick McFarquhar, the secretary of the Highland Fund) have a particular interest in the Highlands.

Short of that, my opinion is that the Highland Development Board, once again, was right to intervene here, trying to act as a catalyst to encourage co-ordinated growth. It is a pity that the Government did not implement the suggestion of the Fleck Committee, that there should be a single authority for the fishing industry; the fishermen themselves were against the idea—but it must be said that fishermen, in the Highlands as elsewhere, are never particularly helpful or foresighted about developing their own industry to the best advantage of all. Schemes for co-operative marketing and processing, that would have created stable employment in the Highland area, have come to grief because of the fishermen's preference to take their catches elsewhere, gambling on a better profit. If any Authority in the future sets up plant installations to encourage a local ancillary industry, the local fishermen will have to play their part by agreeing to supply it adequately.

Essentially and ultimately, the basic reason for the establishment of the Highland Development Board in 1965 was the growing importance of, and need for, industrial development. There had been numerous small official or semi-official agencies at work. The *Scottish Country Industries Development Trust*, a Development Commission agency financed by the Treasury to the tune of some £60,000 a year, was set up to encourage the establishment and expansion of industrial activity (including crafts and craft-based industries) in country towns and rural areas; it provides small loans, and technical and financial advice to firms employing not more than twenty skilled workers.

The *Scottish Agricultural Organisation Society Ltd*, a semi-government agency founded in 1905 to promote co-operation among farmers, gets a grant of nearly £30,000 a year from the Department of Agriculture and Fisheries and devotes much the greater part of its expenditure to the Highland area, trying to stimulate new agricultural industrial enterprises.

The *Highland Fund* is now another semi-government agency. It was launched in 1953 by the late Lord Malcolm Douglas-Hamilton to provide low-interest loans to establish or extend small industries, in an attempt to deal with the chronic lack of investment capital in the Highlands. The great bulk of its loan fund of £139,222 was donated by the late Herbert Ross. In its first 12 years of existence, fostered by John Rollo, the Bonnybridge industrialist who is now vice-chairman of the Highland Development Board, the Highland Fund lent out £416,831— that is to say, the original loan fund has been turned over nearly three times; loans are given on 'character-security' alone, and so far the percentage of bad debts has been only 1·8. Of the various Highland areas, Harris and Lewis have benefited most (£73,153), followed by Skye (£51,269) and Sutherland (£44,371), with Orkney bringing up the rear (£2,494).

The projects assisted by the Fund have been extremely varied, from buying crofts and livestock to building slipways, slaughter-houses, and small factories—and even helping the twenty-seven miners of the Highland Colliery at Brora to buy their mine from the N.C.B. and run it as a co-operative. In October 1953 the Government took a hand (shortly after the Duke of Edinburgh had become patron of the Fund) by asking it to administer a £150,000 Treasury Loan fund for new buildings, plant and equipment. By the time the Highland Development Board was established in November 1965, thereby effectively removing the need for a separate loan fund, £115,192 of this money had been loaned out, mainly on tourist enterprises (£45,215), service industries (£35,250) and manufacturing industries (£34,727). Despite the relative smallness of the capital involved, the Highland Fund played an important part in Highland affairs; the psychological effect of being able to borrow on security of character alone did much for Highland morale, and the loans also served to prime the pump for much larger Government grants and loans—in the Outer Isles Fisheries Training Scheme, for instance, the Highland Fund provided deposit-loans totalling £24,000 to help eleven of the twelve boats get under way.

One other agency should be mentioned in connection with industrial development in the Highlands—the *Scottish Council (Development and Industry)*, based in Edinburgh, a pressure group financed mainly by industry and local authorities. It is not unfair to say that its chief concern since the War has been to build up a strong industrial base in the Central Belt of Scotland from which the rest of Scotland might eventually benefit, lobbying vigorously for improved communications, a greater share of research contracts and modern technological development. Its interest in the Highlands was largely philosophical, although it took an active share in some of the more spectacular developments, like the protracted negotiations that eventually brought Wiggins Teape to Fort William to establish the new pulp mill. In February 1965, however (spurred by local criticism that it wasn't doing enough for the Highlands), the Scottish Council established an area office in Inverness (there are two others, in Aberdeen and Dumfries). A Highland Officer (Douglas Shaw), with a secretariat of precisely one, started working on individual Highland problems, providing consultative and advisory services and feeding back to the Scottish Council headquarters in Edinburgh information about Highland opportunities, which are discussed at regular monthly meetings. The Council helps Highland manufacturers to sell their products in England and abroad (through exhibitions and trade missions), encourages existing firms to diversify their products, does surveys to point opportunities for new firms, and does general publicity work. Before the arrival of the Highland Development Board, it worked closely with the Development Officers appointed by individual County Councils; now its role in the Highlands is rather ambiguous.

I said earlier in this chapter that the establishment of the *Highlands and Islands Development Board* was the most important single development in Highland administration this century, in my opinion. But the surprising thing is that it should have taken so long to arrive. The extraordinary anomalies created by the incoherent nature of Highland administration had been apparent for long enough, and the failure of all these makeshift expedients to solve the problem had been just as obvious all along.

As long ago as 1928 the Liberals had advocated the setting up of a Highland Development Commission to co-ordinate the efforts of public departments and 'to prepare and carry into effect a comprehensive scheme for developing the full resources of the Highlands'. This suggestion appeared in one of the 'Tartan Book' series published on behalf of the Scottish Liberal Federation; twenty years later, a similar proposal was passed by the Scottish Liberal Party conference at Dundee in 1948.

In 1936 the Highland Development League, which had been formed in January of that year at a large public meeting in Glasgow, passed a resolution at its first annual delegate conference calling for the formation of 'an administrative or central board for the Highlands'. Again in 1945 the league (then under the chairmanship of the Rev. T. M. Murchison) pressed this proposal on all Parliamentary candidates in Scotland.

Just before the War, the most comprehensive expression of this idea was formulated by the Scottish Economic Committee, which had been established in 1936. In consultation with the then Secretary of State for Scotland, the late Sir Godfrey Evans, a Highlands and Islands Committee was formed, under the chairmanship of Major E. L. Hilleary (the father of Iain Hilleary of Skye, an Inverness-shire County Councillor). Its remit was: 'To examine economic conditions in the Highlands and Islands and the possibilities of development of local industries therein.'

The Committee reported in 1938, and their recommendations, fully endorsed by the Scottish Economic Committee, were put before the Government; the central recommendation was the immediate appointment of a Development Commissioner for the Highlands and Islands, who would make a comprehensive survey of the area, create a special Central Marketing Agency for all Highland produce, reduce freight charges, develop piers and harbours for the fishing fleet, plan industrial developments based on hydro-electric power, and examine the possibility of land reclamation and forestry projects for crofting townships; and for this he was to have as free a hand as possible—'granted wide discretionary powers with regard to the framing and initiation of schemes involving new functions, such as the development of industry'.

Soon afterwards, in 1939, Sir Alexander MacEwan and John Lorne Campbell of Canna published a stirring plea advocating a Highland Development Board, in a pamphlet called *ACT NOW for the Highlands and Islands*. It was to have four paid members, one of whom must be a Gaelic speaker, and the chairman was to be a Highlander. The job of this Highland Development Board was to give additional grants for roads, water supplies and drainage, to set up Land and Sea Training Centres, to organise co-operative schemes, to carry out land settlement schemes and land reclamation, and 'generally to act in any other way which they may consider to be beneficial to both the economic and social life of the Highlands and Islands'. This programme was to be completed within ten years, at an estimated cost of £500,000. The Board was also to be allowed to make loans not exceeding £50,000 a year—and the Government was urged to float a £5,000,000 Loan repayable in sixty years.

But when the time came, after the War, it was not a Highland Development Board that was appointed, but a *Highlands and Islands Advisory Panel*. Despite the pleas of the Scottish Council (Development and Industry) for a powerful executive agency that could stimulate industrial development, the Government preferred to use the existing administrative machine with a strong advisory panel as the co-ordinating link; it was to be a licensed critic of the Government within the administration, but the Government relied on its discretion not to be too embarassing. (In this, it was certainly successful under its first chairman, Malcolm Macmillan, the M.P. for the Western Isles; it was not until Lord Cameron took over as chairman in 1954 that the Highland Panel really began to make its mark, and eventually succeeded in embarrassing the Government quite seriously by threatening to resign *en bloc* if the Beeching rail cuts in the north were allowed.)

The White Paper on Highland Development in 1950 came and went, and still no Development Board was appointed. But it was now becoming increasingly clear that a pastoral economy would not stop the Highland drain, and that the Highlands had to have some sort of industrial core. So in the early fifties, when they had lost office, the Labour Party began to hammer this line. In 1953 the executive committee of the Scottish Council of the Labour Party published a 'Programme for the Highlands and Islands', calling for a Highlands and Islands Development Corporation with wide financial and executive powers—powers of ownership and control of the use of all land and land-resources, power to grant loans, reorganise crofting townships, establish marketing centres, create more tourist accommodation and facilities, set up a Mineral Development Commission and build factories. Its members were to be elected representatives from the county councils, and representatives appointed by the Government.

The Scottish Trades Unions Congress seized on this policy of industrial development and aired it forcefully at five Highland conferences at Inverness in 1953, 1955, 1957, 1960 and 1963. But an inhibiting note was sounded by the Royal Commission on Scottish Affairs in 1954 (the Balfour Report), which rejected the idea on the ground that it would erode the position and functions of the local authorities: 'If the Highland Development Authority were to act effectively it would be bound to displace local authorities to a greater or lesser degree, or to interpose itself between them and Government departments. If the Development Authority were to assume a substantial propor-tion of the functions of local authorities it would become in-creasingly difficult to get people of the right calibre to serve as town and county councillors in the Highlands.'

This was enough to scare the local authorities off the idea (in 1952, Sutherland County Council had asked the Highland Panel to urge the Secretary of State to set up a special authority for the northern Highland counties).

But the Labour and Liberal Parties were not letting go. Labour promised a Highland Development Board in 'Sign-posts for Scotland'; the Liberals did the same in 'Highland Development'. As the General Election of 1964 began to loom closer, the Conservatives realised that they were losing political capital heavily in the face of this onslaught in the Highlands, and hastily organised a regional planning survey. But it was too late; the Conservatives had lost the Highlands, and more than two out of three voters favoured candidates who were advocat-ing some form of Highland Development Board.

The part played by the Highland Panel had been, on the whole, a fairly subtle one. Its task was not to get cross with the Government and other Government agencies, but to persuade them. It acted as a sort of conscience, gently pricking the Board of Trade or British Railways or BEA or the Post Office (particularly the Post Office, whose mail contracts kept transport to the islands alive) to shoulder unremunerative functions at a time when Government policy was to make the nationalised industries self-supporting and to avoid giving subvention on a 'social-clause' remit. It was self-delusion, of course—but no more so than most political expedients; because it was apparent that the Highland Panel was merely bolstering an inadequate and ramshackle sort of structure. In the areas where it really mattered, in the attraction of new industry or the development of tourism, the machinery simply did not exist. The Board of Trade had neither the machinery nor the power nor the money to tempt industry into the Highlands—only special regional incentives could conceivably have done that; and short of giving the Tourist Board an enormous grant, there was no way of encouraging tourist development, for the county councils could not be wheedled (like the nationalised industries) into providing services for tourists, and hoteliers were not going to invest development capital without greater forms of incentives than were available elsewhere in Britain.

In the early sixties, the dismal record of industrial development in the Highlands was causing increasing concern, even in government circles. Less than 9 per cent of the working population was employed in manufacturing industries, compared with 20 per cent in primary industries (14 per cent in agriculture), and 70 per cent in service industries (11 per cent in construction). Then the Highland Panel visited Norway in September 1961, and had their eyes opened to a country that accepted its northern regions not as a darned nuisance but an integral and useful part of the whole nation. From then on, the Highland Panel's attitude towards the Government hardened perceptibly, and its proposals showed a new awareness of the necessity for planning comprehensively.

And at the same time, it began to be clear that there was, after all, an economic land use in the Highlands that really did suit national requirements—timber-growing and its ancillaries.

The demand for timber products, particularly paper and board, was growing at tremendous speed—and the Highland forests were approaching their first harvest. The removal of tariffs within EFTA on imported paper meant that the British paper-making industry had to become more economic—and one way of doing this was to have unified pulp and paper-making production. The Government moved in with a massive loan to Wiggins Teape for a pulp mill at Fort William, after many years of quiet discussion and negotiation; a big industrial development was under way at last, an industry that made sense in its context. And with the statisticians predicting an increase in the United Kingdom population to 70 million, it was becoming imperative to make the best possible use of available space within Britain. The way was now logically clear for the Highland Development Board, an executive agency that would try to bring in other forms of industrial development and co-ordinate the planning required to cope with the population movement predicted for the next decades. But the Conservatives abhorred the idea of an executive agency, and the chance was lost to them.

And yet, if they had only succeeded in overcoming their reluctance to allow social subvention, a reasonable alternative had been to hand all the time. With only a small adjustment in the existing machinery, they could have accomplished the same kind of thing in a way more suited to their ideological stance. They could have used the *North of Scotland Hydro-Electric Board*, and they could have used *MacBraynes*.

The Hydro Board, as it is affectionately called, was set up as a result of the Hydro-Electric Development (Scotland) Act of 1943, the brainchild of the late Thomas Johnston, Secretary of State for Scotland. There was very little hydro power in the Highlands then; a small hydro station had been brought into operation by the monks of Fort Augustus Abbey in 1890, the British Aluminium Company had built a much larger one at Foyers in 1895, there were further developments at Kinloch-leven (1906) and Lochaber (1921), and the Grampian Electricity Supply Company had created, in the thirties, public supply stations at Rannoch, Tummel and Loch Luichart. The Hydro Board's task was to harness the water-power resources of the Highlands (which it estimated in 1944 to be 6,274 million units of electricity from 102 potential projects), and thereby to revitalise the area by creating an improved social and economic atmosphere. The mere statistics of achievement are impressive enough: 188,000 consumers in 1947 have now grown to 430,000, output has increased from 427 million units to 2,900 million (nearly half the estimated potential of the Highland waters), and 94 per cent of all premises in the Hydro Board's area are now supplied with electricity. More than 110,000 of these 430,000 consumers live in remote rural areas (about 16,500 crofts are now connected). The capital investment involved over the years has been about £173,000,000, employment has been given to an average of 5,000 constructional workers a year, and some £50,000,000 has been paid out in wages in the Highlands; 460 new homes have been built in dying communities, and 400 miles of roads have been built or rebuilt—about 100 miles of which are public roads.

But has the investment been put to the best use? No one can deny the immense psychological boost that the Hydro Board gave to the Highlands, just by *connecting* people to a modern amenity that is elsewhere taken for granted. No one can deny its value to the development of farming and tourism, both of which require ever-increasing supplies of electricity. In addition, the Board claims that since 1948 some 3,500 industrial consumers have been connected to the mains, thus helping to ensure employment for over 13,000 people. But the fact remains that in its other allotted task, that of attracting new industrial consumers to the Highlands, the Board has only succeeded in creating something like 2,000 new jobs in its area.

It would be unfair to blame the Board for this relative failure. There were those who, in the early days, wanted to see the Hydro Board given the kind of over-all economic function of a Tennessee Valley Authority, so that it could act as a Development Authority on its own; but this was watered down into the familiar 'social clause' of so many other bodies. And anyway, the intimidating cost of connecting new consumers in the remoter areas (each new consumer in an outlying district now creates a loss of some £500 a year) drains its capital resources and forces up the charges to existing consumers. So the really crucial potential inherent in the Highland waters—abundant *and cheap* electricity, as in Norway, to attract industry—was never properly realised.

Yet at any time, when the pressure for some sort of coherent industrial attraction policy was growing, the Government could have turned the Hydro Board into such an agency by the simple expedient of relieving it of the crippling financial burden of supplying *social* electricity, in order to allow it to supply *industrial* electricity much more cheaply than it could be bought elsewhere. This would have been infinitely more effective than a cumbersome system of grants and loans to incoming industry— for industry, anyway, is uneasy over grants policies that may not last. With the weapon of cheap electricity, the Hydro Board could have stimulated industry at the time it really mattered—ten or fifteen years ago.

In the same way, while the Government was trumpeting the virtues of tourism as one solution to the problem of Highland development, it ignored the method of achievement that lay to hand—MacBraynes. Like the Hydro Board, this had the virtue, from the politicians' point of view, of requiring only a modification of the existing structure, instead of a revolution.

With its fleet of ships and coaches, MacBraynes were the obvious agency to build up the tourist trade in the Western Isles and the western coastline. Private enterprise simply wasn't interested, for the risks were too great and sporting and landowning interests were pulling the opposite way. Mac-Braynes could have developed a linked coach–boat–hotel service if it had been given the chance; but MacBraynes, that legendary scapegoat of island ills, was allowed instead to stagnate into an emasculated non-company where the incentive towards profit and adventurous management was stifled by a system of government subsidies that denied it profit and paid off its losses (to the tune of about £350,000 a year). At any time, the flaccid, ramshackle MacBraynes organisation could have been rationalised along the lines that the Transport Holding Company (a government agency that holds 50 per cent of the shares) is vigorously advocating at the time of writing; but once again, political timidity missed the opportunity when it could have done most good, and instead of a healthy and sensibly subsidised agency to promote tourism, the Government let itself become hopelessly entangled in a system of ever-mounting subsidies for ever-decreasing efficiency. And meanwhile, in bold black type in the 1959 White Paper, the Government proudly announced a £4,500,000 Highland tourist road programme over five years, building roads from nowhere to nowhere; and MacBraynes were lassoed into a new sea-transport system that encouraged hordes of tourists to take their cars to islands that had no hotels in which to accommodate them. It was a classic example of non-planning.

Little wonder, then, that when the Highland Development Board was announced in the Highlands and Islands Development (Scotland) Act of 1965 it was greeted with such undisguised relief and optimism (even the Conservatives who opposed the Bill on obscure doctrinaire grounds could scarcely conceal their secret pleasure that something positive had been done at last). The new Labour Government, untrammelled by the agonised loyalties to landowning and industrial interests that had bedevilled the Conservative administration, was able to endow the Board with powers that had never been conferred in Britain before; and it was launched on a wave of idealistic fervour to navigate its own way through the clogging Sargasso Sea of Highland administration. Its powers were mainly discretionary, admittedly; it had to be careful not to supersede existing authorities, but merely to co-ordinate them; yet here at last, it seemed, were the 'teeth' of real authority that the Highlands had needed so long.

Not unnaturally, perhaps, the honeymoon period of co-operation has not lasted very long, and the gravest doubts have arisen about the way in which the Board has been using its teeth. Much of what had to be done had, perforce, to be unpopular; the Board muscled in on Highland tourism when it found how ineffective the Scottish Tourist Board has been in that field. It has superseded, with a vengeance, the efforts of the Scottish Council (Development and Industry) where industrial development is concerned—in an area where only 9 per cent of employment is in manufacturing and productive industry, it has concentrated on providing prompt pump-priming grants and loans to the tune (according to its first annual report) of £1,600,000 to produce an estimated employment of some 1,650 jobs. It has encroached purposefully on the austere domains of the fishery agencies (eight new grant-aided boats for the Isles were due to be launched in 1967), MacBraynes, the Forestry Commission, the Board of Trade (it has at last supplied the £50,000 advance so urgently required by the Cairngorms Winter Sports Development Company)— and the traditionally taboo areas of Highland sentiment, like Glencoe.

In the public mind, however, the good things done by the Board so far have been overshadowed by the truly appalling blunders that have been made, and by the growing evidence of a distressing lack of communication both between the Board and the area it serves, and between the Board and central government. In certain major areas of development, its touch and expertise has been lamentably uncertain, substituting bluster for sureness of judgment, optimism for realism. Its public relations have been almost too dreadful to be true—a gross failure to explain what the Board is about. The Board as a whole, in its first few months of existence, has failed to work together harmoniously, and has conspicuously lacked the kind of wise and balanced leadership, the kind of firmness at the top, that was surely necessary.

And yet it must be stated firmly that the Highland Development Board remains the only rational and potentially effective instrument of Highland administration yet forged, an instrument still blunt and lacking in sophistication but one which, given time and experience, may still mature—and, one feels, *must* mature, if the problem of Highland administration is ever to be solved. For despite the traumatic experiences that the Board, and the Highlands, have suffered, despite the policy blunders, despite the lamentable lack of communication with the Scottish Office (a reflection, surely, of the irrational world of Highland administration I have tried to demonstrate in these pages), the Board has at least shown the way and established new patterns of thinking that will assuredly bear fruit in the future.

FIGURE 1

Highland County Councils: Population (mid-1965 estimates)

	Landward	Burghs	TOTAL
Argyll	34,609	24,918	59,527
Caithness	11,815	16,573	28,388
Inverness-shire	47,167	34,522*	81,689
Orkney	10,175	8,070	18,245
Ross and Cromarty	43,201	14,239	57,440
Sutherland	12,281	959	13,240
Zetland	11,834	5,680	17,514
TOTALS	171,082	104,961	276,043

* Includes Inverness Burgh, at 30,716.

FIGURE 2

Highland County Councils : Area in Acres

Argyll	1,990,521
Caithness	438,833
Inverness-shire	2,695,094
Orkney	268,527
Ross and Cromarty	1,977,248
Sutherland	1,297,914
Zetland	352,337
TOTAL	9,020,474

FIGURE 3

Highland County Councils: Rateable Valuations

	Landward	*Burghs*	TOTAL
Argyll	£601,763	£489,058	£1,090,821
Caithness	£162,210	£210,997	£373,207
Inverness-shire	£695,246	£788,250 *	£1,483,496
Orkney	£92,742	£86,240	£178,982
Ross and Cromarty	£439,465	£345,748	£785,213
Sutherland	£185,309	£23,440	£208,749
Zetland	£52,429	£71,441	£123,870
TOTALS	£2,229,164	£2,015,174	£4,244,338

* Includes Inverness Burgh, at £703,000.

FIGURE 4

Highland County Councillors : Age ; Length of Residence in County, and Length of Service

	Average Age	Average length of Residence	Average years of Service
Argyll	57·76	38·91	10·63
Caithness	55·76	42·45	15·46
Inverness-shire	55·62	42·39	11·33
Orkney	59·54	47·73	8·80
Ross and Cromarty	61·86	40·68	12·56
Sutherland	57·06	47·60	11·45
Zetland	56·40	46·80	10·50

FIGURE 5

Highland County Council Profiles: Occupation

	Argyll	Caithness	Inverness	Orkney	Ross	Sutherland	Zetland	TOTAL
Landowner	4	1	9	—	7	—	1	22
Farmer	10	13	9	14	7	8	1	62
Doctor	4	1	—	2	—	1	—	7
Teacher	—	2	3	—	3	—	—	9
Minister/priest	3	1	7	—	4	—	—	15
Other professional	1	—	4	1	1	1	1	9
Ex-Armed Services	1	—	3	1	1	—	1	7
Businessman/company director	7	—	4	5	9	1	5	31
Hotelier	4	2	3	1	2	4	—	16
Private means	1	—	—	—	—	—	—	1
Public/civil servant	2	4	4	3	1	1	2	17
Supervisor/sales/white collar	5	2	4	—	5	1	6	23
Technician	—	10	1	—	—	—	—	11
Shopkeeper/merchant	3	2	19	—	1	2	7	34
Crofter	—	—	8	—	4	—	8	20
Manual	7	3	5	—	1	1	3	20
Housewife	1	1	1	5	4	—	1	13
TOTALS	53	42	84	32	50	20	36	317

Index

(Matter included in the Selected Bibliographies which follow individual chapters is not indexed below.)

302